BURNING DOWN THE HOUSE

Burning Down the House explores the political, economic and cultural landscape of 21st-century Latin America through comics. It examines works from Argentina, Brazil, Bolivia, Chile, Uruguay, Perú, Colombia, México and Spain, and the resurgence of comics in recent decades spurred by the ubiquity of the Internet and reminiscent of the complex political experiences and realities of the region.

The volume analyses experimentations in themes and formats and how Latin American comics have become deeply plural in its inspirations, subjects, drawing styles and political concerns while also underlining the hybrid and diverse cultures they represent. It examines the representative and historical images in a state of emergency and political upheaval; decolonial perspectives and social struggles linked to ethnic and sexual minorities. It looks at how Latin American comics are made right now – from a diverse and autochthonous Latin American perspective.

With a wide array of illustrations, this book in the Global Perspectives in Comics Studies series will be an important resource for scholars and researchers of comic studies, Latin American studies, cultural studies, English literature, political history and post-colonial studies.

Laura Cristina Fernández is a head professor in the Faculty of Arts and Design, Universidad Nacional de Cuyo (UNCU), Argentina. She holds a PhD in Social Sciences and an MA in Latin American Art. She is actively involved in several research projects concerning comics, recent memory and crisis and has co-directed research projects on independent comics, fanzines and discourses on gender and sexual dissidence. Her most recent works as a comic artist are *Ruptures. Les bébés volés du Franquisme* (*Ruptures. The stolen babies of Francoism*, with Laure Sirieix, Bang Editions, 2022) and *Turba. Memorias de Malvinas* (*Peat. Memories of Malvinas*, Editorial Hotel de las Ideas, 2022).

Amadeo Gandolfo holds a History degree and a PhD in Social Sciences. He was granted postdoctoral scholarships by the Ibero-American Institute of Berlin in 2019 and by the Humboldt Foundation in 2020. He curated several comics exhibitions in the city of Buenos Aires. He edited *Kamandi*, an online magazine of comics criticism (www.revistakamandi.com) alongside Pablo Turnes. His research focuses on Ibero-American graphic humor from a transnational perspective and on authorship and collaboration conflicts in the field of American comics. He currently lives in Berlin.

Pablo Turnes is a History Professor and holds a PhD in Social Sciences. He teaches at the Universidad de Buenos Aires (UBA) and is a researcher of the Instituto de Investigaciones Gino Germani (UBA). He currently lives in Berlin as a postdoctoral fellow at the Alexander von Humboldt Foundation. His research, under the direction of Dr. Stefan Rinke (LAI-Freie Universität Berlin), focuses on the topic of contemporary Latin American comics and their relationship to memory, trauma and recent Latin American history.

Global Perspectives in Comics Studies
Series editor: Harriet E.H. Earle
Sheffield Hallam University, UK

Global Perspectives in Comics Studies focuses on comics as an international form, with histories as rich and complex as the stories that fill the pages. We bring together original scholarship on a wide range of themes and theoretical concerns that span the globe. These texts present outstanding bold interventions into existing scholarly conversations, with the freedom (indeed, explicit encouragement) to collocate works by creators from different national and analytical traditions, as well as genres within the form. The books in the series are concerned with offering fresh perspectives on established concepts and theories through the comics form. Our aim in this series is to forge links across the field, to foreground artistic and academic contexts that are underrepresented, and to give attention to comics in all their various guises. Ultimately, this series wants to encourage readers to challenge their existing perspectives on a form that is central to the reading lives of so many.

Books in the series

Cartooning China
Punch, Power, & Politics in the Victorian Era
Amy Matthewson

Burning Down the House
Latin American Comics in the 21st Century
Edited by Laura Cristina Fernández, Amadeo Gandolfo and Pablo Turnes

Comics and Migration
Practices and Representation
Edited by Ralf Kauranen, Olli Löytty, Aura Nikkilä and Anna Vuorinne

For more information about this series, please visit: www.routledge.com/Global-Perspectives-in-Comics-Studies/book-series/GPCS

BURNING DOWN THE HOUSE

Latin American Comics in the 21st Century

Edited by Laura Cristina Fernández, Amadeo Gandolfo and Pablo Turnes

LONDON AND NEW YORK

Cover image: © Ignacio Minaverry

First published 2023
by Routledge
4 Park Square, Milton Park, Abingdon, Oxon OX14 4RN

and by Routledge
605 Third Avenue, New York, NY 10158

Routledge is an imprint of the Taylor & Francis Group, an informa business

© 2023 selection and editorial matter, Laura Cristina Fernández, Amadeo Gandolfo and Pablo Turnes; individual chapters, the contributors

The right of Laura Cristina Fernández, Amadeo Gandolfo and Pablo Turnes to be identified as the authors of the editorial material, and of the authors for their individual chapters, has been asserted in accordance with sections 77 and 78 of the Copyright, Designs and Patents Act 1988.

All rights reserved. No part of this book may be reprinted or reproduced or utilised in any form or by any electronic, mechanical, or other means, now known or hereafter invented, including photocopying and recording, or in any information storage or retrieval system, without permission in writing from the publishers.

Trademark notice: Product or corporate names may be trademarks or registered trademarks, and are used only for identification and explanation without intent to infringe.

Disclaimer: Every effort has been made to contact copyright-holders. Please advise the publisher of any errors or omissions, and these will be corrected in subsequent editions.

British Library Cataloguing-in-Publication Data
A catalogue record for this book is available from the British Library

ISBN: 978-1-032-00348-1 (hbk)
ISBN: 978-1-032-14831-1 (pbk)
ISBN: 978-1-003-33329-6 (ebk)

DOI: 10.4324/9781003333296

Typeset in Bembo
by Apex CoVantage, LLC

CONTENTS

List of figures	*ix*
List of contributors	*xii*
Series editor's preface	*xvi*

Burning Down the House – Introduction   1
Laura Fernández, Amadeo Gandolfo & Pablo Turnes

PART I
Politics, protest and memory   17

1. Intertextuality and iconic images in Lucas Nine's "Borges, inspector de aves"   19
   Tania Pérez Cano

2. The comic as a form of memory of two student movements in contemporary Mexico: the case of Grito de Victoria by Augusto Mora   35
   Laura Nallely Hernández Nieto

3. The memory of Trauma under the dictatorship as portrayed in contemporary Chilean comics. A comparative perspective with Spain   51
   Elena Masarah Revuelta and Gerardo Vilches Fuentes

viii Contents

4 Historical graphic novels in Uruguay 2000–2020   67
   María Victoria Saibene

5 Between comics and memories, other stories of Brazil   82
   Marilda Lopes Pinheiro Queluz

6 Black visualities in Brazilian comics: a historical overview   105
   Ivan Lima Gomes

7 And you will come marching with me: the Chilean comics
   after the social mobilization   117
   Hugo Hinojosa Lobos

PART II
Genre and sexual dissidence   **147**

8 Approaches to remember the bodies in two Latin
   American comics: "Notas al Pie" by Nacha Vollenweider
   and "Las Sinventuras de Jaime Pardo" by Vicho Plaza   149
   Jorge Sánchez

9 Resisting imposed lines: (Feminine) territoriality in the
   work of Chilean comics artist Panchulei   166
   Jasmin Wrobel

10 Bolivian comics and the subalternity   183
    Marcela Murillo

11 Emancipated behavior: the body and art in the work of
    Águeda Noriega and Ale Torres   193
    Carla Sagástegui Heredia

12 Comics as a means to illustrate sexual dissidence:
    Guadalupe and Poder Trans   207
    Janek Scholz

13 Pervertion through funny comics: the case of Diego Parés'
    Sr. and Sra. Rispo   221
    Rodrigo O. Ottonello

Index   238

FIGURES

1.1	Cover of the 2017 Hotel de las Ideas edition of *Borges, inspector de aves*. All images are reproduced with authorization from the author, Lucas Nine.	131
1.2	The first six panels of *Borges, Poultry Inspector*. In the upper right corner, a caption introduces the reader to the "origin story" of how the writer became a man of action and went to investigate the Argentine chicken underworld. The caption contains both a historical fact and the alternative history of Borges as "poultry inspector."	20
1.3	Collage that combines a photograph with a parodic, apocryphal advertising message by Borges.	25
1.4	References to Borges's literature are transformed into visual artifacts by subverting the onomatopoeic device, normally a standard sound effect in comics.	27
2.1	On the left: Cover of Los Agachados, with the photograph taken by Armando Lenin Salgado. On the right: the drawing of *Grito de Victoria* is based on the same image.	132
2.2	On the left: Gray scale to Victoria. On the right: to Valentín.	40
2.3	The point when both stories intertwine.	41
2.4	Drawings of the interviewees and their testimonies.	44
3.1	Full-page scene in *Los años de Allende*.	57
3.2	An intellectual finds tortured people in a basement in *Pinturas de guerra*.	60
4.1	Rodriguez Juele, A. (2011). *La Isla Elefante*. Malaquita Ediciones.	72
4.2	Santullo, R., & Aguirre, M. (2012). *Zitarrosa*. Grupo Belerofonte, Estuario Editora.	133

4.3	Leguisamo, P. R., & Fernández, L. (2015). *Tupamaros, la Fuga 1971*. Loco Rabia y Dragón Comics.	134
4.4	Peruzzo, N., & Serra, G. (2016). *Rincón de la Bolsa*. Ninfa Comics.	135
5.1	Luli Penna. Pages 10–11. *Sem Dó*. 2017b.	89
5.2	Luli Penna. Page with scenes of Lola ironing clothes. *Sem Dó*, 2017b.	90
5.3	Marcelo D'Salete. A sequence that depicts slave ships crossing the Atlantic. *Angola Janga*, 2017, p. 114–116.	95
5.4	Marcelo D'Salete. Pages with symbolic manifestations. Angola Janga, 2017. p. 38 and p. 204.	96
5.5	Marcelo D'Salete. Dara sees the urban future of Brazil. *Angola Janga*. 2017, p. 390–392.	97
6.1	(Left): Sophia Martinez Andreazza, published in September 17, 2018.	136
6.2	(Right): Renata Nolasco, published in September 19, 2018.	137
6.3	Caetano Cury, 2018.	138
6.4	Recreation of Africa: material culture and symbolisms (D'Salete, 2018a, 176).	112
7.1	Gaspar Ortega, "Por qué nos movilizamos" (*Why do we mobilize?* 2011).	121
7.2	Nicolás Cruz y Quique Palomo, *El golpe: el pueblo 1970–1973*.	123
7.3	Guido "Kid" Salinas and Sebastián Castro, *Los Guardianes del Sur* (2019).	139
7.4	Ibi and Marz, Pesadillas y ensoñaciones en estado de Rebeldía (2019).	139
7.5	@artichokat [María Gazale Carinao], *Brígida* N. 7 (2020).	140
8.1	Nacha Vollenweider. The migrant body. *Notas al Pie* (2017).	153
8.2	Nacha Vollenweider. "Every object in your house tells a story." *Notas al Pie* (2017).	156
8.3	Vicente Plaza. Bodies as sketches. *Las Sinaventuras de Jaime Pardo* (2013).	159
8.4	Vicente Plaza. Poor figurative representations of memory. *Las Sinaventuras de Jaime Pardo* (2013).	160
9.1	Powerpaola (2013 [2011]): *Virus tropical*. Barcelona: Mondadori, p. 91.	171
9.2	Panchulei (2020 [2019]): "La matria y la cacerola," in: *ManosManifiesto*. Barcelona: self-published [fanzine], p. 25.	141
9.3	Baldachin from Tost (c. 1220), Museu Nacional d'Art de Catalunya. https://commons.wikimedia.org/wiki/File:Baldachin_from_Tost_-_Google_Art_Project.jpg (last accessed 20 June 2021).	142
9.4	Panchulei (2020 [2019]): "La matria y el canino," in: *ManosManifiesto*. Barcelona: self-published [fanzine], p. 26.	143

9.5	Antependium from the Chapel of Sant Quirc de Durro (mid-twelfth century), Museu Nacional d'Art de Catalunya. https://commons.wikimedia.org/wiki/File:Frontal_d%27altar_de_Durro.jpg (last accessed 20 June 2021).	143
11.1	Happy Mother's Day (Villar 166).	195
11.2	Camille (Águeda s/n).	198
11.3	La fuerza de tres (Águeda s/n).	200
11.4	Day Dreaming (Torres 30).	203
11.5	Feliz día de la Marmota (Torres 1).	204
12.1	Angelica Freitas/Odyr: *Guadalupe* (2012), no page numbers.	212
12.2	Angelica Freitas/Odyr: *Guadalupe* (2012), no page numbers.	213
12.3	Edo Brenes: "Garçon," in: *Poder Trans* (2018), pp. 76–77.	144
13.1	Characters from *El Sr. y la Sra. Rispo* (2009). *El Sr. y la Sra. Rispo* blog (29/10/2009).	145
13.2	Diego Parés, "Daily life," *El Sr. y la Sra. Rispo*. Illustration posted on Diego Parés' official Facebook site (2010).	227
13.3	Diego Parés, "Horacio," *El Sr. y la Sra. Rispo*. Illustration posted on Diego Parés' official Facebook site (2010).	229
13.4	Diego Parés, *El Sr. y la Sra. Rispo*. Illustration posted on Diego Parés' official Facebook site (2013).	146
13.5	Diego Parés, "Tomorrow, there's no tomorrow." *El Sr. y la Sra. Rispo* blog (January 31, 2010).	234

CONTRIBUTORS

Tania Pérez Cano is an assistant professor of Spanish in the Department of Global Languages and Cultures at the University of Massachusetts Dartmouth. Her research and teaching interests focus on Cuban, Latin American and Caribbean literatures and cultures, Ecocriticism and comic and graphic novels in the Hispanic world. She published a translation of Rubem Fonseca's short story collection *Pequenas criaturas* in 2004; in 2005, she wrote the prologue for the Cuban edition of his novel *A grande arte*. She has recently published several articles about comics: "*Athena*: nuevas armas para una diosa antigua, o los nuevos territorios de la historieta cubana" (2020), "La memoria como espacio de libertad: autobiografía y testimonio en las narrativas gráficas *Cuba, my Revolution*, de Inverna Lockpez y *Adiós mi Habana*, de Anna Veltfort" (2020), "Graphic Testimonies of the Balsero Crisis of 1994: Narratives of Cuban Detainees at the Guantanamo Naval Base" (2019). Also in 2019, she coordinated a monographic issue of the journal *Mitologías Hoy* entitled, *Cómics: Intertextualidades, discursividades y paratextos en el arte secuencial de América Latina*. Her book *Imposibilidad del beatus ille: Representaciones de la crisis ecológica en España y América Latina* was published by Almenara Press in 2016.

Gerardo Vilches Fuentes holds a PhD degree in History from Universidad Nacional de Educación a Distancia (UNED). He is a professor in the Education Department of the UEM and in the master's program Comics and Education at the UV. He wrote Breve historia del cómic (2014), El guión de cómic (2016) and La satírica transición. Revistas de humor político en España (1975–1982) (2021) and coordinated Del boom al crack: la explosión del cómic adulto en España (1977–1995) (2018). He has published in scholarly journals and various books, participated in conferences and given lectures and workshops related to comics. Since 2013, he has been the codirector of CuCo, Cuadernos de cómic.

Ivan Lima Gomes is an adjunct professor of Modern and Contemporary/Latin American History at the Universidade Federal de Goiás (UFG). He holds a PhD in Social History from Universidade Federal Fluminense (UFF), which was supported by funding from CNPq. His research interests concern the historiographic study of cultural practices, focused on the aesthetics, history and theory of comics, publishing history, visual culture and Latin American history. He is the author of *Os Novos Homens do Amanhã: Projetos e Disputas em Torno dos Quadrinhos na América Latina (Brasil e Chile, anos 1960–1970)* (Prismas, 2018).

Carla Sagástegui Heredia holds a PhD in Art, Literature and Critical Thinking from the Universitat Pompeu Fabra (UPF) of Barcelona. She has published fiction stories in magazines and anthologies; with Jesús Cossio, she is the author of the graphic novel *Ya nadie te sacará de tu tierra, un comic sobre la Reforma Agraria en Perú* (2019) and is the author of *The new woman* (2022), about the political history of Peruvian poet and activist Magda Portal. Her research on comics and graphic novels can be found in academic reviews, the catalog for *La historieta peruana 1: los primeros ochenta años (1887–1967)* (2003) and in the chapters about the Peruvian comic history in *Redrawing the Nation* (2009); *Bumm! Historieta y humor gráfico en el Perú: 1978–1992* (2016) and *Comics Beyond the Page in Latin America* (2020).

Laura Nallely Hernández Nieto holds a PhD degree in Art History from the Universidad Nacional Autónoma de México (UNAM). Her research interest focuses on Mexican graphic narrative. She has published several articles and book chapters and attended several conferences related to comics. She is part of the network of Latin American Graphic Narrative Researchers (RING). At the present, she is the chair of the Comic Art Working Group of the International Association for Media and Communication Research (IAMCR).

Hugo Hinojosa Lobos is a doctoral candidate at the Pontificia Universidad Católica de Chile (UC) and an academic in the Department of Elementary Level Education at the Universidad Academia de Humanismo Cristiano (UAHC). He is a founding member of the network of Latin American Graphic Narrative Researchers (RING) and La Otra LIJ. He is also a member of the editorial boards for the publication *Neuróptica* and an organizer for the UNICOMIC conference in Spain and *Dibujos que Hablan* in Santiago, Chile.

Marcela Murillo is an assistant professor in the Department of Humanities and Foreign Languages at Santa Fe College, Florida. She holds a PhD from the University of Florida (UF) in Spanish Literature and a master's degree in Women's Studies, Gender and Sexualities. Her research focuses on femininities, gender, representation and Andean literature. She published articles on sartorial empowerment and indigenous representation in comics.

Rodrigo O. Ottonello (PhD) studied Sociology and Social Sciences at the UBA and at the Universidad Nacional de San Martín (UNSAM). He is a CONICET Researcher at the Laboratorio de Investigaciones en Ciencias Humanas of the Universidad Nacional de San Martín, an associate professor at the Universidad de Belgano (UB) and a professor at the Universidad Nacional de las Artes (UNA). He is the author of *La destrucción de la sociedad. Política, metafísica y crimen desde la sociología de Durkheim* (Miño y Dávila, 2016), and his ongoing investigations focus on the birth and rise of contemporary myths.

Marilda Lopes Pinheiro Queluz holds a degree in History and in Art Education from the Federal University of Paraná (UFPR), a master's degree in Social History from the same university and a doctorate in Communication and Semiotics from the Pontifical Catholic University of São Paulo (PUC-SP). She is a researcher and a professor of the Post Graduate Program in Technology at the Federal University of Technology – Paraná, in a research program called Mediations and Cultures. She is the leader of the research group *Design and Culture*. She investigates the history of graphic arts and graphic humor in Brazil; design, technology and culture; and Brazilian art history.

Elena Masarah Revuelta holds a university degree in History and a master's degree in Contemporary History. She is a PhD candidate in Modern and Contemporary History, Universidad de Zaragoza (UZ). Her thesis deals with the subjects of history, Francoism's memory and comics in Spain during the 20th and 21st centuries. She is a professor in the Education Department at Universidad Europea Madrid (UEM) and also teaches in the master's program Comics and Education at the Universitat de Valencia (UV).

María Victoria Saibene holds a humanities degree from the Universidad de Montevideo (UM). She is a high school teacher and an assistant professor in the chair of Universal History (UM). She has worked in several editorial projects related to comics, teaching with comics and historical graphic novels, both as a consultant and as a researcher.

Jorge Sánchez has a PhD in Philosophy, with a mention in Aesthetics and Art Theory, Universidad de Chile (UCh). He teaches comics and image theory at the Universidad de Santiago de Chile (Usach). He belongs to the research group RING. He has published several articles and book chapters referring to the problem of memory and the body in Latin American comics. His current doctoral research (as a CONICyT fellow) focuses on the conditions of time representation in comic strips in Latin American productions.

Janek Scholz studied Romance languages and literature, German as a foreign language and English linguistics in Jena and Naples and spent one year at the Universidade Federal do Ceará (UFC), Fortaleza. He holds a PhD in Brazilian

Literature from the Universität Wien. Currently, he works as a research assistant at the Portuguese-Brazilian Institute at the University of Cologne. His Post-Doc project focuses on trans* narratives in contemporary literature from Brazil and Argentina; other interests include Brazilian and Luso-African comics, narrative hegemony and Luso-Italian literary relations. He co-edited a dossier on the Poetics of Dead Protagonism in Brazilian Literature and several books on a variety of topics.

Jasmin Wrobel studied Spanish and Comparative Literature at the Ruhr Universität Bochum (RUB) and holds a PhD in Latin American Studies from the Freie Universität Berlin (FU). At present, she is a Research Track-Postdoc and academic coordinator at the Cluster of Excellence "Temporal Communities: Doing Literature in a Global Perspective," FU Berlin. She is the author of the book *Topografien des 20. Jahrhunderts: Die memoriale Poetik des Stolperns in Haroldo de Campos' Galáxias* (2020). She edited the volume *Roteiros de palavras, sons, imagens: Os diálogos transcriativos de Haroldo de Campos* (2018); co-edited the dossiers "Experimental Poetry Networks: Material Circulations" (2019 in *Materialities of Literatures*; with P. Bachmann) and "Archives of Resistance: Picturing the Black Americas" (2022 in *Amerikastudien/American Studies*; with D. Breitenwischer and R. Reid-Pharr). She has published in international journals and compilations on topics such as Latin American comics and graphic narratives, Brazilian concrete poetry and Latin American baroque and neo-baroque literature.

SERIES EDITOR'S PREFACE

Burning Down the House: Latin American Comics in the 21st Century
Edited by Laura Cristina Fernández, Amadeo Gandolfo and Pablo Turnes

Comics and graphic novels have been at the forefront of political and social storytelling across the world and nowhere more so than Latin America. The comics scene in the twenty-first century has seen the coming together of a wide range of inspirations, subjects, artistic styles, and political concerns. At the same time, the rise of the internet as a means of publication and publicity, the graphic novel as an emerging format, and the inclusion of the comic in state-supported cultural and educational projects have influenced the changes in readership and cultural perception.

This collection brings to the fore the ways in which comics engage with the histories of Latin America during the transition from dictatorship to democracy. The authors explain how comics are made in twenty-first-century Latin America from a diverse and autochthonous perspective. Our scope is continental and includes contributors from Argentina, Brazil, Bolivia, Chile, Uruguay, Perú, México, Cuba, Spain and Germany.

From local expressions of manga to native superheroes, through the adaptation of the North American independent comic and the emergence of abstract comics, Latin American comics production plays and explores with the different languages and styles made possible by the form. I am delighted to introduce this book, which will bring new and important voices to the conversation on Latin America's contribution to comics.

Harriet E. H. Earle
Sheffield Hallam University, UK

BURNING DOWN THE HOUSE – INTRODUCTION

Laura Fernández, Amadeo Gandolfo & Pablo Turnes

When we speak of Latin American comics in the last 20 years, we are addressing a complex and multiple universe. And this is due both to *mestizaje*, the hybrid and diverse cultures that are often reduced to a simplifying or picturesque concept of "the Latin American," and to the convulsed realities and the traumatic marks of the dictatorial pasts that affect it.

For this volume, we have brought together Latin American and European scholars to analyze the discourses, experiences, innovations and challenges of comics, comic strips and graphic novels in various Latin American countries. We consider it necessary to approach Latin American productions from local voices that offer an interpretation close to their contexts of emergence, as an alternative to the "Outsider" (or "external") perspective. This does not suggest a cloistered position but, on the contrary, to be able to open debates that non-Latin American approaches tend to avoid, such as decolonial perspectives, the discussion on recent memory and social struggles linked to ethnic and sexual minorities. Furthermore, this volume acknowledges and values previous and recent academic research on Latin American comics, even if our perspectives are not necessarily the same, and thus, open for debate (Foster, 1989; Fernández l'Hoeste & Poblete, 2009; Catalá Carrasco et al., 2017; Scorer, 2020).

The contributions of this volume will focus on two main axes: politics, protest and memories on the one hand and gender and sexual dissidences on the other. These are burning topics in current Latin American narratives, intertwined by the tensions of our realities in permanent crisis.

A political/economic overview (2000–2020)

The 21st century has so far been one of turmoil and changes in Latin America, in line with the historical processes of each of the countries that integrate it. It started

DOI: 10.4324/9781003333296-1

with the failure of the neoliberal governments which had steered the economic and political landscape throughout the 1990s. These governments had cut heavily on public spending, privatized a large amount of public services, taken large sums of debt from the IMF and other international organizations and adjusted the labor laws to reduce worker's rights and diminish the quality and stability of employment. As a result, Latin American countries, in the long run, experienced a growth in poverty and unemployment rates, a descent in the quality of privatized services and an increasing misalignment in the balance of payments, which ultimately led to widespread economic crises. These economic crises started in México in 1994, then in Brazil in 1998–1999, Argentina in 1999–2003, Uruguay in 2000–2001, Ecuador in 1998–1999 and Perú in 1999. These crises were marked by devaluation of the currency, a loss of international reserves and the implementation of IMF backed austerity programs. In some cases, such as in Argentina, they were compounded by social uprisings and unrest.

The exception when it comes to neoliberal governments in Latin America was Hugo Chavez´s. While at the start he also followed the IMF mandates and encouraged the entrance of foreign investment in the country, it slowly started adopting populist measures and turning to left-wing policies which ultimately sparked the conversion of his administration toward a "21st Century Socialism." After an attempted coup in 2002, this process gained momentum and also sparked a turn toward a more complete control of the State by Chavez and members of his party. In 1999, his government was almost a peculiarity in the continent (considering the necessary reference of the Cuban experience), but starting in 2002 with the election of Lula Inácio Da Silva in Brazil a swift turnover took place which positioned "populist governments" at the helm of most Latin American countries: Néstor Kirchner in Argentina (2003), Tabaré Vazquez in Uruguay (2005), Evo Morales in Bolivia (2006) and Rafael Correa in Ecuador (2007). To these we can add, with certain caveats, the administrations of Michelle Bachelet in Chile (2006) and Fernando Lugo in Paraguay (2008). These movements coalesced in the 2005 Summit of the Americas in Mar del Plata (Argentina), where the Mercosur governments (Paraguay, Uruguay, Brazil and Argentina) plus Venezuela opposed the Free Trade Area of the Americas, the free trade agreement that was spearheaded by the United States (under the George W. Bush administration), causing the summit to fail to reach an undestanding. This marked the transition of the populist wave from a national phenomenon to a regional stance, which signaled a larger cooperation between the Latin American countries. We cannot fail to mention the influence that the Cuban government has had and continues to have on the imagery of Latin America's left-wing parties. With the process of left-wing governments that began in this period, a channel of dialogue was opened between Cuba and the rest of Latin America, which had been blocked for decades.

To write about Latin America history is to face a particular conundrum: while most Latin American countries have experienced similar political and economic processes, these have been filtered by the particular characteristics, history, social qualities and economic realities of each country. In this regard, we take a page from

Waldo Ansaldi and Veronica Giordano, who aim toward "thinking, understanding and explaining Latin America as a totality. But said totality it is not the same as an abusive homogeneity or generalization . . . Latin America is a reality composed of many diversities" (Ansaldi & Giordano, 2012, p. 25).

This is equally right for the "pink tide" of populist governments that dominated Latin American politics between 2002 and 2015. All had several characteristics in common: an economy that was heavily dependent on exports of commodities (oil in Venezuela, soybean in Argentina and minerals and gas in Bolivia), a focus on human rights, an expansion of welfare programs for the poor and childhood, an attempt to recuperate the State as a great leveler between social classes and as a provider of services, an attempt to strengthen university education among the poor and underprivileged and heavy subsidies on public services to make them affordable for the population. They also shared a difficulty with diversifying exports and with securing a stable fiscal policy.

The results of these governments were heavily positive while the commodity boom remained solid and growing. The middle classes flourished, social programs and welfare reached a larger number of beneficiaries, Argentina managed to reopen the judiciary processes against those accused of Human Rights violations during the last military dictatorship (1976–1983), and economic growth was impressive and unusual for most countries. The problems started when the commodity boom hit its ceiling around 2010 and the injections of money from said boom started to dry up, causing problems with the heavy spending employed on social programs and, in certain countries, leading to an exchange rate lag which introduced several distortions on the macroeconomy.

These processes also encountered difficulties securing successors for its highly influential leading figures. In Brazil, Lula da Silva was succeeded by Dilma Roussef, his chief of staff. After a relatively uneventful and popular first term, Roussef came to be accused of administrative misconduct and of doctoring the budget, alongside accusations that stemmed from *Lava Jato* (*Car Wash* in Portuguese, after the name the police gave the operation that meant to track a chain of car wash establishments supposedly used for money laundering, which involved government-related businessmen and politicians), leading to her impeachment in 2016 and ultimately removing her from office that same year. In Argentina, Cristina Fernández de Kirchner failed to secure her succession in the form of presidential hopeful Daniel Scioli in 2015, ushering in Mauricio Macri's presidency. In Ecuador, Rafael Correa was succeeded by Lenín Moreno, his vice-president, but trouble between them started almost as soon as he was elected, and Moreno distanced himself from Correa. In Bolivia, Evo Morales employed every tactic available to avoid stepping down from office and was ultimately ousted in a coup d'etat in November 2019 after a new election had granted him a new term. In Chile, Michelle Bachelet's party gave way to Sebastián Piñera's neo-neoliberal government. In Colombia, the election of Iván Duque in 2018 represented a turn away from the attempts at a lasting peace with the FARC and other insurgent guerrilla groups engineered by conservative Juan Manuel Santos Calderón. More recently, the triumph of banker Guillermo

Lasso in Ecuador and lawyer Luis Lacalle Pou in Uruguay strengthens this wave of right-wing, neoliberal governments in the region, which in every speech strives to highlight the supposed death of "21st-century Socialism." Even the promising exceptions that have arisen in the last two years (Luis Arce in Bolivia and Gabriel Boric in Chile) are constrained by the power of the right-wing parties.

This turn toward governments which could be characterized as right-wing or center-right-wing can be explained by a number of factors. First and foremost, by a downturn in economic activity. The commodities boom ended in the late 2000s, and the economy of Latin America never recovered. The end of the boom signaled that these countries hadn't given much thought to (or hadn't been able to) diversify the economy. No country experienced the consequences of these decisions in a harsher way than Venezuela. When oil prices started to crash in the late 2000s, this sparked a crisis marked by huge inflation, product shortages, starvation, rising crime levels and rising corruption in the elites. The crisis has only worsened since 2010, when it began, and millions of Venezuelans have fled the country to Colombia, Ecuador, Argentina, Chile, the United States and Europe.

In other countries of Latin America, the crisis did not manifest itself in such a severe manner, but the years between 2015 and 2019 were marked by a decrease in growth, inflationary crisis, increased austerity and the presence of the IMF in several Latin American countries. This process of economic crisis has been compounded with a soaring social unrest. Protests of indigenous peoples in Ecuador, of the middle class in Brazil related to the public transport fare, against a reform of the retirement system in Argentina, and the huge and still continuing process of unrest and protest that gripped Chilean society since October 2019. In certain countries, such as Argentina, Uruguay, Colombia and Brazil, this has also led to a constant polarization in society between those who support and defend the pink tide governments, and those who see them as the cause of the economic woes (and sometimes even the "moral decay") the continent is experiencing.

The second characteristic that marked these years of crisis has been a frontal clash between the executive branch of the government and the judiciary. This clash can start during the years in which the executive branch is in office, as was the case in Brazil, or after the fact, when politicians belonging to the pink tide have stepped down. Interpretations around this process are as polarized as the process itself. One part of the political spectrum refers to Charles Dunlap's (2001) concept of "lawfare" to define the process of opening new judicial processes against notable members of the political class: the term is a joining of the words "law" and "warfare." From this point of view, it is argued that the processes opened against Latin American politicians who come from the left is a form of "war" in which the law is used against them without taking into account their rights and the due process. From the other side of the aisle, politicians and citizens who are disillusioned with the governance of the politicians of the pink tide argue that these processes are simply a way to find out the truth about the many allegations of corruption and mishandling of funds that have been lobbied against them.

It was within this context of economic hardship, heavily polarized societies and a high dose of social unrest that the COVID-19 pandemic hit Latin America. After a brief moment in which these societies experienced something akin to a surge in patriotic pride and a sense of purpose which many leaders likened to fighting a war, the economic and sanitary costs of handling a pandemic exposed the cracks in countries in which the provision of social services and basic health, transportation, housing and education infrastructure is sorely lacking. According to the Social Panorama of Latin America published by the Economic Commission for Latin America and the Caribbean of the United Nations, the GDP of Latin America will fall by 7.7%, poverty has risen from 30.5% to 33.7% and extreme poverty will go up from 11.3% to 12.5% (pp. 15–16). This means that more than 30 million people who previously weren't poor have become poor during 2020 and that 8 million more people have become extremely poor. This process seems to smash all the advancements made by the pink tide governments in their efforts to grow the Latin American middle class, retracting poverty levels to those experienced 20 years ago.

To this dire economic situation, we must add the criminal mishandling of the pandemic by Brazilian president Jair Bolsonaro, the most extreme of all the new leaders who have come from the right in Latin America. As a result of his denial of the pandemic and his refusal to impose stricter restrictions on circulation and quarantines, Brazil is producing new strands of COVID-19 which are more contagious, impact heavily on the younger population and cause reinfections affecting not only Brazil but also neighboring countries.

It's a new world for comics

How does this political and economic process impact our topic: comics? The last two decades have witnessed a renewal in the Latin American comics scene. This has been driven by the exchange habilitated by the Internet; by the growing interrelation between scenes previously considered only as "national"; by the experimentation in topics and formats and by the incorporation of authors that come from different artistic activities (illustration, graphic design, visual arts, advertising, animation, etc.).

Twenty-first-century Latin American comics are deeply plural in its inspirations, subjects, drawing styles, political/social concerns and formats. At the same time, its evolution in this century has been marked by the emergence of three phenomena, often articulated with each other: the Internet as a means of publication and publicity; the graphic novel as a privileged format and organizer of the narrative; and, finally, the inclusion of the comic in state-supported cultural and educational projects.

This growth often clashes with the economic reality of Latin American graphic production, made within an increasingly precarious context. The absence of a stable industry, the creation of comics in fragmentary form and the impossibility of artists to live off their trade are key factors. When we speak about a "post-industrial" landscape, we should, however, be wary: not every country in Latin

America had a comics industry, a phenomenon which could be circumscribed to Argentina, México, Brazil and Chile. In other countries, like Colombia, Perú and Bolivia, a comics industry was never a possibility. These are countries which never had a huge periodical publication industry, and therefore a specialized comics scene was out of the question. The reasons are varied: in some cases, such as the Bolivian one, the illiteracy rates were high throughout the 20th century, and therefore the reader market was limited. In other cases, such as the Colombian one, printing and transport difficulties made it extremely expensive to institute an editorial industry. These countries also lacked comprehensive laws and institutions on the State level which encouraged and protected book production. In the case of Perú, such a policy was not implemented until 2016. In the case of Colombia, the Book Law passed in 1993 explicitly excluded comics from the tax exemptions aimed at increasing book production. They consumed what was printed in Argentina, Mexico and Spain which were, traditionally, the Spanish-speaking countries with a thriving editorial industry. In Argentina, what was left of the comics industry collapsed between the 1990s and the 2000s. In Brazil, all that's left is the publications of Mauricio D'Souza. In Chile, there is a growing independent comic scene, but the most popular and significant publications died out in the 1970s. In México, after experiencing a similar worldwide phenomenon usually known as the emergence of "adult comics" during the 1960s and 1970s (Hinds & Tatum, 1992); the industry started a slow decline in the 1980s due to the arrival en masse of superhero comics and manga, which wiped out the local production, reducing it to a handful of independent initiatives. These phenomena, which could be thought of as obstacles or impossibilities for production, have nevertheless prompted alternative solutions or even conceptually, technically and formally disruptive proposals.

This is due, in a great part, to the rise of the Internet and social networks. First through blogs, and then through Facebook, Twitter, Tumblr and Instagram, local artists from all over Latin America were able to share their work and find readers in a much wider area than before. Latin American artists had always had a close relationship. If we delve on the transnational links between comic scenes of the 1950s, 1960s and 1970s, we can find a lot of connections. So this was not a new phenomenon, but the emergence of the Internet helped make collective projects a much easier reality. For example, the magazine *Cábula*, edited by Ernán Cirianni, the blog *Historietas Reales*, or the magazine *Larva* from Colombia, and Carboncito from Peru, which published cartoonists from all over Latin America. Or the Latinotoons project, spearheaded by Juan Navarrete, who successfully organized several publications and shows which mixed comics with indigenous art.

As a counterpoint to the spread of digital initiatives, we can mention the growth of the graphic novel as a privileged format for the collection of comics. Some anthology magazines still exist, particularly in Argentina. In this country, *Fierro* magazine, although it does not have the centrality of its times of glory (1984–1992 and 2006–2017) continues to provide a space of visibility for many authors. This publication's editorial orientation is often a source of disputes and dissatisfaction from the "young turks" who want to modernize the scene and its topics.

Nevertheless, the magazine functions as an engine in much the same way as floppies in the American comics industry do: the possibility of serializing stories in it (and getting paid while doing it) helps offset the cost of their production before eventually being collected in a book. But the norm has become to edit long-form works in book format. This not only opens up avenues of possibility for artists but also presents new challenges. On the one hand, it allows for longer, more ambitious works to be drawn and published. Latin American comics have (mostly) abandoned the episodic nature that characterized them for most of their history, and artists scramble to find the next big topic for their graphic novels. However, the graphic novel format is time consuming, and the making of a book is usually a slow and painstaking process, during which most artists must find an alternative way of earning a living which leaves them with even less time to work on their graphic novels. It also, sometimes, allows for a paradoxical situation in which artists who are not ready to commit to a long-form project end up doing it anyway, and the results are usually a mixed bag when it comes to quality. The graphic novel format has also allowed for a small quantity of independent publishing houses to spring up, which have proven to be surprisingly resilient.

The third main development has been the growth of comic book conventions, events and spaces of sociability, which have taken the relationships that were grown and fostered on the Internet and turned them into real encounters and exchanges. Any list is incomplete, but we can mention: Montevideo Comics (Uruguay, 2002–present), Viñetas Con Altura (Bolivia, 2002–present), Crack Bang Boom (Argentina, 2009–present), Viñetas Sueltas/Comicópolis (Argentina, 2008–2017) and Entreviñetas (Colombia, 2010–present). To these, we must add a series of conferences and academic events which also have a strong artistic presence: Viñetas Serias (Argentina, 2010–2014), Histórias Em Quadrinhos (Brazil, 2012–present) and Dibujos Que Hablan (Chile, 2015–present). These events all occupy a place between a traditional convention, an academic conference, a social gathering and a marketplace. Friendships are fostered, books are sold and questions are posed about the future of the art form. In a way, these conventions are a reflection of the interdependence and interrelation between Latin American countries that had been one of the main characteristics of the "pink tide," with the growing importance that it gave to multilateral institutions such as Mercosur and Parlasur. But they were also signs of the autochthonous dynamics of the field, in which countries with a strong comics tradition such as Argentina have become beacons for a transnational community of comics creators and audiences. However, the central place of Buenos Aires has been quickly disputed by Santiago de Chile, Medellín and Bogotá as the hometowns of some of the most interesting initiatives. Something which is also a testimony to the growing importance and vitality of the comics scenes in those countries.

The growth of these initiatives is also linked to the growing interrelation between comics and state-sponsored projects that deal with literacy, education and, in some cases, a retelling of history. Most of these events have the support of the State in some capacity, either by a direct investment or through logistical supply. But several

Latin American States have also sponsored initiatives through which comic book artists have found the possibility of earning money from their activity, trying to reach a larger audience that they would normally reach. These can be divided into two categories: those collections and initiatives that employed comic book artists in wide-ranging initiatives aimed at boosting literacy (Leer Es Futuro, Argentina, 2013–2015; Suplemento Telam de Historietas, Argentina, 2011–2015 and Bandas Orientales/Bandas Educativas, Uruguay, 2012–present); the incorporation of comics in diverse schemes for the funding of the arts (Fondo Nacional de las Artes, Argentina; Programa de Ação Cultural, San Pablo-Brazil; Fondos Concursables para la Cultura, Uruguay and ProChile, Chile); and the incorporation of comics as a legitimate and independent category in several contests and competitions (Concurso de Letras FNA, Argentina; Prêmio Jabuti, Brazil and Premio Novela Gráfica Ciudades Iberoamericanas, Spain-Madrid). The presence of Spain and France has also been important in these initiatives as sponsors and central countries that invest money and cultural capital in fostering good relations with the Latin American comic scene. They are also important markets for Latin American artists, who aim to publish their works and to win residencies in both countries.

Brazil, on the other hand, presents a particular case of talent export: many Brazilian artists have found enormous success in the US comics industry. Some names are familiar for superhero fans: Ivan Reis, Joe Bennet, Eddy Barrows and Mike Deodato. But there are also noteworthy examples of Brazilian artists going for a more indie route: Rafael Grampá, Fabio Moon and Gabriel Bá.

To this, we must add the multiplicity of inspirations and worldwide comic traditions that are present in our diverse yet shared continent. From local expressions of manga to native superheroes, through the adaptation of the American independent comic and the emergence of abstract comics, Latin American comics production plays and explores with the different languages and styles made possible by the medium. These are processes of resignification and adaptation of these narratives and styles to the discursive requirements of Latin American realities (Martín-Barbero, 1991, 2015).

We aim to explain how comics are made in 21st-century Latin America from a diverse and autochthonous Latin American perspective. Our scope is continental, and we count with contributors from Argentina, Brazil, Bolivia, Chile, Uruguay, Perú, México and Cuba; as well as European specialists, dedicated to Latin American productions.

The origin of comic studies in Latin America can be traced back to the 1960s, when under the influence of structuralism, Marxism, scholars such as Umberto Eco and art critics like Gérald Gassiot-Talabot, the first approaches to comics were produced through a semiotic perspective. In Argentina, Oscar Masotta (1930–1979) performed a short-lived yet seminal intervention in what would eventually become a field of studies between 1967 and 1970. His activities included academic articles, the organization of the First World Comics Biennial at the Di Tella Institute, the avant-gardist comics magazine *LD* and his most famous work, *La historieta en el mundo moderno* (*Comics in the Modern World*, 1970). Oscar Steinberg would follow in his footsteps by publishing yet another seminal work, *Leyendo Historietas* (*Reading Comics*) in 1977. With the return of democracy, along with the renewal of Latin American studies (mainly with the development of cultural studies with a postcolonial or decolonial perspective), we also find in Argentina the contribution of Anibal Ford, Jorge Rivera and Eduardo Romano, *Medios de comunicación y cultura popular* (*Media and Popular Culture*, 1985), including comics alongside with radio theater, chronicle, etc. The work aims to rethink "popular" as a means of resistance inscribed in the Peronist tradition, an idea that will be crucial to comprehend most of the discourses of the cultural field during the post-dictatorship period (Rivera, 1992; Sasturain, 1993). Starting in the late 1990s, a new set of scholar researchers would revitalize the field of comics studies, trying to rebuild the ties with the pioneers (Vazquez, 2010; von Sprecher & Reggiani, 2010; Berone, 2011; Fernández, 2012; Levín, 2013; Cosse, 2014; Scarzanella, 2016; Burkart, 2017; Turnes, 2018, 2019; Gandolfo, 2022).

Also in 1970, in Brazil, journalist and comics enthusiast Álvaro de Moya published *Shazam!*, a take on comics through communication studies, which could be understood as part of the structuralist turn that humanities were taking in the Western hemisphere. Brazil would also experience a rebirth of comics studies during the 21st century (Júnior, 2004; Vergueiro & dos Santos, 2005; Vergueiro, 2017; Fernandes, 2011; Ramos, 2011; Lima Gomes, 2018; Chinen, 2019). But without a doubt, it was Ariel Dorfman and Armand Mattelart's *Para leer al Pato Donald* (*How to Read Donald Duck*), published in 1971 during Salvador Allende's socialist government in Chile, which made a mark and caused a series of polemics that turned into a document of the 1970s *Zeitgeist* in Latin America. From a Marxist perspective, the authors interpreted Disney comics as one of the most effective tools that US imperialism had made use of to effectively colonize the imagination and the minds of the masses of the continent. Imperialism wasn't just about political influence and primary resources exploitation; it also meant the constant imposition of a foreign culture as "natural" through entertainment. This was far from being a novelty, since both right-wing and left-wing nationalism had been pointing fingers at the United States as the cause of the alienation of Latin American people from their own culture and traditions for decades.

But Dorfman and Mattelart made their intervention in a critical moment during the region's agitated political times, proposing a methodological approach that mixed communications studies with direct political intervention, far from the first, more scholarly semiotic approaches. An echo of this approach can be found in Juan Acevedo's *Para hacer historietas* (*To Make Comics*, 1978). The Peruvian cartoonist proposed the idea of popular workshops where the comics form could be reappropriated by the workers, in a way that would transform the ideological and aesthetic possibilities of comics. This had already been tried during Salvador Allende's government in Chile, after the buyout of Zig Zag publishing house (the one that published the Disney comics Dorfman and Mattelart had taken into account in their work); now renamed Quimantú publishing house (in Mapudungún, "sun of knowledge"). The idea of an assembly model which included the workers (such as printers) to produce comics closer to the workers' reality and needs was disrupted by the 1973 military coup, but part of that experience was compiled in the lesser known second part of *How to Read Donald Duck: Superman y sus amigos del alma* (*Superman and His Soul Friends*, Dorfman and Jofré, 1974). The field of Chilean comics studies, however, has also been revitalized through a series of researchers spearheaded by Jorge Montealegre, himself a former political prisoner of Pinochet's regime (Montealegre, 2011; 2013, p. 201; Hassón, 2015, 2017; Rojas Flores, 2016; Domínguez Jeria, 2017).

This first wave of comic studies would be cut short by the series of military coups that imposed extremely violent, repressive regimes all through the Southern Cone. The forced exile of many scholars, as well as the killing and persecution of intellectuals, the interventions of universities and the actions against the students, would interrupt many lines of research. Comics, however, would discreetly fly under the military radar and kept on being discussed through specialized journalism, often carried by comics authors (writers in particular). It wouldn't be until the late 1990s, and especially the early 2000s, that comics studies would slowly but steadily grow, exponentially revitalizing the field of studies and increasing the academic works on comics during the last 10 years.

Not just renowned academia figures such as Oscar Steimberg, Miguel Rojas Mix or Néstor García Canclini would keep on writing about comics, but new waves of scholars would retake the interrupted lines of study while being influenced by more contemporary authors such as Scott McCloud and Thierry Groensteen, among many others. This, of course, presents a double-edged sword: on the one hand, the access to new sources of information and knowledge has allowed to improve comics studies in Latin America and broaden the field's perspectives and objects of study. On the other hand, Latin American studies are clearly still too constrained by European and North American resources and perspectives, which added to the impoverished and restricted access to academic life in the region, making it more difficult to develop a field in its own terms.

In this sense, and going back to what we discussed at the beginning, this volume presents itself as a question: how can we decolonize our academic perspective and allow Latin American comics studies to flourish and advance beyond both historical and current restrictions? This doesn't mean turning inward, but rather valuing the development of regional nets and knowledge exchange through events, shared projects and collaborative interventions. Also, it means placing these questions in other non-Latin spaces where similar issues are being brought up, as to enrich the dialogue both within and without academic spaces. As García Canclini (2001) has proposed, if hybridization is key in understanding comics, then there is already a historical characteristic that ties the medium with Latin American history, itself a result of the hybridization of Ameri-Indian and European culture. Not without conflict, of course, but that is the point: not to overlook the Gordian knot of violence that crosses our history, but to face it in full without "dodging" the thorny issues, developing new tools that will allow us to better think and contribute to our field of studies.

The never-ending struggle: an overview of contents

This volume contains contributions from researchers from Argentina, Bolivia, Brazil, Chile, Germany, Mexico, Perú, Cuba, Spain and Uruguay. When we first started putting it together, it was our ambition to cover as much ground as possible and to shed light on the biggest number of national scenes and artists. Alas, some areas presented problems when we tried to cover them. We particularly regret the absence of Colombia, one of the most interesting, diverse and thriving comics scenes of recent note in Latin America. Colombia has emerged in the last two decades as a hub of production which comprises both punky looking anti-establishment comics and thoughtful considerations into Colombian history and politics (Suárez & Uribe-Jongbloed, 2016). Sadly, and despite our efforts, we were unable to secure a contribution from the different Colombian academics we contacted. Ecuador also represents a similar case, with a nascent and growing comics production, which shows a heavy focus on educational comics. We experienced the same difficulty getting in touch with people to cover it. However, the figure of Ecuadorian-Colombian author Powerpaola hovers over many of the articles included here, and her presence and influence are vital to explain not only the growing Colombian comics production but also the rising diversity on the Argentine scene.

Other countries, such as Paraguay and Venezuela, still have a pretty low comics production. In the case of Venezuela, one must also factor the ongoing political and economic crisis that the country has experienced for the last decade, and which has disrupted the lives of its citizens and made the development of any cultural industry enormously difficult.

When we started putting the book together, we noticed something that struck us heavily: the majority of articles dealt with works which auscultate the past like a throbbing open wound. Memory is one of the privileged topics of 21st-century comics, and works like *Maus*, *Persepolis* and *Fun Home* and figures like Joe Sacco cast a large shadow. However, we were stunned by such a decisive need to settle scores with the past and to revisit traumatic events which ended with a decisive loss for popular struggles. In a way, we felt as if these texts and the comics they analyze have a need to rewrite history in such a way as to make sense of historical defeats and to bring light and hope through artistic activity. What politics and history undid, comics are trying to sew together again.

The book is divided into two parts, which comprise the two main fields of research on comics studies in Latin America in the last decade: Politics, Protest and Memory; and Genre and Sexual Dissidence.

The first section concerns itself with the different ways in which comics and graphic novels have dealt with the Latin American past, with the remembrance of lost struggles toward social justice and with newer processes of social protest which are reshaping the political landscape of our continent. It opens with Tania Pérez Cano's article about "Borges, Inspector de Aves," Lucas Nine's masterful reimagining of Jorge Luis Borges as a private eye on the Dashiell Hammett vein, who solves crimes related to Argentina's literary circle of the time. Perez Cano's article analyzes not only the way Nine's reimagining rewrites the history of Argentinian literature but also the political coordinates of the traditionally anti-Peronist Argentine literary and art scenes. It also analyzes the way that Nine constructs a symbolic syncretism between high modernism and populist politics.

The volume continues with Laura Nallely Hernández Nieto article on *Grito de Victoria*, a graphic novel by Augusto Mora. Through the lens of the graphic novel, Hernández Nieto reckons with the way the Mexican State has never had a true politics of memory, and the way different episodes of State violence remain unexamined and kept apart from the official governmental narrative. The article also sheds light on the continuity of violence that still afflicts Mexican politics.

This is the same thematic locus that is covered by Elena Masarah Revuelta and Gerardo Vilches Fuentes in their article, which focuses on the way Chilean and Spanish comics have dealt with the long-term consequences and lingering traumas from two of the longest dictatorships imposed on Spanish-speaking countries. The political systems of both Spain and Chile after Francisco Franco's and Augusto Pinochet's regimes, respectively, were built on the notion that the crimes of those years were not to be reevaluated and prosecuted. They imposed a reconciliatory politics which left torture, disappearance and death as festering wounds under the new political regimes. Masarah Revuelta and Vilches Fuentes cast their eyes over a vast swath of comics on both countries whose authors took upon themselves to return to those years in replacement of clear politics of memory at the State level.

This is a similar approach to the one that's unearthed by María Victoria Saibene in her article on historical comics on Uruguay. Here, too, the post-dictatorial politics were those of reconciliation rather than justice and memory. The interesting aspect is that, through the availability of a series of public funds that artists were able to acquire in open competition, the State became an indirect promoter of a series of graphic novels which dealt with the 1970s, the actions of the Tupamaros and the internal exile of political activists. This article illustrates perfectly how important are the actions at the State level to sustain comic production in Latin America.

From there we move on to Brazil, which is touched upon in two different essays. Marilda Lopes Pinheiro Queluz's articles casts its eye on two graphic novels which deal with social history as a way to recuperate the experiences of the downtrodden. On the one hand, Luli Penna's *Sem Dó*, which focuses on the history of a group of women in 1920s São Paulo, and the way fashion, art, culture and city life function as ways to escape oppression and reaffirm identity. On the other hand, *Angola Janga* by Marcelo D'Salete and the way this renowned graphic novel, perhaps the most important one produced in Brazil in recent years, recuperates the secret history of the slave societies of 17th-century Brazil.

This thread is picked up by Ivan Lima Gomes' article, which juxtaposes a comic produced in the 1950s with the work of Marcelo D'Salete to reconstruct a history of blackness in Brazilian comics. This blackness has often been suppressed, not only in the official History of the country but also in its comics. Lima Gomes questions this erasure in historical, aesthetical and ethical terms and poses questions of utmost importance if a diverse future for comics in Brazil is to be had.

Finally, we close this section with Hugo Hinojosa's article which deals with "hot" images produced during the heady days of protest and social change in Chile from 2019 onward. Hinojosa's article rescues poignant images and the way they dialogue with the history being written on the streets. It is an article about a still open process, which had its most recent episode on the December 2021 elections that made Gabriel Boric, a political activist that came to notoriety during the 2011 student protests, the youngest ever President of Chile. That's why we believe it's a fitting closure to this first section.

The second part, titled "Genre and Sexual Dissidence," deals with the way comics and graphic novels in Latin America have incorporated the demand for more diversity, for female and sexually diverse authors and for a representation in which they are present. The section opens with the article by Jorge Sánchez, which turns its eye toward two graphic novels: *Las Sinaventuras de Jaime Pardo* (*The Non-adventures of Jaime Pardo*) by Chilean author Vicente Plaza; and *Notas al Pie* (*Footnotes*) by Argentine author Nacha Vollenweider. Both works deal with the changes and inscriptions that memory leaves on the body, as well as the often complex relationship between memory and history. This article serves as a bridge between sections, as it's interested both in memory and in the body, history and sexuality.

The section follows with Jasmin Wrobel's article, which continues the ongoing work of reconstructing feminist genealogies for Latin American comics production, a task that has also been undertaken by artists collectives such as Chicks on Comics and researchers such as Cintia Lima Crescêncio (2018), Mariela Acevedo (2019), Estefanía Henao and Lina Florez (2021), among others. Through a precise and punctilious reading of images, Wrobel traces a chronology that starts during the Spanish Empire and finishes with Chilean artist Francisca "Panchulei" Cárcamo Rojas as a representative of this genealogy.

Then, we turn our attention to two countries with a growing production and importance in the Latin American comics scene: Bolivia and Perú. In Marcela Murillo's chapter, we confront the different faces of the Bolivian "Chola," the traditional indigenous woman who, according to the long-standing liberal political gospel of the Andean country, must be modernized or left behind. Murillo rescues several comics which attempt to present a positive version of the "Chola," in accordance and in synchronicity with the new policies of cultural identity spearheaded by the governments of Evo Morales in particular and the MAS (acronym for *Movimiento al Socialismo*, Morales´ political party) in general.

Carla Sagástegui Heredia, on the other hand, reflects on the way two female artists from Perú, Águeda Noriega and Ale Torres, represent the behaviors and bodies of women who are stigmatized as "improper." Sagástegui Heredia reframes these behaviors as emancipated and shows how these new comic artists are picking up the torch left by Marisa Godinez, one of the few Peruvian women who dedicated themselves to this profession during the 20th century, to carve their own space of liberation and reflection, away from societal norms.

The section turns to sexual dissidence in Janek Scholz's chapter, which also serves as a way to highlight the way transnationalism is a major issue in 21st-century Latin American comics, linking political, diasporic and gendered stories and experiences across borders. His analysis of *Guadalupe*, a comic created by Brazilian artists Angelica Freitas and Odyr, but which makes Mexico and Mexican mythology its thematic locus, shows how sexual dissidence is incorporated into Latin American comics, even though some of the graphic novels infused with this topic still do not grapple with it completely.

Finally, the book closes with Rodrigo O. Ottonello's chapter about Diego Parés and the psychosexual stories of *El Señor y La Señora Rispo* (*Mr. and Ms. Rispo*). In this chapter, Ottonello traces back the novelties and progresses of Argentine comics in the 21st century to the collapse of the canonized standards during the 1990s. It also deals with that maligned juxtaposition: the reader of comics as sexual pervert and lowlife. In this article our ambition comes full circle: from the dank pits of stigma and low culture, to the lofty heights of memory work and political relevance, Latin American comics, nevertheless, are still made of the same substance and should be treated as a continuous attempt to depict our village, our country and our continent, in ever thriving, colorful and deep tones.

Bibliography/Literature

Acevedo Fernández de Paredes, J. (1978). *Para Hacer Historietas*. Editorial Popular.

Acevedo, M. (2019). *Sextualidades gráficas: Sexualización de lenguaje y expresiones de la diferencia sexual en la revista Fierro, 1984–1992 y 2006–2015*. Universidad de Buenos Aires, Facultad de Ciencias Sociales.

Ansaldi, W., & Giordano, V. (2012). *América Latina: La construcción del orden Vol. 1*. Ariel.

Berone, L. (2011). *La fundación del discurso sobre la historieta en Argentina: De la 'Operación Masotta' a un campo en dispersión*. Escuela de Ciencias de la Información, Facultad de Derecho y Ciencias Sociales, Universidad Nacional de Córdoba.

Burkart, M. (2017). *De Satiricón a HUM®: Risa, cultura y política en los años setenta*. Miño y Dávila.

Catalá Carrasco, J. L., Drinot, P., & Scorer, J. (2017). *Comics and memory in Latin America*. University of Pittsburgh Press.

Chinen, N. (2019). *O negro nos quadrinhos do Brasil*. Editora Peirópolis.

Cosse, I. (2014). *Mafalda historia social y política*. Fondo de Cultura Económica.

de Moya, A. (1970). *Shazam!*. Editôra Perspectiva.

Domínguez Jeria, P. (2017). "La representación de cuerpos femeninos en el discurso multimodal del cómic." *Revista Isla Flotante*, n° 6. Retrieved on September 16, 2022 from La representación de cuerpos femeninos en el discurso multimodal del cómic (academia.cl).

Dorfman, A., & Jofré, M. (1974). *Superman y sus amigos del alma*. Galerna.

Dorfman, A., & Mattelart, A. (2007). *Para leer al Pato Donald*. Siglo XXI Editores.

Dunlap, C. J., Jr. (2001, November 29). "Law and military interventions: Preserving humanitarian values in 21st conflicts." Prepared for the Humanitarian Challenges in Military Intervention Conference, Carr Center for Human Rights Policy/Kennedy School of Government/Harvard University, Washington, DC.

Eco, U. (1984). *Apocalípticos e integrados*. Lumen.

Fernandes, G. (2011). "Humor e identidade: Brasilidade em Laerte e Mauricio de Sousa." *Revista USP*, n. 60, pp. 60–72.
Fernández, L. C. (2012). *Historieta y Resistencia. Arte y Política en Oesterheld: 1968–1978*. Editorial Universidad Nacional de Cuyo/EDIUNC.
Fernández l'Hoeste, H. D., & Poblete, J. (2009). *Redrawing the nation. National identity in Latin/o American comics*. Palgrave Macmillan.
Florez, L., & Henao, E. (2021). "Apuntes para la construcción de una genealogía feminista de la historieta colombiana." *Revista de la Red Intercátedras de Historia de América Latina Contemporánea*, 15, pp. 87–112.
Ford, A., Rivera, J., & Romano, E. (1985). *Medios de comunicación y cultura popular*. Legasa.
Foster, D. W. (1989). *From Mafalda to los Supermachos: Latin American graphic humor as popular culture*. Lynne Rienner Publisher.
Gandolfo, A. (2022). *La oposición dibujada. Política, oficios y gráfica de los caricaturistas políticos argentinos (1955–1976)*. Tren en Movimiento.
García Canclini, N. (2001). *Culturas Híbridas: Estrategias para entrar y salir de la modernidad*. Paidós.
Hassón, M. (2015). *Pin-up: Comics Picarescos en Chile*. NautaColecciones.
Hassón, M. (2017). *Sátira política en Chile (1858–2016): Catálogo de 150 años de publicaciones de humor, sátira y política*. Nauta Colecciones.
Hinds, H. E., & Tatum, C. M. (1992). *Not just for children: The Mexican comic book in the late 1960s and 1970s*. Greenwood.
Júnior, G. (2004). *A guerra dos gibis: A formação do mercado editorial brasileiro e a censura aos quadrinhos, 1933–1964*. Companhia das letras.
Levín, F. (2013). *Humor político en tiempos de represión: Clarín, 1973–1983*. Siglo XXI.
Lima Crescêncio, C. (2018). "As mulheres ou os silêncios do humor: uma análise da presença de mulheres no humor gráfico brasileiro (1968–2011)." *Revista Ártemis*, 26, N. 1, pp. 53–75.
Lima Gomes, I. (2018). *Os novos homens do amanhã: Projetos e disputa em torno dos quadrinhos na América Latina (Brasil e Chile, anos 1960–1970)*. Prismas.
Martín-Barbero, J. (1991). *De los medios a las mediaciones. Comunicación, cultura y hegemonía*. Gustavo Gili.
Martín-Barbero, J. (2015). "¿Desde dónde pensamos la comunicación hoy?" *Chasqui, Revista latinoamericana de comunicación*, n° 128, pp. 13–29.
Masotta, O. (1970). *La historieta en el mundo moderno*. Paidós.
Montealegre, J. (2013). *Coré: El tesoro que creíamos perdido*. Asterión.
Montealegre, J. (2014). *Carne de estatua: Allende, caricatura y monumento*. Mandrágora.
Montealegre, J., & Jiménez Cortés, L. (ed.). (2011). *Apariciones y desapariciones de Luis Jiménez*. Asterión.
Ramos, P. (2011). *Faces do Humor – Uma Aproximação entre Tiras e Piadas*. Zarabatana.
Rivera, J. B. (1992). *Panorama de la historieta en la Argentina*. Libros del Quirquincho.
Rojas Flores, J. (2016). *Las historietas en Chile 1962–1982: Industria, ideología y prácticas sociales*. LOM Ediciones.
Sasturain, J. (1993). *El domicilio de la aventura*. Colihue.
Scarzanella, E. (2016). *Abril: un editor italiano en Buenos Aires, de Perón a Videla*. Fondo de Cultura Económica.
Scorer, J. (ed.). (2020). *Comics beyond the page in Latin America*. UCL Press.
Steimberg, O. (1977). *Leyendo Historietas*. Nueva Visión.
Suárez, F., & Uribe-Jongbloed, E. (2016). Making comics as artisans: Comic book production in Colombia. In *Cultures of comics work*. Palgrave Macmillan.

Turnes, P. (2018). *El exilio de las formas: Alack Sinner de Muñoz y Sampayo*. Tren en Movimiento.

Turnes, P. (2019). *La excepción en la regla: la obra historietística de Alberto Breccia (1962–1993)*. Miño y Dávila.

Vazquez, L. (2010). *El Oficio de las Viñetas. La industria de la historieta argentina* (1era ed.). Paidós.

Vergueiro, W. (2017). *Panorama das Histórias em Quadrinhos no Brasil*. Peiropolis.

Vergueiro, W., & dos Santos, R. E. (2005). *O Tico-Tico: Centenário da Primeira Revista em Quadrinhos do Brasil*. Opera Graphica.

Von Sprecher, R., & Reggiani, F. (ed.). (2010). *Héctor Germán Oesterheld: de El Eternauta a Montoneros*. Escuela de Ciencias de la Información, Facultad de Derecho y Ciencias Sociales, Universidad Nacional de Córdoba.

PART I
Politics, protest and memory

1
INTERTEXTUALITY AND ICONIC IMAGES IN LUCAS NINE'S "BORGES, INSPECTOR DE AVES"[1]

Tania Pérez Cano

In 1946, Argentine writer Jorge Luis Borges (1899–1986)[2] was forced by the government of Juan Domingo Perón (1895–1974) to leave his appointment at the Miguel Cané Library.[3] He was offered a position as "poultry and rabbits inspector"[4] in the municipality of Buenos Aires. Borges had already published many of his most well-known short stories, such as "Tlön, Uqbar, Orbis Tertius" and "The Circular Ruins" (both in 1940); "The Garden of Forking Paths" (1941) and "The Aleph" (1945). He was also an outspoken anti-Peronist. It is said that the Argentine Society of Writers (SADE), outraged at the way Borges was being treated, held a formal dinner to celebrate him. During that dinner, Borges read a text that contained his famous phrase: "dictatorships promote oppression, dictatorships promote servility, dictatorships promote cruelty; more loathsome is the fact that they promote idiocy" (1946). Borges, of course, never accepted the job as a municipal inspector, and instead went on to reassert his position as a public speaker and intellectual.

In *Borges, Poultry Inspector*, comic artist Lucas Nine (Buenos Aires, 1975)[5] creates a fictional speculation about how Borges accepted the position offered to him by the Peronist government and became a happy "poultry inspector" dressed with a trench coat and fedora *à la Humphrey Bogart*, trying to solve crimes at municipal fairs. More precisely, this fictional speculation is an example of *alternative (or alternate) history*, that is, a fictional narrative in which one historical fact is selected, and then altered, to offer an imagined, different outcome and a different set of causes and consequences (see Figure 1.1).[6]

Nine dives into his fictional uchronia right at the beginning of his sequential narrative, when he offers the reader both a historical fact and the alternative version of Borges as "poultry inspector" (Figure 1.2): "Did you know that the great Argentine writer was designated "Municipal Poultry and Rabbits Inspector" in 1946? The following is one of his adventures, which happened while he was performing his duties and in full possession of his mental faculties" (Nine, 2017: 9).

DOI: 10.4324/9781003333296-3

20 Tania Pérez Cano

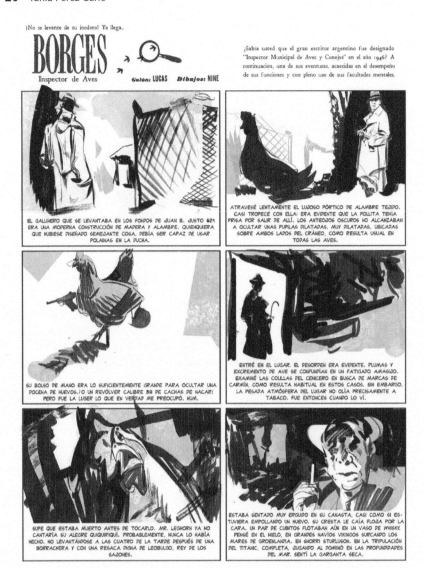

FIGURE 1.2 The first six panels of *Borges, Poultry Inspector*. In the upper right corner, a caption introduces the reader to the "origin story" of how the writer became a man of action and went to investigate the Argentine chicken underworld. The caption contains both a historical fact and the alternative history of Borges as "poultry inspector."

Lucas Nine's *historieta*[7] presupposes the existence of a cultural icon, the writer Jorge Luis Borges, and his defining role in the culture and politics of 20th-century Argentina. Making Borges the protagonist of a comic provides the vehicle that makes it possible to revisit this cultural and political history and transform it into an ironic, satirical, sequential narrative that also constitutes an example of uchronia or alternative history. I argue that intertextuality[8] and iconic images are the central creative practices that give shape to the graphic narrative in *Borges, Poultry Inspector*.

Mariana Casale O'Ryan (2014) defines *cultural icon* as "an empty vessel into which a culture pours its anxieties and questions about identity" (7), arguing that Borges occupies that position, and that the writer's image embodies the most important contradictions and debates that configured Argentina as a nation over the past century. She affirms that her work "proceeds by deconstructing certain oppositions surrounding the figure of Borges in order to expose the ways in which dichotomous notions such as popular/high culture; centre/periphery or nationalism/Euro-centrism are played out on the construction of certain images of the author" (5). Her analysis closely follows that of Beatriz Sarlo, who wrote about the "the empty space called Borges" and explained that the writer became: "a practically limitless space, as if his work were a culture, a system of myths, a typology of characters, and a form of rhetoric. But also, so much more: attributions, anecdotes, likely or unlikely declarations documented or simply attributed to the 'locus Borges'" (2015: 33).

Borges then became a sign, a cultural artifact.[9] Nine takes that "empty space" that is Borges and fills it with other iconic objects and images from film *noir*, journalism, mass media, popular culture, oral traditions and tango lyrics. This mixing of codes and genres adds to the ever-expanding universe of intertexts and discourses that the mythic figure of Borges produces, to enter as a comic character into a universe of parody, satire and the absurd. As a result, a new iconic image is forged: the figure of Borges as a film *noir* detective in a hilarious plot filled with feathers and scarecrows. The archival repertoire of images, anecdotes, photographs, cartoons, and interviews that made Borges an icon, "a widely recognized and well established" image,[10] functions as a colossal intertext. Lucas Nine, for his part, is perfectly aware of this intertextual process. He makes it the center of his narrative, which is also a reflection on how the Argentine comic tradition and history influence his ability to tell stories using the sequential medium. The artist articulates this in an interview with Juan Pablo Cinelli for the *Tiempo Argentino* newspaper (2017):

> To mention Borges, at least in Argentina, means somehow alluding to Perón and the issues that representatives of the elite always had with mass culture. . . . But, if I propose that my fictional Borges accepts the position of poultry inspector – which the real Borges, as we know, never did –, I have to acknowledge the beginning of an ideological change in the character. This is something that is not so alien to Borges if we recall that story of his, "El Sur," in which the writer splits into an alter ego that leaves the bookish world to end up accepting the knife that a countryman offers him in the middle

of *la pampa*. In my book, that knife would come to be his designation as a poultry inspector.

Pablo Brescia (2006: 48) discusses the notion of Borges as a "literary object" and explores what happened when Borges was *written*[11] by analyzing two stories, "La entrevista" ["The Interview," 1979], by Argentine writer Mempo Giardinelli (1947), and "Borges el comunista" ["Borges the Communist," 1977], by Mexican writer René Avilés Fabila (1940–2016). Brescia concludes that both texts illustrated the tension between tradition and innovation, and the "anxiety of influence" because the resulting new texts were parodic and employed writing strategies that reproduced those of Borges. In sum, Brescia asserts that Borges was the first to "call for the death of the author, to understand the author-function, to become a character in his own stories, and to be irreverent with him. He began to 'dis/de-authorize' himself and became, in the process, a literary object" (51).

It is also not the first time that Borges appears as a character in a comic strip. *Perramus*, by Juan Sasturain (1945) and Alberto Breccia (1919–1993), published in Argentina between 1985 and 1989, depicts a Borges who receives the Nobel Prize in Literature (something that never happened) and is a supporter of the *montoneros*, a leftist urban guerrilla group that was active between the 1950s and 1970s.[12] In 1986, Osvaldo Soriano (1943–1997) called *Perramus*, "The first masterpiece about the Argentine dictatorship" (2016: 9). *Borges, inspector de aves* is both a tribute and a parody of *Perramus*. If in the post-dictatorship comic the author helps the protagonist, Perramus, challenge the "Marshals," who represent the repressors, in Nine's narrative the *perramus* is just a brand name for our "poultry inspector's" trench coat, a nod to American *film noir*. In my interview with Nine (2019), the artist acknowledged the intertextual connection with *Perramus*, particularly regarding his drawing style and use of *collage*:

> In *Borges . . .*, I reused photographic collage in certain parts, in backgrounds, especially, sort of emulating Alberto Breccia's collages, of whose work this cartoon is both a tribute and a parody (in such a way that the serious "Breccism" of the image collides with the absurdity of the intrigue).
>
> (255)

On the other hand, Borges has had a significant presence in graphic media, and his influence on comic and popular culture has a global reach. Mariana Casale O'Ryan (2014) offers information about caricatures of the writer that appeared as early as the 1920s:

> Several cartoon depictions of Borges appeared in the press in the Southern Cone, the earliest one of which is thought to be in Buenos Aires's magazine *Caras y Caretas* in the 1920s. But it was only in the 1970s that both Montevideo and Buenos Aires began to see more frequent drawings of the now world-famous author in their pages. In 1973, for example, Argentine

newspaper *La Opinión,* which was considered "mandarín absoluto del mundo cultural"[13] of the city of Buenos Aires, published a cartoon which shows a resigned Borges holding an umbrella to shelter from adverse criticism represented as raining words. It is an accurate depiction of the writer's position at the center of fundamental debates taking place on both sides of the Río de la Plata. Headed by Uruguayan critics Angel Rama and Emir Rodríguez Monegal, these debates concerned the place and responsibilities of literary production in the socio-political configuration of Latin America.

(115–116)

Casale O'Ryan (2014:116–121) also documents the drawings of Borges made by Uruguayan-Argentine cartoonist Hermenegildo Sábat (1933–2018), published in *La Opinión,* some of which became part of the volume *Georgie Dear* (1974).[14] As an intertextual reference, Borges and his work are ubiquitous in the world of comics. Pablo Turnes (2015) analyzes the ways in which in *Un tal Daneri,* by Alberto Breccia and Carlos Trillo (1943–2011), the atmosphere of the city and the themes with which the story deals, "inevitably refer to the works of J.L Borges" (189). The title itself reveals the connection with Borges, as the name is that of the character Carlos Argentino Daneri in the short story "El Aleph."

It is impossible not to mention the adaptation of Borges's story "Historia del guerrero y la cautiva" in *La Argentina en pedazos,* authored by Ricardo Piglia (1941–2017), with drawings by Alfredo Flores and adaptation by Norberto Buscaglia. *La Argentina en pedazos* started being published in the first issue of the *Fierro*[15] magazine, in 1984 (Pérez del Solar, 2011: 59) in a post-dictatorial context. It is a combination of brief essays by Piglia, followed by the comic adaptation of selected texts of Argentine authors. As Piglia himself states:

> *Argentina in Pieces.* A history of Argentine violence through fiction. Which story is that? The reconstruction of a plot in which one can decipher or imagine the traces left in literature by power relations, by forms of violence. Marks on the body and on the language, which allow the reconstruction of the figure of the country that the writers hallucinate. That story should be read against the light of the "true" story and as its nightmare.
>
> (1993: 8)

Javier de Navascués (2017) dedicates an article to the analysis of the "hidden influence" of Borges in Hugo Pratt's graphic novel *Tango,* published in Argentina in 1985 under the title *Y todo a media luz* (165). *Todo a media luz* is a famous tango popularized by Carlos Gardel, with lyrics by Uruguayan writer Carlos César Lenzi (1895–1963) and music by Argentinian composer Edgardo Donato (1897–1963). According to Navascués, Italian cartoonist Hugo Pratt (1927–1995), who created the character Corto Maltés, denied Borges's influence on *Tango* because of the writer's statements in favor of the Argentine dictatorship (167). Navascués also refers to Cristian Palacios' study of the intertextual dialogue between Borges and

Fontanarrosa (1944–2007), and the mark the Argentine writer left on British scriptwriters and cartoonists such as Alan Moore, Neil Gaiman, Peter Milligan and Grant Morrison (159–160).

To this list, I would like to add the graphic novel *Trazo de tiza* (published in English as *Streak of Chalk* in 1994), by Galician comic artist Miguelanxo Prado. Prado includes a quote from "Tlön, Uqbar, Orbis Tertius" at the beginning of his novel. It is the well-known passage in which Borges and Bioy talk about the "execution of a novel in the first person" that "incurred various contradictions, which allowed a few readers . . . the prediction of an atrocious or banal reality" (Borges, 1999: 264). The hint points to the creation of imagined worlds, invites the reader to doubt the "simplicity" of Prado's narrative, and to look for clues to a fantastic plot.[16] It is important to note that Prado includes a tribute to Hugo Pratt at the end of *Streak of Chalk*.

In all the texts and *historietas* we have revisited, the intertextual references to Borges center around the writer's poetics or politics. What stands out is that even when imagining Borges "not as he was, but as he should have been" (De la Calle, 2016: 6), none of these intertextual approaches subverts the position of the writer as a canonical authority that needs to be taken "seriously." Pablo Brescia quotes Sylvia Malloy (2008) in a second article that discusses Borges as a "literary object." He says: "Borges is read with respect (or with resentment, which is another form of respect) but not with the respect he deserves: that of irreverence" (25). Hence our "poultry inspector."

The "poultry inspector": flying across gutters

Nine published his *Borges* as a book by Hotel de las Ideas[17] in 2017, after it appeared as a series in the magazine *Fierro* in 2012. There are three main narrative lines in *Borges*, all of them centered on the cases the inspector tries to solve. The first narrative line (pp. 9–10) that introduces the reader to the precise moment in time in which the uchronia or alternative history is located – as I previously mentioned – deals with a rooster that had been involved in the sex trafficking of hens. Our inspector's second adventure is titled, "The Parrot Who Knew Too Much" (pp. 11–12). In it, Borges confronts his friend, writer Adolfo Bioy Casares (1914–1999), while investigating the murder of a parrot called Pedrito. The bird was known for singing the Peronist March. The confrontation plays with the famous friendship between Borges and Bioy Casares. Just a few examples of their long-lasting collaboration include working under the pseudonym of H. Bustos Domecq with writer Silvina Ocampo (1903–1993) on the *Antología de la literatura fantástica* (1940) [*Anthology of Fantastic Literature*], published in English as *Book of Fantasy*. They also authored a collection of detective stories titled *Seis problemas para Don Isidro Parodi* (1942) [*Six Problems for Don Isidro Parodi*]. In Nine's graphic novel, Borges discovers Bioy's involvement in the assassination of Pedrito, the parrot. The fictional Bioy Casares, in turn, discovers that this "other Borges" uses foul language and is an enthusiastic Perón supporter. The story's last panel is an irreverent, ironic commentary on the designation of Borges as a "poultry inspector," about his relationship with the mass media, with obscenity and, of course, about the intellectual's position in society. The panel reproduces a photograph inserted in a form under a headline that reads: "Be part of the future," with Borges addressing the readers and trying to recruit them for inspector jobs:

> Yes, my friends. I used to spend my afternoons locked in my bathroom translating the beautiful Danish *kennigars* into Spanish with one hand, when I decided to accept my destiny, encrypted in that designation that fell from the sky. My life changed completely, you can believe it! That can be your story, too! Just fill out the attached form.
> Yes, I want to be part of law enforcement as a:
> A- Hog inspector
> B- Empanada filling inspector
> C- Dice and dice cup inspector

FIGURE 1.3 Collage that combines a photograph with a parodic, apocryphal advertising message by Borges.

The third narrative line is entitled "Operation Scarecrow" (pp. 13–157) and is the most complex of all three storylines. In this saga, writer Oliverio Girondo (1890–1967) is Borges's archenemy in an upside-down world in which Girondo, who in real life was married to writer Norah Lange (1905–1972), becomes a sinister figure who has created golems made of "mud and literature" (Nine, 2017: 133, 138). Girondo has kidnapped artist Xul Solar (1887–1963) and forced him to create golems who resemble scarecrows. Each of the automatons corresponds to a poem in Girondo's book *Espantapájaros (al alcance de todos)* [*Scarecrow (Within Everyone's Reach)*, published in 1932 (Hazelton, 2018: xxxi). Girondo commands his scarecrows, who help him execute his plan to dominate the world. Both characters, Borges and Girondo, fight for the love of Norah Lange, Borges using his authority as a poultry inspector and Girondo his ability to fly.

In Nine's graphic fiction, Girondo is the antagonist of a sentimental Borges, who supports Perón and is capable of risking everything for the woman he loves. The evil golems who obey Girondo recite a poem from Girondo's book *Scarecrow* when they are going to die. The huge *papier mâché* doll that the actual Girondo used to publicize his book, his "academic scarecrow,"[18] is transformed into an automaton that threatens Borges when he manages to sneak into a party held by Girondo and Norah Lange at their home.[19]

Borges, of course, disguises himself as a chicken. The party scene deserves attention because it is a sequential representation of the Bakhtinian carnival, complete with costumes, masks, and ritualistic invectives against literature and authority, including that of Borges himself. There are panels full of "gags" typical of silent film comedy such as a multitudinous fight among the attendants and a duel between Girondo and Borges, all seasoned with insults such as: "Death to engagé art!" (78). To summarize, all these are manifestations of what Bakhtin described as the carnival, with its comical negation of official culture and solemnity.[20]

Although it is true that Nine creates a character that is, in many respects, an image in negative of the writer's mythic figure, the "poultry inspector" retains his obsession with encyclopedias, mirrors and labyrinths; he meets the gaucho Gauna, who guides him to Girondo's mansion; rescues his friend Xul Solar and makes fun of his fellow writer, Witold Gombrowicz (1904–1969). Our "poultry inspector" constantly acts in a way that parodies Borges's persona – for example, if he drinks, he orders the drinks in alphabetical order.

Because the narrative is simultaneously an adventure novel, a detective story, a melodrama, a fantasy, an uchronia, and a parody of all those genres, the hero needs a villain capable of rising to the challenge. Writer Oliverio Girondo (Figure 1.4) is "el lechuzón" [a big owl] with hypnotic eyes, "big eyes, eyes like hard-boiled eggs, that stare" at Inspector Borges (36). It is impossible not to see in Girondo's character and his ability to fly a reference to one of his most famous prose poems, "No se me importa un pito" ["I don't give a damn"].[21] For the same reasons, and because of its author's metatextual awareness, Nine's sequential narrative breaks with the conventions of comics by giving an unusual pre-eminence to the texts, and the narrative voice of the character, Borges. According to Nine, the graphic novel is a form open

Intertextuality and iconic images **27**

to experimentation that can adapt to different narrative needs and topics, and even "rescue" forgotten or lost forms:

> There are formats that have been lost, and the graphic novel, insofar as it is not reduced to a label, could rescue: for example, the illustrated book, today

FIGURE 1.4 References to Borges's literature are transformed into visual artifacts by subverting the onomatopoeic device, normally a standard sound effect in comics.

relegated to the world of children. There are lots of possible combinations between the image and the word that have been lost in time and in this sense the graphic novel label could be a viable way of rediscovering them rather than inventing something really novel.

(Pérez Cano, 2019: 257)

The literary work and the biographies of Borges, Girondo, Lange and other icons of the avant-garde become a parodic game in which literary matter is transformed into visual artifacts: mirrors, labyrinths, calligrams and the scarecrows themselves. The same happens with tango lyrics, the streets of Buenos Aires, and that fateful knife that the gaucho Gauna offers Borges, not to challenge him to a duel but to give him a sandwich. The subversion of the onomatopoeic device, for example, is representative of this practice, when instead of *pow!* or *bang!*, Inspector Borges's punches are signaled by *tlön!* and *uqbar!* (30), as seen in Figure 1.4.

References to cinema are important, too, both in the narrative's visual aesthetics and in the parodic dimension of the texts. Although represented mainly through the image of Borges, dressed as Humphrey Bogart/Philip Marlowe, there are many allusions to Hitchcock and his films *The Man Who Knew Too Much* (1956) and, of course, *The Birds* (1963). With black and white images, expressionist lines that accentuate the story's unreal and fantastic atmosphere, or the absurd humor of some its situations, Nine combines iconic images from the Latin American avant-garde with the *film noir* tradition. In a sequence that takes place in a mirror maze, the identifiable literary motifs are as significant as the shootout scene in *The Lady from Shanghai* (1947).

The novel ends with an Epilogue (pp. 158–159) that takes the form of a letter dated August 1949 from Borges to Norah Lange. The narrative's fictional time is framed between 1946, the year in which Borges was appointed "poultry inspector," and 1949, the year in which he published the volume of short stories *El Aleph* and, according to Brescia (2008: 139), "when Borges had already begun to be Borges." Nine's narrative is faithful until the end to the world turned upside down, so Inspector Borges writes to Lange that he is enjoying the benefits of the countryside, doing physical work, and that "he has begun his novel" (Nine, 2017: 159).

Of course, the panel that closes the novel belies Inspector Borges's bucolic rhetoric. This last panel consists of a photo of the city of Buenos Aires and a sign in the foreground that says "Avenida General Paz." The General Paz Avenue separates the city from the Province of Buenos Aires, that is, it represents the limit between "civilization" and "barbarism," with the writer's supposed hut situated in the middle of these "mythical territories" of Argentine culture and history. To accentuate the ambiguity further, a narrative box in the panel asks the question: "Is it possible?" The question not only points to the infinite possibilities in which the story can be read, but is a reference to the ending of *The Eternaut*, by Héctor Germán Oesterheld (Buenos Aires, 1919–1977). The last panel of *The Eternaut* wonders if it is possible to avoid "the horror" by telling a story, the story of the future. It is worth noting that in a famous interview with Carlos Trillo and Guillermo

Saccomano, Oesterheld talks about reading Borges, and about *la historieta* having a bigger readership than Borges.[22] On the other hand, we know that Borges never wrote a novel, that he did not consider it a literary form that he wanted to develop, just as we know that the photos he supposedly sends to Norah Lange are not of the Argentine countryside; rather, they seem to be of landscapes from a European countryside. We go back to the beginning, then, in this never-ending circle, like in "The Aleph." It is all ambiguity and indeterminacy. Nothing is established, just like in the endless readings of Borges's mythic figure that, this time, receives the irreverence it deserves.

Notes

1 My first approach to Nine's graphic novel was a review published in *Variaciones Borges* no. 46 (2018). Later, I presented a version of the present chapter at the International Comic Arts Forum conference, held at St. Ambrose University, Iowa, United States, April 4–6, 2019.

I would like to express my gratitude to Lucas Nine for authorizing the reproduction of images for this article, and for sharing with me his insights about comics. The same goes to this volume's coordinators for their support during a year that has been a challenge for everyone. Finally, I would like to acknowledge Daniel Balderston, Director of the Borges Center at the University of Pittsburgh, for sending me a copy of *Borges, inspector de aves*. On a personal note, this graphic novel brings together two subjects that are dear to me, the first one, reading Jorge Luis Borges. As Alfredo Alonso Estenoz points out in his book *Borges en Cuba* (2017: 9), the edition of Borges's *Páginas escogidas* [*Selected Pages*] in 1988 was the first opportunity for our generation to read Borges, who, as Alonso Estenoz explains, had been "one of those excluded" from the post-revolutionary "canon of reading" until then (9). I, too, read Borges for the first time without having any idea about who he was. As the adolescent that I was then, I remember being impressed and moved by his poems, especially the verses from the "Poem of the Gifts": "In shadow, with a tentative stick, I try/The hollow twilight, slow and imprecise/I, who had always thought of Paradise/In form and image as a library" (Di Giovanni, 1972: 129). I bought the reissue of *Selected Pages* in 1999, a book that has accompanied me in all my great and lesser exiles since I left Cuba. The second topic dear to me is the study of comics as a form of expression that deserves serious academic attention. In Cuba, what I remember is that they were considered children's readings, or a weapon of imperialism's "ideological penetration." I consider myself fortunate, then, to be able to bring together these two fascinations, which are no longer secret.

2 A short biography of Borges in English and Spanish can be found at the website of the Jorge Luis Borges Manuscript Collection at the University of Pittsburgh: https://digital.library.pitt.edu/islandora/object/pitt%3AUS-PPiU-LATINAMER201801/viewer. A Timeline Bio-bibliography can be found at the Borges Center's website: www.borges.pitt.edu/.

3 In his "Palabras" (1946: 14–15), published in *Sur*, Borges says he worked as "an auxiliary third at a municipal library in the Southern slums" (All translations are by the author, Tania Pérez Cano, unless otherwise noted).

4 Daniel Balderston (2018) points out the following regarding this incident in Borges' life: "1946 is a landmark in his personal history –he resigns that year from his position at the Miguel Cané Municipal Library, supposedly because some mischievous Peronist appoints him as Poultry and Rabbits Inspector in the municipal market." Jorge B. Rivera (1935–2004), in "Borges, Ficha 57.323" (2000), points out that there is no formal proof that Borges was actually forced to resign by the Peronist government or offered the humiliating position.

5 Born in Buenos Aires in 1975, Lucas Nine is a comic artist, illustrator, and director of animated films. He has published the graphic novels *Dingo Romero* (Spain, 2004; France, 2008), *El Circo Criollo* (Argentina, 2009), *Thé de Noix/Té de Nuez* (France, 2011; Argentina, 2015), *Les contes de suicidé* (script by Lautaro Ortiz, France, 2016; by the title of *Quiroga*, Argentina, 2018), *Borges, inspector de aves* (Argentina, 2012, 2017; France, 2018; Ecuador, 2020) and *Budapest (ou presque)* (France, 2019). His works have appeared in books, journals, and magazines in Argentina, Bolivia, Chile, France, Spain, Germany, Mexico, Brazil, Italy and Japan, in different publications, such as *Télam*, *Clarín*, *La Nación*, *Caras y Caretas*, *Billiken* and *Fierro*. His illustrations for children's books have been exhibited at the Children's Book Fair in Bologna, Italy (1995) and received awards from ALIJA (Association of Children and Youth Literature of Argentina) in 2005 and 2007. Nine worked as scriptwriter and director in a segment of the film *Ánima Buenos Aires* (2012), which received awards at several animation festivals around the world that year (for example, the Annecy International Animation Festival and the New Latin American Cinema Festival, where it won the First Coral Prize in the animation category). He has collaborated with publishing houses like Alfaguara, Norma, Sudamericana, Richmond, De Ponent, Random House, Les Reveurs and Warum. (Taken from the author's website https://lucasnine.mystrikingly.com/ and updated via email with Nine on June 28, 2021).

6 Paul Alkon (1994: 68) defined *alternate history* as "essays or narratives exploring the consequences of an imagined divergence from specific historical events." Both Amy J. Ransom (2010) and Monique Villen (2019:199) work with the definition offered by Alkon of *alternative history* or *uchronia*. Villen points out in her essay that: "Official history is not denied, but instead, takes a different course that generates a variable of the world where an error or injustice are corrected, a better world is proposed, or a polemic is launched."

7 *Historieta* is the term used in Argentina for comics.

8 As I have pointed out previously, I prefer the term *intertextuality* because it is the more widely used, even though *interdiscursivity* describes more accurately the confluence of discourses present in comics: texts, images, fine arts, photography, film and elements from oral and performative cultures, such as popular music, jokes, slang and sayings. In our Call for Papers (Pérez Cano, Tullis, & Merino, 2019b) for a monographic volume on Latin American comics for the journal *Mitologías Hoy*, we clarified the distinction between *intertextuality* and *interdiscursivity*, following Cesare Segre's definition included in the *Diccionario de retórica, crítica y terminología literaria* by Marchese and Forradellas (2000). Segre explains such distinction as follows: "Because the word *intertextuality* contains *text*, I am of the opinion that it should be used with greater precision to designate relations between a text and another text (written texts, and particularly, literary texts). On the contrary, I would propose the term *interdiscursivity* for the relations that any text, oral or written, maintains with all utterances (or discourses) registered in the corresponding culture and ideologically organized" (2000: 218). See www.academia.edu/38515416/CFP_Mitolog%C3%ADas_Hoy_Latin_American_latino_comics_docx.

9 Lucas Nine uses the apocryphal critic Franco Della Imagine to subscribe to this perspective when he refers to Borges as "our most precious curio" (2017: 5) in his Prologue to *Borges, Poultry Inspector*. Since the very beginning, then, Nine incorporates a textual practice that refers to Borges's literary universe.

10 Definition of *icon* by the Merriam-Webster dictionary: www.merriam-webster.com/dictionary/iconic.

11 Italics in the original.

12 For more information about Montoneros, and their organization and editorial projects, consult Esquivada, Gabriela (2010). *Noticias de los montoneros: la historia del diario que no pudo anunciar la revolución*. Buenos Aires, Editorial Sudamericana, and Gandolfo, Amadeo (2020), "Un intelectual de los márgenes: las historietas de Oski en el diario *Noticias de Montoneros* (1974)," in *Iberoamericana*, vol. 20, no. 73, pp. 173–201.

13 "Absolute Mandarin of the cultural world."

14 The *Clarín* newspaper, in its online version (06/14/2021), reproduces some of the cartoons that Sábat made of Borges. They can be viewed here: www.clarin.com/fotogalerias/jorge-luis-borges-hermenegildo-sabat-grande-visto-grande_5_i8ARz3e5a.html.
15 *Fierro* appeared first from 1984 to 1992, starting almost immediately after the return of democracy to Argentina, following seven years of the State of terror imposed by the military *junta*, from 1976 to 1983. His first title was *Fierro. Historietas para sobrevivientes* [*Fierro. Comics for Survivors*]; its second run lasted from 2006 to 2017. Gabriel di Meglio (2005: 97), writes about the significance of *Fierro* as a cultural project: "*Fierro* was, without a doubt, the most important Argentine comic journal, not only because of its quality and the dissemination it achieved in the world of creators and readers of comics, but mainly because it represented a broader cultural project at a key moment of recent Argentine history." The Historical Archive of Argentine Journals, AHIRA [Archivo Histórico de Revistas Argentinas] highlights the fact that *Fierro* created a space that combined tradition and innovation: "The journal's strategy was to present itself as a publication that articulated 'tradition and experimentation': an inherited tradition to which many members of the editorial board subscribed; and the experimentation accumulated in years of work, both in the country and during the exile years. At the same time, [*Fierro*] was able to combine the professional experience of those coming from graphic humor and those closer to the so-called 'serious comics'" (https://ahira.com.ar/revistas/fierro/page/3/).
16 I dedicated a chapter to the study of *Trazo de tiza* and *Gustavo*, by Max (1956), in my book *Imposiblidad del beatus ille: Representaciones de la crisis ecológica en España y América Latina* (2016, pp. 153–166).
17 The catalog of Hotel de las Ideas can be consulted here: https://hoteldelasideas.com/.
18 In a well-known episode of the Argentine, avant-garde, Oliverio Girondo paraded a huge *papier mâché* doll representing his academic "scarecrow" through the streets of Buenos Aires to publicize his book. Hazelton recounts the incident as follows: "The event itself was a work of public performance art that satirized commercialization at the same time as exploiting it. Girondo constructed a nine-foot high *papier mâché* statue of his scarecrow, an academic-looking dandy in a black coat, white gloves and a top hat, complete with a pipe and monocle, which is now in the Museum of the City of Buenos Aires. He then went to a funeral parlor and hired a six-horse carriage piled high with funeral wreaths, together with two coachmen and a footman in livery, placed the figure within it, and arranged to have it driven around downtown Buenos Aires for several weeks in order to announce the book to all. At the same time, he rented a shop staffed by young women to sell the book on the city centre. Within a month, all five thousand copies of the book had sold out. Girondo's plan was to burn the statue, which represented all that he considered lifeless and stultifying in literature, on the twenty-fifth anniversary of the first issue of *Martín Fierro*, but his wife, Norah Lange, finally convinced him not to" (xxxii).
19 The party actually took place, and celebrated the publication of Norah Lange's novel *45 Days and 30 Sailors* (1933). A photo of the event I found online shows Norah Lange disguised as a mermaid and a group of assistants (among them, Girondo and Pablo Neruda) disguised as sailors. See it here: www.girondo-lange.com.ar/norah-lange/galeria-de-fotos/index.html.
20 Bakhtin writes about the meaning of laughter and carnival in Medieval culture: "The infinite world of the forms and manifestations of laughter was opposed to the official culture, to the serious, religious and feudal tone of the time. Within their diversity, these forms and manifestations – carnival public festivals, comic rites and cults, buffoons and 'fools', giants, dwarfs and monsters, clowns of various styles and categories, the vast and multiform parodic literature, etc., have a unity of style and constitute unique and indivisible parts and zones of popular comic culture, mainly carnival culture. The multiple manifestations of this culture can be subdivided into three large categories: 1) Forms and rituals of the spectacle (carnival festivities, comedic performances in public squares, etc.);

2) Verbal comic works (including parodies) of various kinds: oral and written, in Latin or in the vulgar language; 3) Various forms and types of familiar and rude vocabulary (insults, curses, popular slogans, etc." (2003: 4).

21 I reproduce a fragment of the poem, translated by Hazelton: "I don't give a damn whether a woman has breasts like magnolias or like dried figs, skin like a peach or a piece of sandpaper. I give zero importance to the fact that she wakes up with breath like an aphrodisiac or an insecticide. I'm perfectly able to put up with a nose that would win first prize in a carrot show; but one thing – and on this I'm unyielding – which I can't forgive under any pretext is that she doesn't know how to fly. If she doesn't know how to fly, she's wasting her time trying to seduce me! (2018: 187).

22 The interview was originally published in *Historia de la historieta argentina* (1980: 103–114), by Carlos Trillo and Guillermo Saccomano. Oesterheld was kidnapped and presumably assassinated and "disappeared" by the Argentine military junta in 1977. Ana Merino (2003: 245–247) details the horror of the kidnapping of Oesterheld and his four daughters, Beatriz, Diana, Marina and Estela.

Bibliography

Alkon, P. (1994), "Alternate History and Postmodern Temporality" in *Time, Literature and the Arts: Essays in Honor of Samuel L. Macey. English Literary Studies* (Ed. Thomas R. Cleary), vol. 61, Victoria, University of Victoria Press, pp. 65–85.

Alonso Estenoz, A. (2017), *Borges en Cuba. Estudio de su recepción*, Pittsburgh, Borges Center.

Bakhtin, M. (2003), *La cultura popular en la Edad Media y en el Renacimiento: el contexto de François Rabelais*, Madrid, Alianza Editorial.

Balderston, D. (2018), "Revelando las falacias del nacionalismo: de 'Viejo hábito argentino' a 'Nuestro pobre individualismo'", in *Variaciones Borges*, no. 46, pp. 135–55.

Borges Center, University of Pittsburgh [https://www.borges.pitt.edu/about].

Borges, Jorge Luis (1946), "Palabras pronunciadas por Jorge Luis Borges en la comida que le ofrecieron los escritores", in *Sur*, no. 142, pp. 114–15. Retrieved on May 20 from https://catalogo.bn.gov.ar/F/?func=direct&doc_number=001218322&local_base=BNA01.

Borges, Jorge Luis (1999), *Páginas escogidas*, La Habana, Casa de las Américas.

Brescia, P. (2006), "Post or Past Borges? The Writer as Literary Object", in *World Literature Today*, vol. 5, no. 80, pp. 48–51.

Brescia, P. (2008), "Borges deviene objeto: algunos ecos", in *Variaciones Borges*, no. 26, pp. 125–44.

Casale O'Ryan, M. (2014), *The Making of Jorge Luis Borges as an Argentine Cultural Icon*, Modern Humanities Research Association. Retrieved on July 2, 2021, from www.jstor.org/stable/j.ctt9qfbdn

Cinelli, J. P. (2017, June 11), "La sátira de un Borges peronista e inspector de aves", *Tiempo Argentino*. Retrieved on May 11, 2021, from www.tiempoar.com.ar/cultura/la-satira-de-un-borges-peronista-e-inspector-de-aves/

De la Calle, Á. (2016), "*Perramus*, o como hubiera sido hermoso que fuera", in *Perramus*, Torino, 001 Ediciones.

Di Giovanni, N. T. (Ed.) (1972), *Jorge Luis Borges. Selected Poems 1927–1967*, London, Allen Lane the Penguin Press.

Di Meglio, G., Marina, F., & Silva Aras, S. (2005), "La Argentina en cuadritos. Una aproximación a la Argentina reciente desde la revista Fierro (1984–1992)", in *Entrepasados*, no. 27, pp. 97–115.

Esquivada, G. (2010), *Noticias de los montoneros: la historia del diario que no pudo anunciar la revolución*, Buenos Aires, Editorial Sudamericana.

Gandolfo, A. (2020), "Un intelectual de los márgenes: las historietas de Oski en el diario Noticias de Montoneros (1974)", in *Iberoamericana*, vol. 20, no. 73. Retrieved on July 2, 2021, from https://journals.iai.spk-berlin.de/index.php/iberoamericana/article/view/2688

Hazelton, H. (2018), "Preface", in *Obras completas/Complete Works* (Oliverio Girondo, vol. 1), Hamilton, ON, Wolsak and Wynn Publishers Ltd, pp. xxiv–xxxviii.

Marchese, A., & Forradellas, J. (2000), *Diccionario de retórica, crítica y terminología literaria*, Barcelona, Ariel.

McCloud, S. (1993), *Understanding Comics: The Invisible Art*, New York, HarperCollins.

Merino, A. (2003), *El comic hispánico*, Madrid, Cátedra.

Navascués, J. de (2017), "Borges, Pratt y Corto Maltés: convergencias y malas lecturas", in *Variaciones Borges*, no. 43, pp. 159–81.

Nine, Lucas (2017), *Borges, inspector de aves*, Buenos Aires, Hotel de las Ideas.

Oesterheld, H. G., & Solano López, F. (2007), *El Eternauta*, Madrid, Norma Editorial (Anniversary edition).

Palacios, C. (2015), "La verdad sobre el Aleph. Contrapunto humorístico entre Fontanarrosa y Borges", in *Pasavento. Revista de Estudios Hispánicos*, vol. 3, no. 2, pp. 393–405.

Pérez Cano, T. (2016), *Imposibilidad del beatus ille. Representaciones de la crisis ecológica en España y América Latina*, Leiden, Almenara Press.

Pérez Cano, T. (2018), "Reseña de Borges, inspector de aves", in *Variaciones Borges*, no. 46, pp. 241–3.

Pérez Cano, T., Tullis, B., & Merino, A. (2019a), "Introducción. El cómic: intertextualidades, discursividades y paratextos en el arte secuencial de América Latina", in *Mitologías Hoy. Revista de Crítica Literaria Latinoamericana*, vol. 20, pp. 11–15. Retrieved on May 15 from https://revistes.uab.cat/mitologias/issue/view/v20

Pérez Cano, T., Tullis, B., & Merino, A. (2019b), "Call for Papers", in *Mitologías Hoy. Revista de Crítica Literaria Latinoamericana*, vol. 20. Retrieved on May 15, 2021, from www.academia.edu/38515416/CFP_Mitolog%C3%ADas_Hoy_Latin_American_latino_comics_docx

Pérez Cano, Tania (2019c), "'Crear el propio lector, un lector nuevo'. Entrevista con Lucas Nine", in *Mitologías Hoy. Revista de Crítica Literaria Latinoamericana*, vol. 20, pp. 253–260.

Pérez Cano, Tania (2021), Email exchange with Lucas Nine (personal email, June 28).

Pérez del Solar, P. (2011), "Los rostros de la violencia. Historietas en *La Argentina en pedazos*", in *Revista Iberoamericana*, vol. LXXVII, no. 234, pp. 59–86.

Photo Gallery (Oliverio Girondo and Norah Lange). Retrieved on May 31 from http://www.girondo-lange.com.ar/norah-lange/galeria-de-fotos/index.html.

Piglia, R. (1993), *La Argentina en pedazos*, Buenos Aires, Ediciones de la Urraca.

Prado, Miguelanxo (2003), *Trazo de tiza*, Barcelona, Norma Editorial.

Ransom, Amy J. (2010), "Warping Time: Alternate History, Historical Fantasy, and the Postmodern *uchronie Québécoise*", in *Extrapolation*, vol. 51, no. 2.

"Retratos únicos. Jorge Luis Borges por Hermenegildo Sábat, un grande visto por otro grande". *Clarín* (online, 06/14/2021). Retrieved on June 20 from https://www.clarin.com/fotogalerias/jorge-luis-borges-hermenegildo-sabat-grande-visto-grande_5_i8ARz3e5a.html.

Rivera, J. B. (2000), "Borges, Ficha 57.323", in *Territorio Borges y otros ensayos breves*, Buenos Aires, Atuel, pp. 23–36.

Sarlo, B. (2015), "Borges después de Borges", in Adriaensen, B., Botterweg, M., Steenmeijer, M., & Wijnterp, L. (Eds.), *Una profunda necesidad en la ficción contemporánea: la recepción de Borges en la república mundial de las letras*, Madrid, Iberoamericana/Vervuert.

Sasturain, J., & Breccia, A. (2016), *Perramus*, Torino, Italia, 001 Ediciones.
Soriano, O. (2016), "Una pesadilla argentina", in *Perramus*, Torino, 001 Ediciones.
Trillo, C., & Saccomano, G. (1980), *Historia de la historieta argentina*, Buenos Aires, Ediciones Record.
Turnes, P. (2015), "La milonga del destino. Héroes y antihéroes en *Un tal Daneri*, de Alberto Breccia y Carlos Trillo." Retrieved on June 17, 2021, from www.academia.edu/11326205/La_Milonga_del_destino._H%C3%A9roes_y_anti-h%C3%A9roes_en_Un_tal_Daneri_de_Alberto_Breccia_y_Carlos_Trillo
Villen, M. (2019), "'Vi un mundo nuevo que se avecinaba velozmente': estudio de la ucronía en *Never Let Me Go* de Kazuo Ishiguro", in *Castilla. Estudios de Literatura*, no. 10, pp. 195–222.

2

THE COMIC AS A FORM OF MEMORY OF TWO STUDENT MOVEMENTS IN CONTEMPORARY MEXICO

The case of *Grito de Victoria* by Augusto Mora

Laura Nallely Hernández Nieto*

Introduction

The aim of this chapter is to analyze the type of memory built around two student movements in two different periods of contemporary Mexican history in the graphic novel *Grito de Victoria* [*Hail Victory*], by Augusto Mora. Using a parallel narrative, the author builds two stories around the student massacre known as the *Halconazo* or "Corpus Christi Massacre," which occurred on June 10, 1971. In the same manner, Mora talks about the protest movement called #YoSoy132, which opposed Enrique Peña Nieto, the presidential candidate for the Institutional Revolutionary Party (PRI); and the protest march of December 1, 2012, the day on which he took office after an election marked by irregularities. Both episodes are intertwined in a single graphic novel to tell the reader what happened during these events. For the author, it is important to rescue the events of 1971, which allows us to understand the events of 2012. According to the proposal of Todorov, this would be an exemplary use of memory, which consists of employing the latter as a model to understand new situations with new agents (Jelin, 2002, p. 33).

In the second part of the book, Augusto Mora utilizes a comic journalism format to produce a graphic chronicle that links the political and social context in which the 1971 and 2012 protests developed. In the specific case of the *Halconazo*, 50 years after the aggression, it is unknown how many people died or were injured. The importance of *Grito de Victoria* lies in that it recovers the testimonies of some of the survivors of 1971 and renders visible a historical event that is little known and investigated. On the other hand, the author narrates his own experience in the 2012 demonstrations and the #YoSoy132 Movement. Comic journalism is a growing creative-informative current in literature: authors seek the truth of an event by approaching the place and verifying it what happened through interviews and

DOI: 10.4324/9781003333296-4

exhaustive documentation, by means of interpersonal contact with the protagonists (Matos Agudo, 2016, p. 260).

The concept of memory refers to how past experiences are reconstructed in the present. This process is an object of political dispute by the different actors involved. That is why researchers dealing with this problem refer to memory as a work, highlighting its dynamic and transformative nature (Jelin, 2002). In this respect, we will observe how the graphic novel can be an instrument for the recovery of memory. Through visual analysis, the reader is able to observe how the author establishes parallels in both movements to build a political reflection of the social context of contemporary Mexico.

Augusto Mora is originally from Mexico City (1986), he studied Graphic Design and works as an illustrator and a cartoonist. He has been a fellow of the Young Creators program (FONCA) and obtained a mention in the III Ibero-American Cities Prize for the Graphic Novel, organized by the Union of Ibero-American Capital Cities (UCCI). Among his works, we can mention the following: *Cosas del Infierno* [*Things of Hell*] (2005); *El Maizo, la Maldición del Vástago* [*El Maizo, the Curse of the Scion*] (2010); *Muerte Querida* [*Dear Death*] (2012); *Tiempos Muertos* [*Dead Times*] (2012); *Fuertes Declaraciones: Diario de un presidente* [*Strong Statements: Diary of a President*] (2015); *En Busca de una Voz* [*Looking for a Voice*] (2015); *Grito de Victoria* [*Hail Victory*] (2017); *Encuentro en la Tormenta* [*Encounter in the Storm*] (2018) and *Québec, Apuntes de Viaje* [*Québec, Travel Notes*] (2019). Mora defines his works as comic journalism.

The massacre of June 10, 1971

The so-called *Halconazo* or Corpus Christi Massacre was an event in which students and paramilitary groups from the State of Mexico were involved. It happened on June 10, 1971, in Mexico City, in the vicinity of the San Cosme neighborhood. The origin of the altercation is related to what happened at the Autonomous University of Nuevo León (UANL). The students of the UANL began to organize themselves to demand parity in the representation between teachers and students in the UANL University Council. The president of the entity, Eduardo Elizondo, sabotaged the movement and, in turn, had the university rector, Ulises Leal, removed from office and imposed Colonel Arnulfo Treviño in his place. The latter dismissed all the managers, which increased the conflict.

The governor gave the order for the police to repress a group of students who were taking over high-school facilities and imprisoned former Rector Ulises Leal. At this point, the federal government, headed by Luis Echeverría, intervened and dismissed both the governor and the rector, Arnulfo Treviño, and reinstated Ulises Leal in office. However, the initial demand for parity in student representation and a reform of the organic law of the University had not been resolved.

Meanwhile, students from the National Polytechnic Institute (IPN) and the National Autonomous University of Mexico (UNAM) in Mexico City expressed solidarity with their peers in Monterrey and organized a demonstration to support the democratization of education. This mobilization would take place within a particular context, since it would be the first after the violent events of October 1968. The plan for the march consisted in setting out at the Casco de Santo Tomás, continuing along Carpio Street, and going out onto the México-Tacuba highway until reaching the Zocalo in Mexico City. However, the students were intercepted at Av. De Los Maestros by a paramilitary group of young people armed with kendo rods and firearms, directed and commandeered by the State of Mexico, who attacked the protesters. This shock group was known as the *Halcones* [Hawks].

The Halcones were formed by soldiers and young recruits from the outskirts of the city. This paramilitary group existed since the 1960s and is even linked to the 1968 Tlatelolco Massacre. Initially, it was created to protect strategic facilities of the State of Mexico, such as the new Line 1 of the Metro, but it soon changed its objective. It was directed by Manuel Díaz Escobar, who was Deputy Director of General Services of the government of Mexico City. The young recruits had received training in martial arts, self-defense and, in particular, in kendo, a Japanese martial art that provides training with a bamboo stick. Participating in its organization and command were Jesús Castañeda Gutiérrez, chief of the Presidential General Staff of the Echeverría government, and Fernando Gutierrez Barrios, head of the Federal Security Directorate.

An estimated of 120 students died – many of these were shot after being chased to hospitals – and there were many missing persons as well. This episode and others, linked to the guerrillas and the repression of the seventies and eighties, are known in Mexico as the Guerra Sucia [Dirty War]. The *Halconazo* has not been clarified, and in 2009, former President Luis Echeverría, one of those responsible for the massacre, was exonerated.

Nonetheless, monuments, memorial plaques, and other markers are now official, and unofficial actors attempt to supply materiality to memories (Jelin, 2017). It was not until 2011 that a sculpture was placed at the entrance of the National Teachers School to commemorate the anniversary of the 1968 Massacre 40 years after the events. This sculpture was unveiled by the Head of Government of Mexico City, Marcelo Ebrard, and by the artist known as Sebastián. In 2019, the Federal Government inaugurated a memorial at the former building of the Federal Security Directorate (DFS), where some young people of that time were abducted, tortured, and disappeared.

The *Halconazo*, a little-addressed event

Various documentaries, series, and movies have been filmed about Tlatelolco – some are fictional love stories – but concerning the 1971 massacre, there have been fewer. Among the exceptions, we can name the documentary *El año de la rata* [*The Year of the Rat*], by filmmaker Enrique Escalona, exhibited during the Second National Independent Film Contest, in 1971. There is also a 2019 documentary entitled *Halcones, terrorismo de Estado* [*Hawks, State Terrorism*], directed by Carlos Mendoza Aupetit.

Regarding fictional movies, *El Bulto* (*The Bundle*, 1991), directed by Gabriel Retes, narrates the conflict of Lauro, a left-wing photographer who is covering the student protest of June 10, 1971. He is beaten by the paramilitaries and left in a coma. Lauro awakes from the coma twenty years later to find that his wife has married another man, that his children are now adults, and that his friends had been "absorbed into the system." In addition, there is *Roma* (2018), the Oscar-winning film written and directed by Alfonso Cuarón. Set in the early 1970s, it narrates the daily life of a middle-class family and of Cleo, their housemaid. One of the main sequences of the film takes place on the day of the massacre: the grandmother takes Cleo – who is pregnant – to a furniture store to purchase a crib. The student protest takes place in the street and is repressed by another group of young people. The persecution of one couple ends in the store, where Cleo recognizes the father of her son among the attackers. He points a gun at her, and that causes her water to break. Cuarón has said, "The *Halconazo* is one of those social scars that we share as Mexicans" (Netflix España, 2018).

Although cinema can be a catalyst for collective memory, as stated by Jorge L. Catalá Carrasco et al. (2017), "comics elicit and mobilize memories in those who read and enjoy them and enable a particular engagement with the past distinct from that which may be experienced through the medium of, say, a film or a battle reenactment" (p. 5).

Eduardo del Río influenced Mora's work, who stated that he always had the intention of addressing social problems thanks to the influence of Rius: "I like it that every comic is a narrative, and through this, I can make a social statement" (El Heraldo de México, 2017). The first – and probably the only – time a comic was dedicated to the Corpus Christi Massacre was in the *Los Agachados* magazine: *Halcones, se sigue investigando* [*Halcones, the Investigation Continues*], published exactly one year after the tragedy. Eduardo del Río aka Rius, whose work was characterized by having a critical, left-wing perspective, formulated the comic based on testimonies and publications in the press, as he notes in the volume presentation. The magazine was published during the presidency of Luis Echeverría, when the events occurred.

In the magazine, Rius retells the murders and political crimes from 1927 through 1971. He concludes – in his time – that these fifty years of official violence have convinced many young people that the only way to change this state of things is by armed struggle. The 1968 Movement demonstrated the urgent need to make changes in order to avoid a violent revolution. Eric Hobsbawm (1998) claimed that the 1960s revealed that young people were not only politically radical and explosive but also uniquely effective in giving national and even international expression to political and social discontent. Even in dictatorial countries, these young people comprised the only citizen group capable of taking collective political action. The reason why 1968 – and the subsequent years of 1969 and 1970 – was not a revolution, was that students, however numerous and active as they were, could not do it alone (pp. 300–301).

On the cover of the magazine, on an orange background, appears what – possibly – is the most iconic photograph of the 1971 Massacre: it shows one of the paramilitary-group members with a kendo rod while he runs to attack the protesters.[1] The image is in black and white, and a yellow letter "H" was placed on the attacker's chest, pointing him out as an *halcón*. It should be mentioned that the author of this photograph is Armando Lenin Salgado (1938–2018), who was tortured for ten days under the orders of Miguel Nazar Haro, then head of the Federal Security Directorate (DFS), in addition to undergoing persecution and censorship (Lenin Salgado, 2015). The reason was that, through his photographs, the operation of the *halcones* came to be proved: that they were armed and shot innocent persons at the National Teachers School in Mexico City. The images contradicted the official version of President Luis Echeverría Álvarez, who had issued assurances that during the day of June 10, 1971, there was only a confrontation between groups of students and that there were no deaths. The images of Lenin Salgado have been reproduced innumerably in the media; these images have never produced any royalties, even though the photographer contributed to social change in Mexico (Miranda, 2018). This image was also a reference for Augusto Mora, who drew the "hawk" on the blank page of the book (see Figure 2.1).

Use of memory narratives in *Grito de Victoria*

In this graphic novel, Augusto Mora addresses the student movements in Mexico: the *Halconazo* and the protests of the #YoSoy132 students. Mora intersperses the events that occurred in the repression of young people in both protests to show the reader the parallels between these student movements.

On the one hand, the graphic novel tells the story of Victoria and Vicente, two young people who participated in the 1971 Student Movement and were victims of the repression of the so-called *Halconazo* on June 10 of that year. On the other hand, it tells the story of Valentín and Vanesa, a young couple who attend the protests against the presidential inauguration of Enrique Peña Nieto on December 1, 2012, outside the Chamber of Representatives in the Mexico City Historical Center. This event would also end with the repression of protesters by the police (Figure 2.2).

To narrate both repressions, the author employs a parallel montage. This cinematographic resource allows the reader to be exposed to two events that occurred in different settings without the need of them happening in the same year or at the same place. In this way, the author alternates images of both situations, creating mental associations in the mind of the reader. In the same manner, Roberto Bartual (2010) notes that, depending on the way the panels are arranged on the page, the author of a comic book can coerce the reader into reading the panels in one way or in the other, and the reader can as well play with the possibility of seeing all of the panels at the same time to create narrative effects beyond the reach of cinema or the literary novel (p. 28).

According to Tzvetan Todorov (2000), the literal use of memory implies turning the memory of past events into something unique or incomparable. Contrariwise,

FIGURE 2.2 On the left: Gray scale to Victoria. On the right: to Valentín.

the exemplary use of memory can mean taking advantage of the lessons of past injustices to favor the fight against the injustices committed in our present (Jelin, 2002, pp. 29–33). In this regard, Augusto Mora creates characters to talk about past and present events in situations that could be real: in this fashion, he manages to afford greater credibility to the story. The names of every character begins with the letter "V," because the letter has a certain symbolism. It is the "V" for Victory, a word repeated extensively, especially in the movements of 1968 and 1970. It has a political meaning due to the demonstrations of those years (El Heraldo de México, 2017).

The story begins with Victoria, a young woman who lives in Colonia Santa Julia, a poor neighborhood in Mexico City that currently does not exist. In her room, Victoria changes her clothes to go to the march and calls Vicente on the phone. She cannot find him and decides to go to the Casco de Santo Tomás, where the demonstration was to take place. On her way there, Victoria eats a *torta* and drinks a soda at a street-food stall. The author narrates that Victoria found out about the march through some flyers distributed at the Faculty of Economics, which days before had announced the resurgence of the student movement: a popular demonstration was called in support of the University of Nuevo León, on Thursday, June 10, at 17:00. As she walked, Victoria noticed many police officers, riot tanks, and other young people with kendo rods.

When she arrived at the Casco de Santo Tomás, many people were there despite fear of the repression that had taken place on October 2, 1968. Victoria

The comic as a form of memory of two student movements   41

sees Vicente, who is one of the organizers of the contingent from the School of Economics. He tells her that there are rumors that people are going to come to cause destruction, but, together with other young people, they begin to move down the avenue. Valentín wears a chain with a "V" around his neck, and he gives

FIGURE 2.3   The point when both stories intertwine.

it to Victoria. Suddenly, the police arrive to block the way, and noise is heard from another part of the avenue. The armed youths enter the scene (the author does not mention the term *halcones*), who begin to beat the students and to throw gas at them. Victoria asks Vicente to leave, but he does not want to. Another friend takes Victoria by the arm to flee the place. The aggressors are joined by an armed group that begins to shoot at them. She remembers the events of 1968 in Tlatelolco.

At the same time, in the other story, Valentín wakes up with a hangover after a night out. He had several missed calls and WhatsApp messages from his girlfriend, Vanesa, asking him if he would be going to the march. In the end, he decides to get up, as different calls were circulating to protest the inauguration of Enrique Peña Nieto as President. He is struck by the fact that some images requested that the students bring sticks and stones to attack. He prints one of the digital calls, takes a shower, makes himself a sandwich, and leaves his house. At the Metro station, he cannot find Vanesa, and proceeds directly to the Chamber of Deputies.

Upon arriving there, Valentín finds Vanesa, and she complains about him not having answered her messages due to him going out partying the night before. He notices the large number of police officers who are heading toward the place of the march. Outside of the Chamber of Representatives, different groups were already protesting. Some were attempting to tear down the iron wall that protected the building. Police officers begin to throw gas, while protesters throw Molotov cocktails. In the smoke, Valentín loses sight of his girlfriend Vanesa. Then he sees that one of the protestors had been wounded with a rubber bullet. Perceiving the climate of violence, Valentín tells Vanesa to leave the area. At noon, they walk to the Mexico City Historical Center, where there are other demonstrations. At that moment, he sees that, on the Internet, there are rumors of a first death. He asks Vanesa if she is still angry, and they continue to argue. Then the police arrive to arrest the young people.

At this point, both stories intertwine, and the characters move forward to 2012. Young Victoria sees an injured man on the street and realizes that it is Vicente. Suddenly, a cry for help brings her back to the present, where she is already an adult and is accompanying young people in the 2012 demonstrations. Vanesa is cornered by the police and asks Valentín to rescue her. Victoria (adult) tries to help Vanesa not be taken away. He also attempts to help Vanesa, but the police start beating him. Victoria intervenes to protect Valentín with her body. In that moment, she remembers the image of Vicente, dead in her arms. The story ends with a full-page panel with Victoria screaming "Basta!"

The narrative begins with an entire page dedicated to Victoria and another to the story of Valentín. As the end of the story draws near, the panels of each narrative are interspersed on the same page, until it finalizes in a full-page drawing which joins the history together. This distribution of panels creates the feeling of the enclosure and closeness of the events. The feeling of impotence is also graphically transmitted in the close-ups of the faces used by the author. Will Eisner (2008) notes that the use of perspective produces a variety of emotional states in the reader: the observer's response to a specific scene is influenced by their position as spectator (p. 92). To differentiate each narrative, the author utilizes shades of gray for Victoria's story and a clear line for Valentín. In both stories, there is the use of photographs as backgrounds or collages to provide dynamism.

To situate the reader in each era, the author draws characteristic elements of the decades addressed. For example, in the first panel, outside the house we find parked a "crocodile" taxi, as it was called at the time: these cars painted green and having a lateral line resembling the reptile's teeth. Victoria's room is decorated with the following posters: of revolutionary icon Che Guevara; of Chilean president Salvador Allende; the film *El Topo* (1970), by Alejandro Jodorowsky, and of Chilean singer-songwriter Víctor Jara. There are also vinyl records and a typewriter.

There are elements that both stories share. While Victoria uses a phone, Valentín has a cell phone. Victoria finds out about the march from a flyer, Valentín sees an image on Internet. Victoria has a *torta* (Mexican sandwich) before going to the march, Valentín eats a sandwich before leaving his home. Victoria is suspicious of the presence of so many policemen at the place; Valentín is also concerned about that fact. Victoria wants to flee from the march, but Vicente does not want to. Similarly, Valentín wants to get away from the area where there's violence, but Vanesa resists this.

The documentary part: #YoSoy132

As mentioned in the Introduction section, to elaborate *Grito de Victoria*, Augusto Mora relied on interviews, documentary research and chronicles to narrate a story that intertwined the past and the present. In the second part, the author gathers the testimonies of the interviews with the survivors of 1971 and explains in detail the events surrounding the most recent student movement in Mexico, that is, #YoSoy132, and the events leading to the repression of December 1, 2012.

The second part of the graphic novel corresponds to a work of journalism: in this aspect, the work of Mora is similar to *Los Agachados* by Rius. Augusto Mora became a reporter and employed the information collected in his research, coverage of the marches, the interviews, and his own experience. Previously, Eduardo del Río rebuilt the history of the political massacres in Mexico and the *Halconazo* with interviews and the few publications that existed at that time. As the Argentine journalist Julián Is Gorodischer (2013) asserts, comic journalism is a zone of the miscegenation of genres, themes, and styles; journalism and script, intimacy and current affairs, text and drawing, are rejected and are attracted to each other but, in the end, they are understood as related to the obsessions of journalism, including territorial contact, urgent current issues, and closeness in time and space.

The second part of the book began with four testimonies of 1971 survivors: firstly Joel Ortega, a survivor of 1968 and of the *Halconazo*. He was a member of Communist Youth and participated in the formation of the UNAM (SPAUNAM) and the STUNAM Teachers Unions. He is the author of books about the student movements, such as *El otro camino: cuarenta y cinco años de Trinchera en Trinchera* (2006) [*The Other Way: Forty-five Years from Trench to Trench*]; *Adiós al 68* [*Goodbye*

Los dirigentes de la marcha, llevada a cabo el 10 de junio, se deslindaron de los líderes del CNH. Después de la matanza en Tlatelolco, cada escuela creó su propio comité de lucha que funcionaba a través de la toma de decisiones en asambleas estudiantiles. Los comités de lucha concurrían en un especie de consejo llamado Comité Coordinador de Comités de Lucha (CoCo). Todas las decisiones emanaban de las asambleas de cada una de las universidades.

Debido a las presiones sociales se derogó la ley universitaria de la Universidad Autónoma de Nuevo León, pero otros puntos que habían sido sumados a la protesta estudiantil no fueron cumplidos: la unión obrero-estudiantil, la libertad de los presos políticos, el derecho de manifestación, una reforma universitaria, la desaparición de las porras de golpeadores y el rechazo a la "apertura democrática" del presidente.

Sobre la democracia sindical, Joel Ortega Juárez dice:

"En México no hay sindicatos reales, en todo el mundo ha habido huelgas generales por la crisis. Aquí en México no ha habido una sola por que no hay sindicatos auténticos. Los que existen son 'charros' construidos desde arriba.

En otros países no hay uno sino varios sindicatos, los trabajadores escogen, pero pueden no pertenecer a ninguno y eso no les impide trabajar. El contrato colectivo no lo administra un sindicato, lo administra una asamblea electa por los Trabajadores (...) Aprendimos con el 68 que solos no podíamos, había que unir fuerzas entre estudiantes y trabajadores".

Joel Ortega Juárez
Ex-miembro de la Juventud Comunista y Partido Comunista Mexicano. Líder en la marcha del 10 de junio. Periodista y escritor.

Entrevista realizada en la Ciudad de México, 12 de junio de 2013.

Libertad a los Presos Políticos
Cárcel a los que reprimen al pueblo

Por otra parte, **Luis Echeverría Álvarez**, había llegado a la presidencia con un discurso de "apertura democrática" y libre participación de la ciudadanía en la vida política.

FIGURE 2.4 Drawings of the interviewees and their testimonies.

to 68] and *La izquierda Mexicana del Siglo XX* [*The Mexican Left of the 20th Century*]. Secondly Luis Fernando, cartoonist and author of graphic novels. Since 1978, he has had his work published in newspapers such as *Unomásuno*, *El Universal*, *La Jornada*, and *Milenio Diario*. He is the author of the graphic novels *Comixtlán*,

Avándaro, la historia jamás contada [*Avándaro, the Story Never Told*] and *La pirámide cuarteada, evocaciones del 68* [*The Cracked Pyramid, Evocations of 68*]. Thirdly Emilio Reza-Araujo, Member of Committee 1968, a biologist from the UNAM Faculty of Sciences, National Autonomous University of Mexico. And lastly Mauro César Enciso-Barrón, Professor at the Higher School of Mechanical and Electrical Engineering of the IPN and former member of Communist Youth and the CNED.

Augusto Mora transcribes fragments from the interviews on two pages. To not make the amount of information that he transcribes monotonous, he utilizes close-ups and mid-shots of the interviewees as they were at the time that they spoke with him. Thus, Joel Ortega is portrayed sitting with a cup of coffee in hand; Luis Fernando appears in his study; Emilio Reza Araujo is on the street in Mexico City, and Mauro César Enciso-Barrón is drawn in front of one of the IPN faculties. In addition, on these two pages, he draws graphic elements that, again, refer to the repression: a federal police officer and one of the snipers who fired on the day of the *Halconazo* (Figure 2.4). This journalistic practice recalls the illustrations penned by John T. McCutcheon (1870–1949), the US newspaper political cartoonist – and winner of a Pulitzer Prize in 1931 for an editorial cartoon – when he was traveling as a correspondent. An example of this is the portrait he made *in situ* of the revolutionary leader Francisco Villa in July 1914, during an interview with him by journalists covering the military occupation in the state of Veracruz during the Mexican Revolution. The headline of the portrait in the Chicago Daily Tribune reads as follows: "Mr. McCutcheon visited the most remarkable man in Mexico" (Ortiz Medina and Hernández Nieto, 2015, p. 204).

The chronicle of 2012, year of elections

The movement known with hashtag #YoSoy132 refers to the movement that followed the protests carried out by a group of students from the Ibero-American University (UIA) in Mexico City during the visit to their campus of presidential candidate Enrique Peña Nieto on May 11, 2012. It has as a background the events that occurred during this visit and the subsequent publication of a video entitled "I am 131," as explained later.

Enrique Peña Nieto, the PRI candidate for the presidency of the Mexican Republic in 2012, visited the Ibero-American University on that date after rescheduling the visit. Since May 10, the organization of a protest against his presence on the campus had circulated in students' social networks. According to the students, the candidate's logistics team committed irregularities in terms of the assignment of seats in the auditorium, which increased the tensions among the protesters inside the university (students) and outside of the campus (supporters and detractors). The visit entertained the format of a forum and, after the intervention of Peña Nieto, a series of critical questions followed. The topics addressed included fighting poverty, the state of Coahuila's public debt, the economic model, his management as former governor, among others, such as the 2006 repression in Atenco.

The mention of this topic upset the audience, and cries of protest were heard, among these that of "murderer." At the end of the forum, the candidate needed to go to the university's radio station booth for an interview that had been agreed upon previously. However, the candidate was rebuked by students who shouted slogans against him. Peña Nieto went into the bathroom and remained there while the protest lasted. Later he was escorted outside the university campus by elements of the Presidential General Staff amid shouting and accusations; meanwhile, his logistics team canceled the interview.

This chain of events unleashed the fury of the press, which accused the students of being intolerants. At the same time, messages of support for the protesters circulated on social networks such as Twitter and YouTube. However, the national press questioned the legitimate identity of the young people at the UIA and even sought out the leaders. Later, those who had taken part in the protest edited a video in response in which their faces and the registration plates accredited them as students. This video was known as "More Than 131" and was broadcast on YouTube on May 14, 2012 (Morales Sierra, 2014, pp. 42–45). The press attacked again, and there were even third parties who threatened the publicly identified protesters.

At that time, the movement ceased to be exclusive to the UIA, and in solidarity, numerous students from various public and private universities began to join it, including UNAM, IPN, UAM, ITAM, UVM and others within the Mexican Republic. The #YoSoy132 Movement arose, its name possibly due to that of a student at the University of Guadalajara known as @achoad and the journalist Denise Dresser (González Villareal, 2016, p. 131).

Henceforth, the movement took the form of a petition and became prominent for its horizontality within its organization. It made the following demands: massive transmission of the second presidential debate; creation of a third debate; participation of its members as electoral observers, and the opening of the information to alternative media. The 132 was related to a violent repression on December 1, 2012 and to the 85 people arrested in the protest against Enrique Peña Nieto as president. However, although #YoSoy132 did call for demonstrations, these had to be "non-violent." Shock groups and infiltrators committed acts of provocation that day, which ended discrediting the movement.

Young people, agents with agency capacity

Grito de Victoria uses different mechanisms to recover the memory of the #YoSoy132 Movement. In comic format, the author addresses the 2012 social mobilizations and the context prior to the presidential election of that year: the "war on drugs" and the disappearance of persons caused by this war was initiated by President Felipe Calderon using the Army and the Federal Police. Employing photomontage and collage, Augusto Mora mixes photographic backgrounds with caricatured characters; in other parts of the narrative, he gives weight to the photographs and uses these as a frame.

Statistics report that in Latin America, 60% of the population is under 30 years of age. However, frequently, the young people represented in public and media discourses continue to be criminalized, infantilized, and shown, in a reductive manner, as problematic individuals or groups whose only aim should be consumption (Gutiérrez Cham and Kaltmeier, 2020, p. 7). To a lesser extent, they are perceived as agents.

In that year, Arab Spring came about thanks to the use of social networks. In Mexico, the media referred to this as the Mexican Spring, similar to the youth movements of countries such as Egypt. The author addresses key aspects that allow us to understand the protest and reveals the aspects that characterized this 2012 Movement. There is a selection of key moments that occurred during that year. This is despite that, in the introduction of the graphic novel, Mora (2013) clarifies that he does not intend to cover each of the important events or protagonists of these, but he does take on the issue from the perspective of just another citizen who had witnessed a social phenomenon (p. 7).

The marches on Paseo de la Reforma Avenue (Mexico City) against the candidacy of Enrique Peña Nieto are cataloged in the graphic novel. Although these protests were not directly related to the #YoSoy132 Movement, these young people were also summoned to participate through social networks. At that time, a certain sector of the population was against Peña Nieto, in that he was the product of a meticulous media campaign promoted by Televisa network, that included the transmission of his wedding on television and spots starring soap-opera actresses.

There are two moments during which the narration changes over to the first person and the author becomes the main character: he is then an author-protagonist (De Cabo and Pereira, 2009, p. 5). On the one hand, there was the demonstration in which young people wore cardboard televisions on their heads and; on the other hand, there was one the day after the electoral fraud.

In this part, the author relates his experience in deciding to take part in the performance, where he was told to travel by subway with "television heads" to two different places in the city. He adds descriptive elements beyond the drawing. An example is a cartoon in which a member of the #YoSoy132 Movement explains how the movement would be carried out. In the cartoon, he adds a laconic sign describing that "his box did not look like a television." Stylistically, he adds collage elements to build the narrative, such as the Mexico City subway map and reproductions of the flyers that he kept while documenting the movement. He registered aspects that he saw and that were not recorded in a formal journalistic chronicle: the media that came to cover the event, and the questions that older people asked them.

The second time the narrator switches to the first person, Augusto speaks of the disappointment he felt when he saw that people declared that they had sold their vote without any shame. The writer Piedad Bonnet (s.f.) wrote that the act of narrating reconciles us with reality, generates dialogue and builds memory, and that if we want to get to the bottom of the social conscience, we must record the testimony in documents or art (p. 45). The author understands this need to register this moment in some way. He narrates how, after his car got stuck in traffic, he realized that the blockage of the avenue on which they were driving was due to a demonstration outside the offices of the Institutional Revolutionary Party (PRI). He and his girlfriend got out of the car to record the testimonies of the people demanding the money they were promised in exchange for voting for Enrique Peña Nieto. Additionally, he edited a video that included his interviews with the protesters and included the link on these pages. He also leaves the transcription of some of these testimonies in the frames.

The author emphasizes the rejection faced by young people who went out to distribute flyers in the subway with slogans against television stations and media manipulation. Mora drew a young woman with a "television head" who went into a subway car to distribute flyers. A girl asks for a flyer, but her mother reproaches her, "leave it if you do not know what it is!" The mother immediately pulls the girl out of the subway. In other panels, the author sketches the information sessions that the young people conducted in the walkways of the subway. Some people talked to them, seeking more information about the movement, and praised their work. Others defended previous governments or questioned their political position. The researcher Rossana Reguillo (2000) claims that the concerns of society are not precisely due to the transformations and disorders that the young people are experiencing, but that they are rather due to their questioning of the lies with which that society arms itself in order to continue believing in normalcy that the political discontent, demoralization, and explosive aggressiveness of young people is unmasking (p. 65).

In addition, Mora highlights the massive actions young people are engaged in, such as the "Festival of the Light of Truth," a protest that took place outside of the *Televisa Chapultepec* television station on June 13, 2012. This company was linked to the media campaign in favor of candidate Enrique Peña Nieto. The author uses photographs of the event as panels; in these, performances and video projections are shown on the walls of the television station. He also recovers the independent candidate debate that was broadcast via the Internet, one of the achievements of the movement.

The graphic novel culminates with the phrase attributed to Salvador Allende: "Being young and not a revolutionary is a biological contradiction." As Karl Mannheim (1993) wrote, young people oriented by the same historical-current problem live in a "generational connection" (p. 223). Through graphic narrative, Augusto Mora demonstrates how social and cultural activism around the #YoSoy132 Movement helped forge a generation.

Conclusions

The main objective of this study was to elucidate whether the graphic novel comprises a tool for the recovery of historical memory. *Grito de Victoria* rescues stories that have not been told or that disappeared in time but that are present in the minds of those who lived them. Augusto Mora also records his memories and gives them a voice in the frames. This chapter presents how two student movements in Mexico are reconstructed by what Tzvetan Todorov calls the exemplary use of memory.

In the first part of the graphic novel, through a resource similar to cinematographic parallel montage, the author intertwines two stories. First, the story of Victoria and Vicente, two young people who participated in the June 10, 1971 Student March, and who were the victims of the paramilitary attack known as *Halconazo*. Second, the story of Valentín and Vanesa, young couple who attended the protests against the presidential inauguration of President Enrique Peña Nieto on December 1, 2012, outside the Chamber of Representatives, in the Historical Center of Mexico City.

In the second part, the author employs comic journalism to provide the reader with testimonies of certain characters who lived through the 1971 massacre. The versatility offered by the graphic narrative allowed the author to utilize drawings, photomontage and collage to recount the origin of the #YoSoy132 Movement to the events leading up to the repression of the march on December 1, 2012.

Another contribution of *Grito de Victoria* lies in rescuing the role of young people as agents of change. Eric Hobsbawm (1998) stated that, in dictatorial countries, young people were often the only citizen collective capable of taking political action (p. 300). Although Mexico did not have a military dictatorship, it also had these repressive practices at the same time South American countries under military dictatorships did: for this reason, the catalyst of historical memory is the war against oblivion. Sometimes the past can be reluctant to being forgotten and can come back and update itself in different ways. This is because persistent social actors do not allow us to forget it and insist on its presence (Jelin, 2002, p. 15). Augusto Mora envisions the intrinsic capacity of the graphic novel to recover the past, and it can function as a means of bringing us in closer proximity to the past.

Notes

* The participation of this author was conducted with the financial support of the Postdoctoral Fellowship Programme of UNAM, advised by PhD Vicente Quirarte Castañeda.
1 Alfonso Cuarón related that when he was a child, he saw the photograph in which a hawk chased a student with long hair and a white shirt. While he runs away, the student turns around with a face of disbelief of what is happening. In the background, there was a furniture store with big windows through which people looked down upon the scenario (Netflix España, 2018).

References

Bartual Moreno, R. (2010). *Poética de la narración pictográfica: de la tira narrativa al comic* [Dissertation]. https://repositorio.uam.es/handle/10486/10334

Bonnet, P. (s.f). Narrar la guerra. *Revista Conmemora*. Centro Nacional de Memoria Histórica de Colombia. www.archivodelosddhh.gov.co/saia_release1/colecciones/co_poc_1_acceso/PA4840.pdf

Catalá Carrasco, J., Drinot, P. and Scorer J. (2017). *Comics and memory in Latin America*. University of Pittsburgh Press.

De Cabo, C. y Pereira, L. (2009). Introducción al estudio del comic biográfico y otros tipos de historietas no funcional. *V Jornadas de Jóvenes Investigadores*. Instituto de Investigaciones Gino Germani de la Universidad de Buenos Aires, Buenos Aires, Argentina. www.aacademica.org/000-089/91.pdf

Eisner, W. (2008). *Comics and sequential art: Principles and practices from the legendary cartoonist*. W.W. Norton & Company.

El Heraldo de México (2017). *Novela gráfica: Movimientos sociales en cómic*. 15 de junio. https://heraldodemexico.com.mx/cultura/2017/6/15/novela-grafica-movimientos-sociales-en-comic-12555.html

González Villareal, R. (2016) Materia, sustancia y forma de la protesta: Flujos moleculares y compuestos molares en #YoSoy132. En Olivier Téllez, M. G. (Coord.) *Educación, política y movimientos sociales*. Universidad Autónoma Metropolitana.

Gorodischer, J. (2013). Reunión Cumbre del periodismo en comic. *Revista Anfibia*.

Gutiérrez Cham, G. y Kaltmeier, O. (2020). *¡Aquí los jóvenes! Frente a las crisis*. Universidad de Guadalajara.

Hobsbawm, E. (1998). *La historia del siglo XX*. Crítica.

Jelin, E. (2002). *Los trabajos de la memoria*. Siglo XXI.

Jelin, E. (2017). *La lucha por el pasado. Cómo construimos la memoria social*. Siglo XXI.

Lenin Salgado, A. (2015). *Una Vida en Guerra: Cuando el genocidio tuvo permiso*. Editorial Paradigma.

Mannheim, K. (1993). El problema de las generaciones. *Revista Española de Investigaciones Sociológicas*. (62). https://doi.org/10.2307/40183643

Matos Agudo, D. (2016). El cómic periodístico como testigo: memoria y desmemoria. En: Lluch-Prats et al. (Editores.) *Las batallas del cómic* (pp. 248–264). Universitat de València. https://roderic.uv.es/handle/10550/58688

Miranda, J. (2018). Armando Salgado: 'He luchado para olvidar, no para entender'. *Revista Proceso*. www.proceso.com.mx/nacional/2018/4/20/armando-salgado-he-luchado-para-olvidar-no-para-entender-203578.html

Mora, A. (2013). *Grito de Victoria*. Muerte Querida Ediciones.

Morales Sierra, F. (2014). *El movimiento estudiantil #YoSoy132: antología hemerográfica* [Dissertation]. http://ri.ibero.mx/handle/ibero/523

Netflix España (17 de diciembre de 2018). Preguntas y Respuestas de #MiROMA con el Director Alfonso Cuarón en CDMX [Video]. *YouTube*. www.youtube.com/watch?v=xZ_SodWzcZY

Ortega, J. (2006). *El otro camino: cuarenta y cinco años de trinchera en trinchera*. Fondo de Cultura Económica.

Ortiz Medina, A. y Hernández Nieto, L. N. (2015). La Revolución Mexicana en el espejo de la caricatura estadounidense. En: Azuela de la Cueva, A. (Editor.) *México: 200 años de imágenes e imaginarios cívicos, Volumen I* (pp. 186–217). Instituto de Investigaciones Estéticas UNAM. http://dx.doi.org/10.22201/iie.9786070274428e.2017

Reguillo, R. (2000). *Emergencia de las culturas juveniles. Estrategias del desencanto*. Norma.

Todorov, T. (2000). *Los abusos de la memoria*. Paidós.

3
THE MEMORY OF TRAUMA UNDER THE DICTATORSHIP AS PORTRAYED IN CONTEMPORARY CHILEAN COMICS. A COMPARATIVE PERSPECTIVE WITH SPAIN

Elena Masarah Revuelta and Gerardo Vilches Fuentes

Introduction

The weight that traumatic past events have on present-day societies in Chile and Spain, where political and public debate continue to be ongoing, can only be understood by analyzing the magnitude of the violent legacy that the dictatorships of Francisco Franco (1936-1975) and Augusto Pinochet (1973-1990) left on their respective countries: 150,000 people murdered during the Spanish Civil War and the post-war period, and over 3,000 dead or missing along with 40,000 victims of abuse and torture under the Chilean dictatorship. The coup d'état on September 11, 1973 in Chile marked the beginning of a state-backed policy of violence in which torture was the regular method taken against dissidents. The ultimate goal was to quell all responses to the new regime's neoliberal political agenda; therefore, this violence cannot be separated from its political objective (Horvitz Vásquez, 2010, p. 99).

As such, recording the number of casualties and analyzing repression mechanisms in both countries has been a priority, not only for historians but also for society as a whole. Historiographical work thus coexists with the demands of collective movements around memory: recognition, recovery and repair. This situation reveals the controversial and complex relationship between history and memory, which are presented as two different means for reconciling with the past. Not only does this point of view spark public debate, only amplified through the media and social networks, but it also sparks an epistemological debate around the limits of each of these concepts and the need to include new sources and methods of analysis.

The politics of memory in Chile and Spain: a comparative perspective

Within this context, comparatively analyzing the politics of memory and recovering testimonies that document repression and seek to remedy victims can help shed

DOI: 10.4324/9781003333296-5

some light on these phenomena. This methodological strategy is one that is repeatedly conveyed in the work of Paloma Aguilar Fernández (2008), Jaume Peris Blanes (2008), Julián Chaves Palacios (2010) and Luis Martín-Cabrera (2016). However, this approach is even more pertinent not only because of the cultural, historical and political ties between Chile and Spain[1] but also because of the parallels we can draw between the two countries. Both coups d'état staged against the democratic governments were legitimized by presenting communism as a dangerous threat. Narratives were created to place blame on these governments and the left-wing and in turn to present the coup leaders as saviors of the nation. Moreover, both transitions to democracy occurred without any rifts, through transformations propelled by the dictatorships themselves. What is even more important is that both in Chile and in Spain, not to mention Argentina, a decision had to be made about what to do with the legacy of the human rights violations inherited from the previous regime (Aguilar, 2008, p. 425). These transitions ensured the impunity of leaders and perpetrators under "pacts of silence" to protect them from being tried for their crimes. In Chile, the Amnesty Law (1978) was promulgated early on, still under the dictatorship. In Spain, amnesty (1977) was granted after the country had already transitioned to a democracy, and it provided protection for all political crimes. In the long run, it was the ideological heirs of the dictatorship who benefited the most (Aguilar, 2008, p. 419).

The Spanish transition thus initiated a period of "urgent memory" (Mainer, 2006, pp. 144–148) which logically arose after a period during the dictatorship (1936–1977) marked by the "denial of memory," then "politics of oblivion" during the transition (1977–1981), and finally the "suspension of memory" during the first democratic governments (1982–1996) (Espinosa, 2006, pp. 171–204). The year 1996 saw the emergence of the "revival of memory," the seed that would later be known as the "movement for the recovery of historical memory" which broke out in 2001 with the mass grave exhumations. This shift occurred thanks to a combination of certain factors among which the existence of a large historiographical corpus, the birth of a sort of politics of memory, the urgency for vindication on the part of many of the survivors (Yusta, 2014, pp. 23–41), and an international context of heightened activism surrounding memory both in Western Europe and in Latin America (Traverso, 2007; Quílez Esteve and Rueda Laffond, 2017, pp. x–xii). Years later, the enactment of the Spanish Law of Historical Memory in 2007 marked a milestone and opened an intense debate around the subject. The political right's resistance to condemning the dictatorship, the rejection of the law by memory associations – "They wanted crimes to be tried, to circumvent amnesty with a conceptualization of imprescriptible crimes, and justice to liberate their grandparents from the status of *just another* missing person" (Rodrigo, 2012, p. 243) – and the inexistence of monuments commemorating the victims (Aguilar, 2008, p. 432) demonstrate the limits, shortfalls and difficulties in the politics of memory.

As for Chile, despite the committees and reports aimed at recognizing and remedying victims,[2] and the politics of memory spaces – with the renaming of sites where political torture or repression took place such as Villa Grimaldi and Estadio Nacional – and the restitution of Allende's figure (Aguilar, 2008, pp. 426–428), the politics of memory have been criticized for letting crimes against human rights go unpunished and for offering a vision of these that disconnects them from neoliberal politics and Pinochet's regime. In fact, a certain viewpoint exists that focuses on human rights and tends to reduce punished activists to their status as victims, and in this way, conceals the political causes for which they were tortured or murdered (Martín-Cabrera, 2016, p. 259).

Memory in images

Enzo Traverso wrote that both memory and history are constructed from the present. The difference is that the former is always subjective. It does not need evidence and "is a construction always filtered by knowledge acquired after the facts" (Traverso, 2007, p. 22). Whereas the latter must tend toward universal truth through an "objective, empirical, documentary and factual verification" of the former (Traverso, 2007, p. 24). For Traverso, memory is constantly being re-created. What he means by this assertion is that the oral testimonies given by witnesses can change the discourse throughout their lives depending on the different personal and social contexts. Yet, it is true that certain testimonies can become fixed and closed when they are written down in the form of a diary or memoir, or even in artistic forms such as novels, music, film or comics. Traverso alludes to Hegel, who asserted that only populations with a written language could have a memory, while all others have a primitive memory "made up of images" (Traverso, 2007, pp. 25–26). Perhaps this hierarchical vision of the relationship between words and images explains the predominance of the former in memory studies. However, since the second half of the 20th century, and most notably in the 21st century, the remembrance society that emerged after the debates surrounding the Holocaust has grown and evolved hand in hand with the images on the big screen (Lipovetsky and Serroy, 2009). As such, we can add a new element to the problematic relationship between history and memory: visual representation. A contemporary interpretation of events given by a witness is followed by, on the one hand, an open process of construction through oral means, and on the other, by a closed process of memory rendering that can be done through written words or drawings. This constitutes visual memory, which requires its own set of analysis methods and tools different from those used for textual memory.

Provided that visuality and language are intimately intertwined despite the fact that they never coincide, as recognized by Keith Moxey (2015, p. 163), and that we create a large part of our world through a dialogue between verbal and pictorial representations, in the words of W.J.T. Mitchell (2017, p. 154), we can conclude that the verbal and visual language of comics is ideal for rendering memory, especially one rooted in trauma. Hillary Chute established a tradition that dates back to Spanish painter Francisco de Goya, who in the 19th century represented crimes committed during the Spanish War of Independence (1808–1812). In one of his prints from the series *The Disasters of War*, he wrote the caption "I Saw It" as a way to vindicate the importance of directly witnessing traumatic events (2016, p. 10). Chute's thesis is that it is the very nature of their language that "connects comics to the practice and possibility of witness, to the expression of realities of lived life and history" (2016, p. 70). From the perspective of memory and testimony, the juxtaposition between images and words creates a layout on the page that revolutionizes the notions of chronology and causality of time and space, "on the idea that 'history' can ever be a close discourse or a simply progressive one" (2016, p. 4).

Authors such as Moxey have already warned that visual objects go beyond linguistic conventions and must be analyzed with other tools (2015, p. 130). When it comes to comics, it is even more necessary to develop a specific methodology that goes beyond just describing the images or analyzing from a cinematic perspective to understand the relationship between verbal and visual elements as a "hybridization," beyond a mere juxtaposition of words and drawings (Davies, 2019, p. 69).

The memory of traumatic events under the dictatorship in Chilean comics

The comics studied in this article can be classified into two main categories. The first is "memory comics," where we can classify *Fuentealba:1973* (2017) by Ricardo Fuentealba Rivera and *Historias clandestinas* (2014)[3] by brothers Ariel and Sol Rojas Lizana. The first work is a type of direct testimony written by the author as an adult – he was born in 1936 – that depicts the coup and the violent repression that occurred during the early days in different parts of his town. The way of approaching testimony and representing it through drawings draws an allusion to Goya, and in fact, the author mentions him directly. First, when he refers to "Goya's dirty war" to make a connection between that conflict and Pinochet's coup (Fuentealba, 2017, p. 24), and second, when he compares a Chilean soldier with one of the riflemen depicted by the painter in his painting *Los fusilamientos del 3 de mayo* (*The Third of May 1808*): "That was when I saw him. A chubby man: blind, like the riflemen in Goya's *The Third of May*, piercing the air with the heavy stomps of his boots, violently raising his Indian hand in the air"[4] (Fuentealba, 2017, p. 26).

As for *Historias clandestinas*, it represents the authors' childhood memory. When the authors were children, their family home became the hideout for Ernesto Miranda, the leader of the Revolutionary Left Movement (MIR), and his partner Veronica. To create this childlike perspective, in most of the book the authors use a naive style, one that conjures up the world of children and draws similarities with graphic novels such as *Persepolis* (2000–2003) by Marjane Satrapi.

The second category corresponds to "history comics": *Los años de Allende* (2018 [2015]) by Carlos Reyes and Rodrigo Elgueta, *El golpe. El pueblo 1970–1973* (2014)[5] by Nicolás Cruz and Quique Palomo and *Anticristo* (2017) by Javier Rodríguez. In all three books, the authors depict events that did not happen to them directly. Furthermore, they fictionalize to different degrees as a strategy for relating testimonies and constructing a memory of repression. This takes on literary codes even though it works with the same memories as a direct testimony in first person. Paradoxically, it can give more solidity to testimonies and memories even when it does so from a stylistic point of view, which is the case of thrillers (Peris Blanes, 2008, pp. 323–324). Not only does fiction end up being more effective than historical linearity in presenting multiple perspectives (Burke, 2015, p. 18), but it also, in instances where it offers up deviations from historical events, "can provide an alternative notion of justice, . . . in its attempt to create an alternative history" (Martín-Cabrera, 2016, p. 4). This thought-provoking idea – proper to post-modernity and which we can see in pop culture such as films by Quentin Tarantino *Inglourious Basterds* (2009) and *Once Upon a Time in Hollywood* (2019) – perfectly explains the mechanism that is used in *Anticristo* by Javier Rodríguez. However, we must point out that, in fact, non-fiction comics have used this same strategy since their very beginnings: as Hillary Chute suggests, Keiji Nakazawa, in his comic *Barefoot Gen* (1973), made his wish of being a witness come true. After the dropping of the atomic bomb on Hiroshima, he bears witness to the barefoot corpses of his family; however, in a prior short comic titled *I Saw It* (1972) – another reference to Goya – the same author remained faithful to the events and narrated that in fact he never had the opportunity to witness this event (Chute, 2016, p. 125). In *Anticristo*, Rodríguez presents a fake investigation around the Corpus Christi Massacre (1987), in which the CNI forces murdered opponents of Pinochet's regime for attempting an attack against the dictator. To give the story authenticity, first the author depicts himself as well as other real characters such as historian Luis Rojas Núñez and Guillermo Teillier, president of the Chilean Communist Party. The first part of the comic adopts many of the tools used in audiovisual language, so much so that at times it seems as though it is representing frames from a television news report – the author has explained that he makes "graphic movies" and that his main inspiration comes from cinema and series (Reyes, 2017). Rodríguez starts by telling the facts we already know, but at one point he introduces a fictitious narrative element suggestive of the horror genre: a vampire has been murdering all the members of the CNI who took part in the operation. In Rodríguez's opinion, the supernatural element is fitting because the real story is so terrifying and brutal that it seems unbelievable: "the elements I introduced can be understood as a way to hyperbolize the time period" (Reyes, 2017). Thus, the desire to take revenge on Pinochet's regime for orchestrating this massacre is fulfilled. It is interesting to point out that the author always maintains a realistic tone in his drawings, with clear photographic references in his portraits of real people, in order to give his work greater authenticity.

This strategy is similar to the one chosen by Rodrigo Elgueta and Carlos Reyes in *Los años de Allende* and by Quique Palomo and Nicolás Cruz in *El golpe. El pueblo 1970–1973*. Their styles do not resemble that of Rodríguez's, but they do use the same realism and reference to photographs. The effect is the same: reinforcing the authenticity of what is being told. Although the historical events depicted in *Los años de Allende* are real and meticulously documented, the authors introduce a fictitious character – American journalist John Nitsch – who creates a common thread throughout the story. As for Palomo and Cruz, they use the story of two fictitious families as a vehicle for relating true events. In recent Spanish comics, it is noteworthy to point out that fiction has not been used, in general, in the same way as in *Anticristo*. The fictitious elements introduced in works such as *El arte de volar* (2009) or *El ala rota* (2017) by Antonio Altarriba and Kim and *Cuerda de presas* (2005) by Jorge García and Fidel Martínez aim to provide real facts with narrative cohesion and even to highlight their crudity and dramatic nature, rather than seeking to offer up a more uplifting alternative version. Nevertheless, there are exceptions that use science fiction to create a version that differs from history: in *Rayos y Centellas* (1996) by David Muñoz and Luis Bustos, an alternative timeline of history is presented in which, thanks to the help of superheroes, the legitimate government of the Republic is able to beat the Nationalist faction during the Spanish Civil War.

As for *Fuentealba: 1973*, we see an operation that is remarkably similar to the one described earlier and used by Keiji Nakazawa. According to the author, the story of "El muchacho héroe del puente Pío Nono" "is the heroic story of a work colleague that I would see from time to time and to whom I pay tribute in these pages" (Fuentealba, 2017, p. 70). In it, the author tells the story of a boy who is killed at the hands of some soldiers who shoot him on a bridge. Fuentealba's expressionist lines suddenly shift to a certain degree of abstraction when, thanks to the power of fiction, the boy manages to escape alive, only to die later in his home. As Michael J. Lazzara explains, "that which is dramatic, nameless and unresolved in this episode leads to a fantasy: the boy who was shot manages to escape and does not die until he reaches his home. In this way, the story – perhaps driven by a feeling of guilt or shame that a survivor often feels as a mere result of having survived – offers this 'proletarian boy' a more dignified death" (2017, p. 10).

We also find a different kind of remedy, in this case one that is purely contained in the graphic art: Ricardo Fuentealba often depicts the soldiers, the perpetrators of repression during the military coup, with blurred faces (Fuentealba, 2017, p. 48), thus negating their identity. This is a sort of symbolic revenge which at one point tries to go even further when the narrator says, "if only I could take a pencil and erase the face of that soldier who received the wrong order, only then would I have peace of mind" (Fuentealba, 2017, p. 36). However, the author buries this wish by sinking into the feeling of defeat that lingers throughout the novel. In the full-page panel, a figure, who can be identified as the illustrator himself, approaches a soldier from behind with a pencil in his hand. However, the illustrator does not manage to go through with his figurative revenge of using his pencil to erase and thus negate the soldier's identity: "killing" in a drawing someone who killed in real life. This operation is similar to what Joan Fontcuberta has called "photo-voodoo": the act of cutting someone's face from a photo or scratching it out until it is unrecognizable as a way of getting rid of the memory of the person or erasing it from a family history (2016, pp. 218–220).

Violence against civilians

The violent repression of civilians plays an interesting role in many of the comics analyzed. Almost all of them represent it in a fragmented way, without it actually being a part of the narrative sequencing. In this analysis, we have detected two fundamental types of violence. The first occurs in public spaces and is more spontaneous in nature: immediate repression in the streets, control of protests, and clashes between political activists and state security forces or radical groups. The second is the violence carried out in private spaces such as detention centers for political prisoners, police stations and clandestine detention centers. This type of

The memory of trauma under the dictatorship   57

FIGURE 3.1   Full-page scene in *Los años de Allende*.

violence is carried out by the system and employs a strategy aimed at instilling terror and eliminating political adversaries. This extreme violence is key in constructing power and in creating new political identities (Peris Blanes, 2008, p. 30). In it, we observe clear gender biases that we will analyze on a case-by-case basis.

Perhaps the clearest examples of violence occurring in a public space can be found in *Fuentealba: 1973*. The fact that the author takes on the role of witness is fundamental in representing the violence the army deployed during the early days of the coup d'état. This is how the comic depicts various scenes where civilians are threatened with rifles and even shot at point-blank range (Fuentealba, 2017, pp. 24, 65–67). Fuentealba's style, of strong pictorial influence, tends toward an expressionist representation of bodies, focusing on the executioners and distorting them until they almost look like dehumanized monsters (Fuentealba, 2017, pp. 30, 45 and 48). The author also talks about the fear felt by those, like himself, who did not directly endure the repression or the torture: "Many of us would not feel the bloody trace of shrapnel on our skin, but we would feel the bullets of fear, the knives stabbed into our lost dreams, the weight of the perpetrator's boot, the contempt, the mockery. Walking blind for many years. Meeting a neighbor's evasive glance" (Fuentealba, 2017, p. 39); "We who were not detained, nor tortured, also suffered during that long night" (Fuentealba, 2017, p. 47). The bodies of the victims, often blurred or distorted, symbolize the fragmentation of Chilean society (Peris Blanes, 2008, pp. 26–27), and, as Lazzara asserts, "the destruction of a political project, the Chilean path to socialism" (2017, p. 10). This fragmentation can also be seen in the constant breaks in the page design, the shapes of panels, words, sentences, and even in the linearity of time, which directly influence how memory is constructed (Sánchez, 2019, p. 58). In fact, according to Peris Blanes, the fragmentation of discourse is a common characteristic among the testimonies given by survivors of violence (2008, p. 63).

In the rest of the comics, the representation of this violence is much more anecdotal and focuses on capturing a moment outside the narrative sequencing. In *Los años de Allende*, it would seem that this direct depiction of violence is deliberately omitted as if it were considered to be an "unbearable image" (Martínez Luna, 2019, p. 49). However, we do see several clashes between the extreme right nationalists from Patria y Libertad and the supporters of Unidad Popular. The most noteworthy clash happens during the Silent March (Reyes and Elgueta, 2015, p. 38), and is shown on a full page. The supporters of Unidad Popular are not victimized and are shown as equals in strength, with a spectacular frame, evocative of superhero comics. Attacks against members of Allende's government are also emphasized, although explicit violence is avoided: For example, the murder of general René Schneider – known as Operation Alpha – depicted in all accuracy, shows the violence of the act but does not show the victim's lifeless body, except for a close-up of his wounded hand in the last panel (Reyes and Elgueta, 2015, pp. 41–42). This same episode is also reflected in *El golpe. El pueblo 1970–1973* with practically the same approach, except here the general's wounded body is not even shown.

However, Palomo and Cruz's comic uses static images to show explicit depictions of those who died as a result of the violence employed by the right. These static panels are never in a sequential order and use the color red to heighten the impact of the blood. These panels recall the way Carlos Giménez represents the dead among the rearguard in the siege of Madrid during the Spanish Civil War of 36–39. *Malos tiempos* (2007, vol. 1, pp. 36, 55): he underlines the indiscriminate violence with black pools of blood and through the horror reflected on the expressions of the survivors and the dead. As for *Jamás tendré 20 años* (2016), Jaime Martín shows a sequence of three nearly mute pages in which the main character finds the bodies of her anarchist comrades who had been murdered at the beginning of the Spanish Civil War, murders we do not see. In this example, the author draws the dead with no blood but with bruises and explicit expressions on their faces, which make them more realistic than those drawn by Giménez (Martín, 2016, pp. 28–30).

Torture

Torture was used during most of Pinochet's dictatorship and sought to eliminate political dissidence and dissolve opposing groups. What is noteworthy is that this subject is present in almost all the Chilean comics analyzed but few of them show it explicitly. The difficulty in narrating the trauma of torture is common to almost all the testimonies. Some of the narrative strategies witnesses most often use are fragmentation, dissolution of the self, or the imposition of an "objectifying distance" (Peris Blanes, 2008, pp. 60–63).

Realistic illustrations intended to explicitly represent atrocious events are forced to use direct graphic rendering. This explains why many of them use ellipses or other strategies to avoid depicting torture in this way, although this is how the latter is found in many written and oral testimonies. In *Fuentealba: 1973*, the narrator alludes to torture without illustrations actually showing it: "the real [story] was being written by the men and women in the torture chairs, in the 'camps' in the middle of the desert, and in the rat nests of silent cities" (Fuentealba, 2017, p. 29). The same thing occurs in *El golpe. El pueblo 1970–1973*, in which a woman talks about the tortures in concentration camps: "children . . . and they would bring them dead . . . torn apart. For some of them, you couldn't even recognize their little faces." In *Los años de Allende*, the authors do not talk about the post-coup period, but they do show a torture victim, a double agent who we see after they have already given him the coup de grâce but without actually being witnesses to the process (Reyes y Elgueta, 2015, p. 112). It is not haphazard that the only comic to show a direct image of this violence is the one that uses the least naturalistic graphic style: in *Historias clandestinas*, we witness an isolated action of torture when two burly men are hitting a detainee tied to a chair. However, the image does not show the moment when the detainee is hit but rather the moment immediately after. The text is what provides all the information: "The torturers hit the prisoners with bars wrapped in wet towels so as not to leave any visible marks on their skin" (chapter 3: Resistencia).

Ariel and Sol Rojas Lizana maintain a distance with torture that does not exist in the best example of how comics depict this question: the work of Spanish author Ángel de la Calle, *Pinturas de guerra* (2017). Although the novel focuses on the memory that a group of Latin American artists have of exile after moving to Paris, the first chapter is set during an unspecified time of Pinochet's reign in Chile. A group of intellectuals met after curfew hours in a house in the outskirts of the capital. At one point in the night, one of them finds in the basement various people who have been brutally tortured, to such an extent that it is impossible to tell which ones are still alive (De la Calle, 2017, pp. 25–27). Although Ángel de la Calle

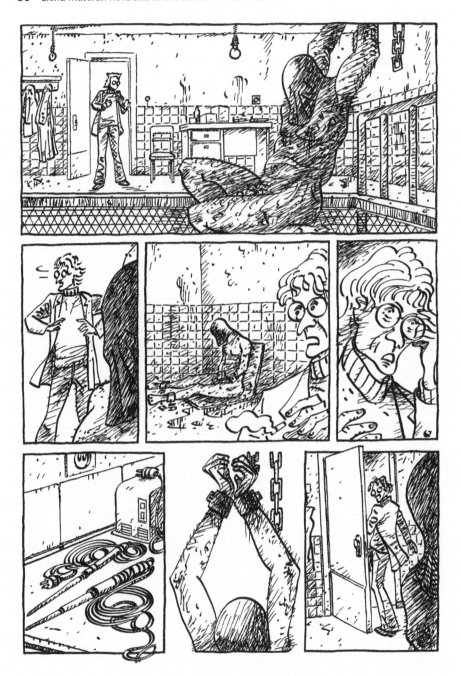

FIGURE 3.2 An intellectual finds tortured people in a basement in *Pinturas de guerra*.

does not directly depict the act, he uses two different strategies to address it. The first is to show the effect on the bodies, reflected in dirty, harsh strokes, without overlooking the details. The second strategy is to use a conversation between two torturers who refer to the most horrific techniques widely documented in survivors' testimonies, including electric shocks, rats and rape (De la Calle, 2017, p. 29). It is worth pointing out that in contrast to the Spanish framework that uses a group of intellectuals, here we see a dialogue between two torturers who speak in a very vulgar Chilean Spanish with expressions such as "conchetumadre," "colisa," "ahueonao," "culiar" and "poronga" (De la Calle, 2017, pp. 29–34).

Spanish comics are not generous when it comes to representing torture during the Franco regime, but there is a good example in *Miguel Núñez. Mil vidas más* (2021 [2010]) by Pepe Gálvez and Alfonso López, which narrates episodes from the life of the well-known anti-Franco guerilla fighter. Captured in 1958, Miguel Núñez was a victim of torture during the interrogation he endured in a police station in Barcelona. During this sequence, the authors stop using the illustration style which is present throughout the entire comic, a style that is based on chiaroscuro, with light lines and a certain degree of caricaturing of the characters but not for the sake of humor. When the torture begins, the lines become expressionist and nervous, with broken lines and exaggerated shapes: In fact, the illustrator does away with panels when the violence reaches a climax (Gálvez and López, 2021, pp. 80–87). To express the horror, the bodies are symbolically distorted: the victim appears as a helpless and disconnected figure, predominantly in white, whereas the killers have black bodies and appear dehumanized. Transformed into grotesque monsters with wild eyes and sharp teeth, they hit the defenseless prisoner without an inkling of pity (Gálvez y López, 2021, pp. 85 and 87). This representation strategy is linked to the use of poetic language that Peris Blanes has analyzed for certain testimonies, and which is used to narrate events otherwise difficult to approach with common everyday language (2007, p. 77). The sequence reflects the intention to "transform the subject into a substance that is moldable by bodily torture" (Peris Blanes, 2007, p. 45) because as Miguel Núñez wrote, "the violence, torture and terror used against them [the people] . . ., sought . . . to convert a decent and exemplary person into an indecent and chastened being" (Gálvez et al., 2010, p. 78).

Violence against women

For Chilean women, the coup and the dictatorship that followed meant a return to the traditional gender model in which their role in society was reduced to being mothers, wives and housekeepers. Beyond a quantitative analysis,[6] the violence used against them, especially when they were victims of political detention and torture, must be analyzed from a qualitative perspective to take into account the gender biases of the repression techniques used on the victims. This concept has been studied in other time periods in history and in other locations, but in order to better understand this situation, we need to overcome the concept of "sexual violence," which is generally understood as "one of the most serious forms of violence" (Comisión Nacional sobre Prisión Política y Tortura, 2004, p. 251). Rather, it is more fitting to use the concrete concept of "gendered repression." Introduced by historian Maud Joly (2002), this term refers to the mechanisms of physical and symbolic violence and repression that directly attack femininity and sex, "sex being understood as the sex organs as well as the parts of the body that our society considers related to sexuality or to sexual appropriation" (Cases and Ortega, 2020, p. 359). As for the Spanish Civil War, which has been thoroughly studied thanks to the recovery of memory in personal testimonies, these punishments refer not only to rapes but also to other questions such as the language used by repressors during trials (Sánchez, 2009) and the act of shaving heads, which many women from the Republican faction were subject to because they met two conditions: they were women and *rojas* (left wing).

The gendered repression that occurred during the early days of the coup appears briefly in *El golpe. El pueblo 1970–1973*: in a short sequence, various soldiers mercilessly cut the hair and trousers of several women, calling one of them "whore." This image reproduces three aspects of violence against women: a physical punishment against femininity (shaving heads), a symbolic punishment against the new clothes progressive women wore (tearing the trousers), and finally an insult ("whore") which refers to their sexual freedom.

In *Fuentealba: 1973*, these concepts are more extensively developed. In a sequence, the author represents a young girl "girl-woman" who has been detained in the street by soldiers. Between fits of laughter, they insult her and call her a "dirty slut." Scissors appear in various panels as a symbolic representation of the repression of women. The soldiers blindfold the young girl as a way to dehumanize her and then proceed with the humiliating punishment: The victimized body of the young girl – who calls out for her mother – is the main focus of one page in which the panel covers up her genitals. In addition to cutting her hair, they destroy her trousers: "they imposed upon women the punishment of traditional skirt wearing, destroying their coquettish trousers with no lack of disgust, in the absurd belief that the trousers turned them into guerilla fighters." Rape as a form of punishment does not appear graphically but is referred to: "there he was, the shady soldier who boasted about those he shaved; the raped teenage girls, while he undauntedly partook in the 'ultimate' punishment" (Fuentealba, 2017, pp. 28–33).

It is worth noting that in the few Spanish comics that have addressed these questions, we find a more direct and less symbolic type of representation. The shaving of heads appears in the first very interesting scenes of two graphic novels. Although the novels are quite different from one another, what they have in common is the exhaustive documentation work put into this subject: *Paseo de los canadienses* (2015) by Carlos Guijarro and *Cuerda de presas* by Jorge García and Fidel Martínez. In the first work, the fictitious memories of an old lady tell of all types of traumatic experiences, including repression, a rape attempt, and the shaving of heads (Guijarro, 2015, p. 81). In *Cuerda de presas*, set in a women's prisons during the postwar period, one of the survivors talks in the present time about how the Falangists would shave all the women's hair (García and Martínez, 2017, p. 29). The representation of prisoners is very brutal and grim. Their shaven heads together with the signs of hunger make them look very sick and dehumanized: "What women? Can't you see they're just prisoners?" (García and Martínez, 2017, p. 80).

This same story also very explicitly represents the brutality of torture: on two panels and in violent expressionist graphic design, the main character recalls how electric shocks were administered to her nipples (García and Martínez, 2017, p. 31). This method, applied using an instrument called "picana" in Latin America, was frequently used to torture political prisoners in Chile. However, even though it frequently appears in written testimonies, the authors of Chilean comics do not represent it in illustrations. *Pinturas de guerra* addresses this more in detail: in a torture scene, Ángel de la Calle represents the naked bodies of various men and women with hoods over their heads – another strategy for dehumanizing them (De la Calle, 2017, pp. 25–27). The condition of women being focused on corresponds almost point by point to some of the stories compiled in the report of Comisión Nacional sobre Prisión Política y Tortura: "They took me to a room. When I entered, I could smell the strong odor of blood. . . . They undressed me and left me there wearing only a hood over my head. They put me on a type of table with my hands and feet tied and my legs open. I felt a very powerful light that nearly burnt my skin. I heard these individuals laughing. . . . Then the interrogator came . . . and ordered them to put electric shocks on my breasts, vagina and knees" (p. 243). Even though various panels show wide angles of one of her breasts and genitals (De la Calle, 2017, p. 27), Ángel de la Calle asserted: "I did not want to sensationalize the suffering of the victims so I limited the illustrations to what was strictly necessary to narrate the horror" (*Cazarabet*, 2019). He talks of this horror in more detail in a later conversation between two torturers who refer to the "picana" as well as the practice of introducing rats into the orifices of the victims' bodies. The conversation also relates the rape of a very young girl in the same degrading words used to talk about the other women (De la Calle, 2017, pp. 30–32).

Some final reflections

The trial of Augusto Pinochet, arrested in London in 1998, marked a milestone in Chilean politics of memory. The violence of his regime was pushed to the forefront and the cause became an international one, thus putting an end to the discourse of the elites justifying the coup, a discourse already eroded by social pressure (Winn, 2007, p. 30). This trial also revealed a convergence with Spanish memory. Both Chilean and Spanish laws prohibited bringing charges against the perpetrators of crimes committed during their dictatorships. Therefore, the charges against Pinochet, brought in Spain by judge Baltasar Garzón, can be seen as a psychoanalytical "shift": "the desire to try Pinochet condenses and 'shifts' the hidden and impossible desire to try Franco" (Martín-Cabrera, 2016, p. 238).

In the 21st century, both Chile and Spain have gone through periods in which there has been a proliferation of testimonies and memories related to the controversy around the hegemonic accounts of the dictatorship and its subsequent transitions. As a result, over the last few years we have seen the emergence in these two countries of citizen and political movements that, within the context of a system in crisis, question its founding principles. This was the case with the 15-M movement in 2011 in Spain and the *estallido social* (social upheaval) in Chile in 2019 which culminated in a new constitutional process. At the same time, in both countries we are seeing the proliferation of political agents who in some cases vindicate the dictatorships or in others refuse to condemn them.

All these questions provide proof of the influence and the connection that the memory of the dictatorships has on the present and current political and social circumstances in both countries. It is therefore not unusual that this connection is made explicit in the comics analyzed, given that this medium has had a long tradition of engaging in political positioning in Chile, especially during Allende's government and the final days of the dictatorship with magazines such as *Trauko* (1988–1991). Prominent authors published in this magazine, even Ricardo Fuentealba, who decades later returned to the places where the events occurred and made illustrations. This act triggers the memory exercise in *Fuentealba: 1973*. In *Los años de Allende*, the connection with the present day appears in its conclusion when the main character returns to Chile 40 years after the coup (Reyes and Elgueta, 2015, pp. 122–123), a period of growing social tension in the country, as also depicted in the plot of *El golpe. El pueblo 1970–1973*. This work draws a clear parallel between the protests during Allende's time and the more recent ones, especially the student protests of 2011: "these are the same streets as forty years ago. The same ones where a collective dream was born and then transformed into a nightmare." As for *Historias clandestinas*, the authors also narrate the events from the present time and in line with Hugo Hinojosa's idea that, "the challenge this work raises is to look at the past, see the broken dreams and aspirations in order to question what we are right now so we can rebuild ourselves" (2018, p. 78).

In fact, all these comics were published between 2014 and 2017 around the 40th anniversary of September 11, 1973. After the difficult crisis that nearly destroyed the Chilean comics industry, the appearance of these graphic novels initiates a sort of recovery process, a perfect example of which being the international success of *Los años de Allende*. By reading these works, we see the importance this medium has in representing the individual and collective memory of an entire country and the need for historiography to definitively incorporate it into the epistemological debates around the controversial relationship between history and memory, to which we can also add images.

Notes

1 Clear ideological connections existed as early as the 1930s and 1940s with publications in Chile related to Francoist ideology and Hispanicism, under the fundamental influence of Ramiro de Maeztu (Jara Hinojosa, 2010, pp. 329–330).
2 In 1990, the Chilean government set up the Comisión Nacional de la Verdad y la Reconciliación (National Commission for Truth and Reconciliation Report) which published the Rettig report in 1991. Twenty years later in 2004, a new report was published by the Comisión Nacional sobre Prisión Política y Tortura (National Commission on Political Imprisonment and Torture Report), also known as Comisión Valech. The Comisión Presidencial Asesora para la Calificación de Detenidos Desaparecidos, Ejecutados Políticos y Víctimas de Prisión Política y Tortura (Presidential Advisory Commission for the

Classification of Disappeared Detainees, Political Executions, and Victims of Political Prison and Torture) was established in 2010 and released its report in 2011.
3 The pages of this book are not numbered, and therefore page numbers are not referenced throughout this article.
4 In Spanish in the original. Unless otherwise noted, this and all the quotes taken from the comics are our own translation.
5 The pages of this book are not numbered, and therefore page numbers are not referenced throughout this article.
6 According to the Comisión Valech's report carried out in 2004, out of the 28,459 people recognized as victims, 12.72% were women.

Bibliography

Aguilar Fernández, P. (2008) *Políticas de la memoria y memorias de la política*. Alianza Editorial, Madrid.
Burke, P. (2015) Puntos de vista: representar la guerra en la pantalla. In Bolufer, M., Gomis, J. & Hernández, T. M. (eds) *Historia y cine. La construcción del pasado a través de la ficción*. Institución Fernando el Católico, Zaragoza, pp. 17–28.
Cases, A. & Ortega, T. M. (2020) La investigación sobre la represión femenina y violencia sexuada en el franquismo. Evolución historiográfica. *Ayer*, n. 118, pp. 347–361.
Cazarabet (2019) *Cazarabet conversa con Ángel de la Calle*. www.cazarabet.com/conversacon/fichas/fichas1/pinturasdeguerra.htm
Chaves Palacios, J. (coord.) (2010) *La Larga Memoria de la Dictadura en Iberoamérica*. Prometeo Libros, Buenos Aires.
Chute, H. L. (2016) *Disaster Drawn. Visual Witness, Comics and Documentary Form*. The Belknap Press of Harvard University Press, Cambridge, MA.
Comisión Nacional de la Verdad y la Reconciliación (1991) *Informe*. Santiago de Chile.
Comisión Nacional sobre Prisión Política y Tortura (2004) *Informe*. Santiago de Chile.
Comisión Presidencial Asesora para la Calificación de Detenidos Desaparecidos, Ejecutados Políticos y Víctimas de Prisión Política y Tortura (2011) *Informe*. Santiago de Chile.
Espinosa, F. (2006) *Contra el olvido. Historia y memoria de la guerra civil*. Crítica, Barcelona.
Fisher Davies, P. (2019) *Comics as Communication. A Functional Approach*. University of Arts, Palgrave Macmillan, London.
Fontcuberta, J. (2016) *La furia de las imágenes. Notas sobre la postfotografía*. Galaxia Gutenberg, Barcelona.
Hinojosa, H. (2018) Una memoria ilustrada: problemas de la narrativa gráfica histórica contemporánea en Chile. *CuCo, Cuadernos de cómic*, n. 11, pp. 52–80.
Horvitz Vásquez, M. E. (2010) Entre la memoria y el cine. Re-visitando la historia reciente de Chile. In Chaves Palacios, J. (coord.) *La larga memoria de la dictadura en Iberoamérica. Argentina, Chile y España*. Prometeo Libros, Buenos Aires, pp. 75–112.
Jara Hinojosa, I. (2010) Imaginarios en contacto: libros, imágenes e ideas políticas de la dictadura chilena y el franquismo. In Chaves Palacios, J. (coord.) *La larga memoria de la dictadura en Iberoamérica. Argentina, Chile y España*. Prometeo Libros, Buenos Aires, pp. 325–342.
Joly, M. (2002) Posguerra y represión "sexuada": las republicanas rapadas por los franquistas (1936–1950). In *Enfrontaments civils: postguerras i reconstruccions. Actas del II Congreso de la Asociación Recerques: Historia, Economía, Cultura*. Pagés, Lleida, pp. 910–921.
Lazzara, M. J. (2017) Retazos de la memoria. In Fuentealba Rivera, R. (ed.) *Fuentealba: 1973*. Pehuén Editores, Santiago de Chile.
Lipovetsky, G. & Serroy, S. (2009) *La pantalla global. Cultura mediática y cine en la era hipermoderna*. Anagrama, Barcelona.

Mainer, J. C. (2006) Para un mapa de lecturas de la guerra civil (1960–2000). In Juliá, S. (dir.) *Memoria de la guerra y del franquismo*. Taurus, Madrid, pp. 135–161.
Martín-Cabrera, L. (2016) *Justicia radical. Una interpretación psicoanalítica de las postdictaduras en España y el Cono Sur*. Anthropos, Barcelona.
Martínez Luna, S. (2019) *Cultura visual. La pregunta por la imagen*. Sans Soleil, Vitoria-Gasteiz/Buenos Aires.
McCloud, S. (1993) *Understanding Comics: The Invisible Art*. Tundra Publishing, Northampton, MA.
Mitchell, W. J. T. (2017) *¿Qué quieren las imágenes?* Sans Soleil, Vitoria-Gasteiz/Buenos Aires.
Moxey, K. (2015) *El tiempo de lo visual. La imagen en la historia*. Sans Soleil, Vitoria-Gasteiz/Buenos Aires.
Peris Blanes, J. (2008) *Historia del testimonio chileno: de las estrategias de denuncia a las políticas de memoria (1973–2005)*. Facultat de Filología, Universitat de València, València.
Quílez Esteve, L. y Rueda Laffond, J. C. (2017) *Posmemoria de la guerra civil y el franquismo. Narrativas audiovisuales y producciones culturales en el siglo XXI*. Editorial Comares, Granada.
Reyes, C. (2017) Anticristo: dictadura, terror y found footage. *Ergocomics*. https://ergocomics.cl/wp/2017/11/02/anticristo-dictadura-terror-y-found-footage/
Rodrigo, J. (2012) El relato y la memoria. Pasados traumáticos, debates públicos y viceversa. *Ayer*, n. 87, pp. 239–249.
Sánchez, P. (2009) *Individuas de dudosa moral. La represión de las mujeres en Andalucía (1936–1958)*. Crítica, Barcelona.
Sánchez, J. (2019) El cuerpo espasmático en "1973 La Tormenta" de Ricardo Fuentealba. *Panambí* n. 8, pp. 53–63.
Traverso, E. (2007) *El pasado, instrucciones de uso. Historia, memoria, política*. Marcial Pons, Barcelona.
Winn, P. (2007) El pasado está presente. Historia y memoria en el Chile contemporáneo. In Pérotin-Dumon, A. (dir.) *Historizar el pasado vivo en América Latina*. Universidad Alberto Hurtado, Santiago de Chile.
Yusta, M. (2014) El pasado como trauma. Historia, memoria y recuperación de la memoria histórica en la España actual. *Pandora. Revue d'études hispaniques*, n. 12, pp. 23–41. https://dialnet.unirioja.es/descarga/articulo/5238920.pdf

Comics

Cruz, N. & Palomo, Q. (2014) *El golpe. El pueblo 1970–1973*. Pehuén Editores, Santiago de Chile.
De la Calle, Á. (2017) *Pinturas de guerra*. Reino de Cordelia, Sevilla.
Fuentealba Rivera, R. (2017) *Fuentealba: 1973*. Pehuén Editores, Santiago de Chile.
Gálvez, P. & López, A. (2021) *Miguel Núñez. Mil vidas más*. Desfiladero, Barcelona.
Gálvez, P., López, A. & Mundet, J. (2010) *Miguel Núñez. Mil vidas más*. De Ponent, Alicante.
García, J. & Martínez, F. (2017) [2020] *Cuerda de presas*. Astiberri, Bilbao.
Giménez, C. (2007) *36–39. Malos tiempos*, vol. 1. Glénat, Barcelona.
Guijarro, C. (2015) *Paseo de los canadienses*. De Ponent, Valencia.
Martín, J. (2016) *Jamás tendré 20 años*. Norma Editorial, Barcelona.
Reyes, C. & Elgueta, R. (2018) [2015] *Los años de Allende*. La oveja roja, Madrid [Hueders, Santiago de Chile].
Rodríguez, J. (2017) *Anticristo*. Ediciones Metales pesados, Santiago de Chile.
Rojas Lizana, A. & Rojas Lizana, S. (2014) *Historias clandestinas*. Lom Ediciones, Santiago de Chile.

4
HISTORICAL GRAPHIC NOVELS IN URUGUAY 2000–2020

María Victoria Saibene

Why historical comics?

This article aims to analyze the specific development during the first two decades of the 21st century of a narrative language that has intermittently maintained its presence in Uruguayan cultural production. Comics in Uruguay kept a marginal place within the cultural system. The Uruguayan market has always behaved inconsistently, so work-for-export was always the way out for those seeking to become professional. During the 21st century, there has been an emergence in Uruguayan production, publishing, and reading markets, all dedicated to historical issues. In the same period, there has also been a rise of state funds that have supported this process, such as the Competitive Funds for Culture. The relationship between these aspects is questionable and a central focus of this paper.

To carry out the analysis of this period and contextualize it within the global framework of comics production, the study begins by carrying out a brief periodization of the production of comics in Uruguay. The last of these stages can be traced back to the first two decades of the 21st century and is the one we will analyze more deeply.

A selection of five works covers some of the aspects of the historical graphic novels in Uruguay. These were published within the 2010–2016 period, and were mostly supported by the Competitive Funds for Culture, as winners of the Graphic Story category. To analyze the link that Uruguayan artists have had with historical comics as a genre, interviews were used as a recuperation of oral memory (Benadiba, 2014) and as a historical source.

The cross dialogue generated from the artists' responses allows us to know the framework in which these works were conceived and the relationship they had with both state policies to support culture in general and with comics in particular,

DOI: 10.4324/9781003333296-6

as well as the debates that they generated *a posteriori* among Uruguayan comic creators.

This article is part of a major research project about the aspects of historical representation through comic language in Uruguay.

Periodization of the Uruguayan strip

Comics in Uruguay have undergone a long fluctuating history since its inception. Throughout the entire 20th century, the production of comics was not always accompanied by recognition from the public or even from the artists themselves. The academic analysis of the comics in Uruguay is journalistic or encyclopedic, comprehensive and not very reflective. An example of this is the book *La Historieta en el Uruguay* (Mainero and Costa, 2012). We can identify a global periodization that allows us to analyze parts of this journey.

With minor production, not artistically valued or properly accredited, this is how the comic strip developed in Uruguay in the early years of the 20th century. Many artists signed with pseudonyms since they did not want to be identified with comic book work. The emergence of the weekly *Mundo Uruguayo* in 1919 changed the projection of the comic strip in Uruguay. "Aventuras de Peneque y Sapito" (Mainero and Costa, 2012, p. 182) first appeared in its second issue of that same year: they were six vignettes in which the dialogue incorporated elements of Uruguayan culture that identified it as national production. The identity of its author is unknown and may be considered the first Uruguayan comic strip. Since then, the comic always had space on the pages of this publication. Main figures of Uruguayan comics developed their career through this publication and through the sale of their work to agencies. Through *Mundo Uruguayo* the comic strip had a large number of readers[1] as Magdalena Broquetas points out:

> Although there is a lack of specific studies on multiple aspects that make up this publication, it does not seem risky to venture that, unlike the illustrated magazines of the beginning of the century, whose circulation was restricted to a much more limited public, *Mundo Uruguayo* was a mass consumption magazine that attracted a wide spectrum of readers.
>
> (Broquetas, 2015, p. 8)

The crisis of the mid-20th century in Uruguay broke the foundations of the epic of "How Uruguay does not exist" and with this, a cultural period was closed in which Uruguayan production was valued in the country. From then on, the economic crisis and the radicalization of political positions around the dominant ideologies after the Second World War led to the politicization of comics' production. Two aspects emerged: comics at the service of the author's political position and other comics with no connection to the political-social-economic reality that the country was experiencing at that time, but which also implied to a certain extent a position taken by their authors.

During the years of political dictatorship,[2] new artists began to work mainly in children's magazines and visiting the science fiction and fantasy genres. In the last years of the dictatorship (1973–1985), at the beginning of the eighties, the cultural movement allowed the birth in Montevideo of graphic humor magazines with a strong political imprint. Thus, *El Dedo* with its seven numbers and then *Guambia*, in its different incarnations for almost 30 years, were a space for growth. Among the artists who participated in these two magazines, Fermín "Ombú" Hontou and Luis "Tunda" Prada were the masters for most cartoonists, from 1993 onwards they jointly carried out a drawing and comic workshop for twenty years, which was that a seedbed for next generations.

In the late nineties, comics gained strength with the emergence of a series of self- published publications. Until that moment, the comic strip in Uruguay had always been part of periodical press publications; however, it was never the central axis of them. There were also no specific publishing houses in the field, or state financial support, and their readership was scarce. Despite this, comics at this point in time engendered several attempts to start their own publishing projects with different results.

A review of these publications can be found in Santullo's article (1999) published in the magazine *Posdata*. It is worth noting the emergence of a trend of self-publishers, as a result of the appearance of the fanzine from Colonia, *Ángel Negro*, by Leandro Di Pascuale. With the format of neighborhood magazines that were sponsored by local businesses, *Ángel Negro* was a magazine of superhero comics, which positioned his creator as a pioneer of the self-published fanzine production in Montevideo. Among these self-managed projects, the magazine *Balazo* coordinated by Gezzio and another magazine, *Montevideo Ciudad Gris* by Rodolfo Santullo and various artists, stand out. It is also interesting to look at the magazine *¡Guacho!*, by José Gabriel Lagos (2011), where he reflects on his role in defining Uruguayan identity for the 21st century.

In 2003, the management of newspaper *La República* entrusted Ardito with the task of putting together a comic book magazine that would include many of the names that were involved in the comic field at that time. The result was *Quimera* magazine. Shortly after, relevant names of self-publishers, such as Pablo "Roy" Leguisamo and Beatriz Leibner with their "Freedom Knights" series or Nicolás Peruzzo and his "Tales of Ciudad Fructoxia," would be published there. The newspaper's publishing move spearheaded the emergence of artists/publishers who went against commercial forecasts and helped to create a reader market. Since then, the comic strip in Uruguay has undergone a boom process with some characteristics that we will analyze later, production growth and expansion, and the consolidation of a consumer/reader market.

In 2000, to mark the milestone at the end of the century, a fundamental work for the national comic strip, *Historiet@s.uy*, was published by Editorial AlmaZen. In this work, five stories by national authors were adapted to the comic format, so it was then the closest thing to a front-page by local artists (Eduardo Barreto, Daniel González-Carlos di Lorenzo, Tunda, Ombú and Renzo Vayra). Based on a group of renowned mainstream artists from the 20th century, comic books/graphic novels in Uruguay were consolidated during the first two decades of the 21st century. Especially with the creation of publishing houses that began to professionalize, such as Grupo Belerofonte in 2005, followed later by Dragón Cómics, led by the aforementioned Roy and Bea, or Peruzzo's Ninfa Cómics.

These authors opened spaces to show themselves to the public. They took part in artists fairs (the Book and Engraving Fair, later known as Ideas+), and the first editions of events dedicated to comics (Montevideo Comics). By showing themselves as a constant presence in these events and through the production of original material that could be found there, they were nurturing the relationship with the specific reading public and expanding it. Every year in these meetings, the public knew that they could find new works, and the publishers could rely on strong direct sales. New releases of graphic novels were gradually linked mainly to these two annual events. In some cases, these publishers and artists allowed themselves to think about entering other markets such as Argentina. Since 2000, Argentina's economic crisis, publishing conditions were similar to Uruguay's. The emergence of publishing houses with a similar profile and regular events on both shores created an unusual level of integration for artists from the Río de la Plata. From this relationship works that combined both Argentine and Uruguayan authors were produced. This also facilitated the entry of Uruguayan authors into the Argentine market. The meeting between Uruguayan authors also generated shared spaces that allowed mutual knowledge and over time fostered collaboration which led in 2011 to the signing of the statutes of the AUCH (Uruguayan Association of Cartoonists).

In 2005, the national Law No. 17,930 of December 2005 in its articles 238 and 250 created the Competitive Fund for Culture. Its implementation was regulated in the following year and since then it has been part of the state support for artistic projects in the country. In the 2007 call, a Graphic Story category was already included, although later, in 2015, the category was shared with Animation and then it became part of the new Editorial Proposals category, losing its specific space. During these years, the possibility of having funds allowed the strengthening and professionalization of this group of Uruguayan authors. The comics that were published from the competitive funds had capital to invest in their edition, something unprecedented for the Uruguayan comic scene. Print quality improved and, above all, allowed authors to charge creation fees beyond the copyright. The winner of the fund should be Uruguayan but nothing prevented the collaboration with foreign artists, which also fostered the already flourishing link between Argentine and Uruguayan comics production.

The boom of the 21st century: historical comics as a phenomenon

It is at this time in the growth of comic production and comics reading audiences that a specific interest in stories of historical nature began developing: comics that dealt with specific events in Uruguayan history; stories that developed fictional accounts complying with the rules of the literary genre but were also immersed in specific historical settings; stories that collected personal experiences in a testimonial way.

Determining the starting point of this genre can be complicated since other previous genres are mixed, such as the *gauchesco* comics. The public used to read comics that had an approach to historical work through the aforementioned *Ismael* from Cortinas, but also in others closer in time like *Las aventuras de Santos Cruz*, the gaucho created by Gezzio. Along these lines, and as a result of the first call for the Competitive Funds (2006), two volumes of the cartoon *Muxica* by Nicolás Rodriguez Juele were published, which tells the life of a fictional character from the *charrúa* tribe. Subsequently, we find prolific output of works that encompass various categories within the historical comic such as *Los últimos días del Graf Spee* (Santullo and Bergara, 2008), *Acto de Guerra* (Santullo and Bergara, 2010), *Cardal* (Betancor and Ginevra, 2012), and *Morir por el Che: 1961* (Leguisamo, Vergara and Di Lorenzo, 2013).

On the other hand, stories about the colonial period have had strong pedagogical content. Taking this into account a project of digital comics called Bandas Orientales, later renamed as Educational Bands, was started. It was the winner of the Funds destined to financing projects related to the celebration of the Bicentennial of the Revolution in 2011. Initially, they were digital comics that narrated the process of the Revolution during the year 1811. Through monthly episodes, the center of the plot was developed as fiction but the historical framework followed the events that took place in that same month of 1811. Given the structure of the project, it allowed the episodes to be narratively independent and to be developed by a great variety of authors. The first year of Bandas Orientales, gathered the vast majority of artists who were active at that time in Uruguay, generating a visually striking project due to the great diversity and artistic quality. Subsequently, the project continued and through the financing obtained by the Competitive Funds, it finished narrating the complete process of the *artiguista* revolution and even advanced in later episodes to reach the historical milestones of the 19th century. The purpose of this project was pedagogical, the comics were available digitally and the spirit was that they could be used as a didactic resource through the governmental Plan Ceibal that provides computers to all primary education students in Uruguay.

But the 20th century was also the topic of comics, now focusing on specific events and not on long-term historical processes. With a historical anecdote as the starting point, there are police stories, adventure stories, etc. In this sense, perhaps the most remarkable work was *The Last Days of Graf Spee*, which obtained a Competitive Fund in 2008, and became the first Uruguayan graphic novel.

Five graphic novels

La Isla Elefante (Rodríguez Juele, 2011), *Zitarrosa* (Santullo and Aguirre, 2012), *Crónicas del Inxilio* (Galizzi and Tolj, 2015), *Tupamaros* (Leguisamo and Fernández,

FIGURE 4.1 Rodriguez Juele, A. (2011). *La Isla Elefante*. Malaquita Ediciones.

2015) and *Rincón de la Bolsa* (Peruzzo and Serra, 2016). In some cases, these works were the product of a writer and artist; in others, of integral authors. The Uruguayan authors were asked a series of fixed questions that made it possible to compare their points of view concerning their approach to the historical comic.

First, a synopsis of each of the works is presented. *Elephant Island* (Rodríguez Juele, 2011), the winner of the Contestable Fund for Culture in 2010, recounts the participation of Uruguayan sailors in the failed rescue of the crew of Admiral Shackleton's expedition in 1916 (Figure 4.1). The author in his double role as script writer and artist, chose the style of the Franco-Belgian school, the "clear line." Drawing Antarctica presents the challenge of drawing emptiness, nothingness. In this sense, there is a clear homage to the cover of *Tintin au Tibet* (Hergé, 1960). In 32 A4-size pages, the odyssey lived by the expedition that left London in 1914 under the command of Commander Shackleton intending to cross Antarctica, from one coast to the other, passing through the South Pole, is recounted. The participation of Uruguayans sailors in this adventure had a bittersweet flavor: they attempted the rescue and came very close to achieving it but had to return to Montevideo because of technicalities. A couple of months later, Shackleton managed to rescue his crew with the help of a Chilean ship. This book is an example of a historical anecdote little known to the public that is reproduced based on rigorous research and historical reconstruction of the event.

Zitarrosa (Santullo and Aguirre, 2012) was also the winner of a Contestable Fund for Culture in 2011. It is part of the trilogy about the military dictatorship in Uruguay that the scriptwriter Santullo developed. This trilogy has very varied styles both from drawing, since each work is made with a different artist, and also in terms of the approach to the subject. *Acto de Guerra* is about the fictionalization of testimonial stories that accompany each episode of the comic; in *Valizas*, the dictatorship is the setting and historical context that triggers a series of personal situations about family relationships. *Zitarrosa* closes this trilogy with a biographical approach to the Uruguayan singer-songwriter, where once again the script writer draws on testimonies and interviews for the construction of the specific episodes that end up telling the life of Alfredo Zitarrosa (1936–1989). The style provided by Argentine artist Max Aguirre is cartoonish, in two colors (black and cyan), inspired by aesthetic design from the 1960s and 1970s, years in which some of the stories developed (see Figure 4.2). The book is not a biography per se and it does not detail situations of the military dictatorship that takes place during any of his stories, it is a selection of specific episodes of the singer's life, where the dictatorship is experience through his exile, and is also about how the popular protest song became an element of political and cultural resistance and what it meant for the Uruguayan people during those years.

Tupamaros: la fuga (Leguisamo and Fernández, 2015) was the winner of the Contestable Fund for Culture in 2013 and was published in December 2015. In this case, it narrates a specific episode: that of the escape of a group of political prisoners belonging to the National Liberation Movement, who escape through a tunnel of the Punta Carretas Prison in Montevideo. The escape took place through a passage dug by the prisoners themselves, which led them to a house that was on the block in front of the prison. The book is a meticulous reconstruction from the historical point of view, based on historiographical research and also on interviews with some of the real protagonists of the event (see Figure 4.3). The drawing was made in full color by Argentine artist Lauri Fernández and also reflects the graphic study of history by representing public figures of recent history. The book has a coda including historical notes that indicate elements that are shown in the story and that demonstrate the research carried out to make it.

Crónicas del Inxilio (Galizzi and Tolj, 2015) was published in 2015 after having won a Contestable Fund for Culture in the previous year. As the author himself establishes in the introduction, the idea of it had arisen a few years ago and its aim was to narrate the vicissitudes of the daily life of young people who lived during the dictatorship in Uruguay; to emphasize, in some way, that all Uruguayans who lived in the country in those years were affected by the irruption of the military dictatorship. Without reaching the extremes of jail, torture or exile, it is a portrait of the daily life of everyone and, above all, of the young people who were affected by the most repressive characteristics of the military regime.

Rincón de la Bolsa (Peruzzo and Serra, 2016) was originally published serially in *Revista Lento*, a Montevideo monthly magazine that gives place on its pages to the national comic, making it a new space conquered by the medium. This graphic novel did not participate in the Contestable Fund for Culture. It is, perhaps, the least historical work included here in the sense of the development of a specific historical event (see Figure 4.4). On the contrary, it focuses on the reconstruction of the circumstances experienced in various towns of Uruguay that grew in the developmental impulse of the mid-20th century associated with industry, and that today remain as ghost towns and abandoned factories, places where the train does not stop at anymore. This work is a historical comic since it represents the spirit of a moment in smaller towns in Uruguay. It's not based on a particular historical episode, but rather on different, smaller slices of life reconstructed by the author. At what point does this story take place? It is not explicit, but from the graphic setting, it can be assumed that the story is set somewhere between the 1980s and the 1990s. It is also interesting on a literary level. Without being a reconstruction of *El Astillero* by Juan Carlos Onetti (1909–1994), it could be understood within the *Onettian* universe even by certain explicit references made as to the name of the factory. The prologue of this graphic novel delves into this point and is written by José Gabriel Lagos.

Why did the artists embrace the historical theme? Each author has a different answer to this question. For some, the issues came to them through personal and intra-family ties. Such is the case of Alejandro Rodriguez Juele (2020), who mentions his love for history and for boats, inherited from his father. This led him to read *Parallel 62, Uruguay in Antarctica* by Ana María De Salvo, the episode that kick-started his book took not more than a few pages. It struck him that there was little public knowledge about the event. And even more, it seemed to him that it was a very interesting moment in the early days of modern Uruguay, worthy of being drawn.

Santullo (2021) reflects on his relationship with the figure that is the center of his book, Zitarrosa. Even when the music of Alfredo Zitarrosa was part of his childhood, he did not pay attention to it until reaching 30, when he started listening to it on his own. But the link was not only with the artistic side. Due to the characteristics of Santullo's personal life, his parents met the singer in Mexico during their exile. Back in Uruguay, Santullo's mother was part of the management of El Galpón Theater, and organized venues for Alfredo Zitarrosa. All these connections were the basis for the anecdotes that give structure to the book.

On an even more personal level of connection with the period of his work, Silvio Galizzi (2021) creates an autobiographical comic book. He understood it could be interesting for younger generations to read about the lives of teenagers during the dictatorship.

On the other hand, some authors of historical graphic novels chose the topic of their works based on non-personal aspects. The objective was making comic books and publishing graphic novels and for that the presence of the Contestable Funds for Culture was a crucial way of making comic book publishing possible. Furthermore, a clarification was added on the selection criteria of the projects that stated: "quality and relevance: the cultural value of the project and contribution to the state of the art, heritage and cultural traditions."[3]

From this, it was understood that those projects related to the traditions and/or history of Uruguay would potentially have a greater possibility of being selected by the Funds to obtain financial support. Although this was an interpretation made by some of the artists of the pre-selection criterion, it was based on the number of projects that in the field of Graphic Story had been awarded and complied with this premise.

Pablo "Roy" Leguisamo (2021), thinks comic books authors have two ways of putting together a book project. One was a personal project with spontaneous topics but with less chances of becoming a published book. The second way to start a project was to think about them specifically for the funds. And in that case, Roy says it was an open secret that could not be verified that projects that treated a Uruguayan historical event or dealt with an issue associated with the Uruguayan being had a better chance of winning.

Was this the necessary stimulus for the increase in projects of a historical nature in the Uruguayan comic strip? From an institutional perspective, it was declared that there was no intention to influence the topics and that the Funds were not to be sought specifically to benefit one genre. However, between 2009 and 2015, when the specific category of Graphic Story existed, an average of 10 works was selected each year, and amongst them all of the graphic novels that could fall within the broad spectrum of the historical comic genre were included.

In contrast, some authors do not see in the Contestable Funds for Culture an intention to reward historical comics, but on the contrary, it was the authors who proposed this approach. As a result, projects of this genre were awarded. When asked about this, Alejandro Rodriguez Juele (2020) said that "the trend towards historical issues came more from the authors and editors than from the public or the Contestable Funds juries." To him, the jury chose from the options given to them, and if the majority had a historical topic, it was by decision of the authors and editors.

Other authors point out that the historical genre was a way of conveying the narration of stories that were part of recent history and that, in some way, were also striving for a diverse audience beyond comic fans. Broadening the spectrum of comic book readers was an objective that the historical comic helped to achieve insofar as the subject would interest people who were not part of the usual consumers of this material. Santullo (2021) shares this opinion, as he points out a process in which the reading public found in the historical comic a legitimation of the language itself. If the theme was serious, the language seemed to become serious too. The historical graphic novels in Uruguay opened the doors of bookstores for Uruguayan comics, and won space in the media. Nowadays, it seems that readers of historical comic books no longer make differences, and read comics probably as a result of a legitimation process.

In line with the above, Rodriguez Juele (2020) adds that historical graphic novels demonstrate that comics are a capable language for serious content and leave behind the prejudice that sees comics as a language for younger readers, or even only for children. He even links this to similar processes in other cultural areas like literature. Post-dictatorship years seems to be a moment of great development for literature, that starts with historical Uruguayan novels to later give way to more subjective matters. But he did not perceive a particular preference for historical comics from the public. He brings up similar examples of historical comics such as *Cardal*, that did not succeed, and other non-historical ones such as *Ranitas*, that did. He also remarks that some specific moments such as the Bicentennial celebrations both in Uruguay and in Argentina, brought the historical narrative to the attention of the press and public opinion. There even was a specific fund with the sole objective of promoting projects around the historical celebration.

Talking with Nicolás Peruzzo (2021), the same idea was brought up: historical comics have been the gateway for many people to the world of Uruguayan comics, at least since the mid-2000s. It was also a genre that gave certain legitimacy to comics that they did not have until then.

According to Peruzzo, graphic humor had a tradition and was familiar to readers, but most of adventure, science fiction or gauchesco comics were published in children's magazines, and that was the only public that consumed them. In the early years of the 21st century, a series of historical graphic novels caught the attention of the public and the press; it was the kickoff for a new, more contemporary generation of creators.

Looking at the growth process of historical comics in Uruguay, it is worth wondering about the existence of similar processes in other comic markets. In this sense, the proximity to Argentina, one of the great centers of comic production during the 20th century, questions and challenges us, since, for example, from the five the graphic novels presented here, three have Argentine artists involved.

In regard to this, Roy (Leguisamo, 2021) explained the participation of Argentine artists as a direct consequence of the Contestable Funds for Culture. These funds gave the opportunity to hire either Argentine or Brazilian artists. And this, maybe, added more significance to the works, thanks to a more developed professional experience on the part of foreign artists than the Uruguayans had. This interpersonal link that we mentioned in the first section between the groups of Uruguayan and Argentine artists during the 21st century, has allowed direct artistic collaboration in several projects that were published in both countries.

Thus, it is worth asking ourselves if the trend that we see around historical comics is a phenomenon limited to Uruguay, or if it encompasses a creative process and a reinterpretation of the reality that is lived on a regional level. The analysis carried out by Berone (2020), in which he studies the development of historical comics in Argentina, is interesting. It is also noteworthy that just as well as Argentine artists are involved when we analyze Uruguayan comics, this is a two-way street. In the study carried out by Berone on Argentine comics, Uruguayan authors such as Santullo and Leguisamo make appearances in their role as scriptwriters. In this analysis, historical comics are part of a production process related to the resurgence of the comic book publishing industry in the hands of independent publishers after the crisis at the end of the 20th century. It seems then that it is a common currency to both sides of the Río de la Plata, which should not surprise us given the constant parallelism of the historical and cultural processes between both countries.

Historical comics is a genre found worldwide; Argentina is immersed in this trend as one of the main producers of comics in Latin America and Uruguay, through this trend, makes viable the increase and legitimation of its production. It is through historical analysis that one of the central points from which to approach historical comics is found: in its quality as a construct of history and the memory that feeds on the collective past. But when historical comics become popular among the reading public, the question arises about the role that history plays in this process. The previous research, the documentation, and above all, how attached to the facts or what historiographical version is reflected in the script of the comic.

The authors decide to tell a story within History, and for this, they must carry out a prior investigation, which allows them to introduce their fictional narrative in a framework that is not flexible; the flexibility should be in the story they want to tell. In this regard, Santullo (2021) has said that he attempts to find "history as a form of a narrative skeleton that fiction 'decorates' with flesh, shape, or consistency." That's how he describes his working method. He emphasizes the graphic novel is ideal to rescue an unofficial type of History and use his experience as a journalist to do the research. The combination of archives, bibliography, interviews with people involved in the topic, gives form to the story in the center of the work.

The personal training of each author and the type of narration is what determines the investigative approach to the period to be reconstructed. In situations closer to personal experiences, such as the case of *Crónicas del Inxilio*, Galizzi (2021) goes back to his own experiences during the dictatorial period in Uruguay and reflects on it. He doesn't feel the necessity to carry out a historiographical investigation or call on anyone to tell him about something he already knows by personal experience. So, he only documented his work with facsimiles of newspapers of the time and historical photographs of Montevideo to assist the Argentine artist.

The historiographic rigor is much more accurate in the case of *La Isla Elefante*, where though there was room to recreate the anecdote and give consistency to the characters, the rhythm of the story and the events were marked by historical events. Rodríguez Juele (2020) says he used the historical events to define a framework within which the fictional story can develop. This made the construction of the story much easier and helped him to write the script. He defined the work of the writer such as the painter painting a landscape. It must detect the underlying structure, the broad lines, to make a synthesis that both reveals and values that structure. He felt it was safer using the structure of history, which has a validating effect when the story comes from a historical fact and not from the imagination of the author.

In the case of *Tupamaros*, the scriptwriter Roy (Leguisamo, 2021) highlights that, on the one hand, because it is a historical fact publicly known, and also because of the research interest of both authors (Lauri Fernández, the Argentine artist, and himself), the process was exhaustive. They pursued academic research. They did a bibliographic search, including press releases, in-depth interviews with *tupamaros* linked to the creation of the plan or the excavation of the tunnel and looked for graphic material.

Finally, in the case of *Rincón de la Bolsa*, by focusing its story on the experience of a character and recreating more of a global environment than a specific moment, it allowed the artist Serra to enrich and expand the storytelling. Against this, graphic research was what had the most weight, with the rescue of emblematic elements of a historical period, (e.g., telephone sets, clothing, and transport). Nicolás Peruzzo (2021) wrote a script with a fairly closed structure, with visual references for various vignettes. Gabriel Serra is a very solvent artist when it comes to visual narrative, so he brought his elements to each page.

So, in the use of history to frame a comic two trends seem to emerge. One, in which the development of the historical event prevails, adheres to the historiographic version. In this cases, we find a meticulous investigation that researches both the visual aspects and the historical narrative. On the other hand, we identify another trend in historical comics in which the fictional story takes the narrative center, and the historical research is submissive to this, generating a particular context in which the central story is framed. This does not imply less historical rigor but rather a different approach since the historiographic event is not the central point of the narrative and it gives the authors greater creative freedom, which in turn allows them to develop both universes and the psychology of the characters more freely. The historical framework, then, is first of all a way of giving credibility to the story itself.

Conclusions

After interviewing the authors, reflecting on comic creation, a vast field of study is revealed on the analysis of their perception to capture popular sentiment and turn it into a cultural expression. The Competitive Funds for Culture seem to have also reflected part of this, even though it was not their explicit objective, generating a circle in which it is difficult to identify the genesis and the consequences. Regarding this point, there is a sum of general aspects that may have influenced both the spirit of the authors when it came to selecting their themes, and the spirit of those who carried out public policies for cultural promotion.

Also, in this period a temporal ban was lifted that allowed, for example, to turn to periods of recent history that had only been approached from historiography but, suddenly, seemed open to fictionalization. On the other hand, political interest in promoting concepts about a new Uruguayan identity was projected through cultural actions. The conjunction of both factors probably generated the height of the phenomenon. Since 2016, the Competitive Funds merged the category of Graphic Story first with Illustrated Album, then with Animation, and finally, since 2020, the comic production can only be presented within the Publishing Proposals category, where all printed formats converge. Of the ten average titles that were published in Uruguay per year, it should be noted that in 2020 there were only two titles published and none of them was the winner of the Competitive Funds for culture 2020, which did not select any work coming from the medium of comics. The disappearance of economic support influenced the abrupt decline in the number of comic book titles (not just historical ones) published in recent years.

In regard to the question, is the historical comic a phenomenon isolated to the Uruguayan case? Everything indicates that this is not the case. Globalization and communication technology not only allows us to quickly discover the work of artists from other latitudes, but it also allows the interrelation of the artists themselves and enables collaborative work without the need for physical displacement. In the Río de la Plata in particular, this fostered the linking and creation of work that crossed the creative processes of both countries.

In conclusion, in terms of the way of working on historical material, two trends are glimpsed, one more formal in terms of its historiographic treatment and the other with stronger personal authorship. In between, some nuances and works were not taken into account in this analysis, but that can undoubtedly be contemplated in the future. Perhaps in a more exhaustive analysis employing quantitative methods, this would allow assessing the flow of works and not only their qualitative characteristics.

Finally, it seems necessary to reflect once again on the vulnerability of comics production in Uruguay, whose abrupt decline is directly related to the end of the economic support of the state. But, unlike other periods in Uruguayan history, this is a time when, despite the low local production, there is a strengthening of the professionalization of Uruguayan artists who gained places in foreign markets and published many titles out of Uruguay.

Notes

1 To learn more about the circulation of *Mundo Uruguayo*, there is an analysis carried out by this author in Saibene (2020), "Comparative study of children's comics in the work

of Julio E. Suárez and Geoffrey Foladori (Fola), 1938–1942" (Unpublished degree thesis) University of Montevideo.
2 About the history of Uruguay in the 20th century and in particular the military dictatorship, see Caetano and Rilla, 1987, 2005.
3 https://fondoconcursable.mec.gub.uy

Bibliography

Anáforas: Mundo Uruguayo (1919–1967). (n.d.). Retrieved June 8, 2021, from https://anaforas.fic.edu.uy/jspui/handle/123456789/20276
Anáforas: Negro Timoteo, El (1876–). (n.d.). Retrieved June 8, 2021, from https://anaforas.fic.edu.uy/jspui/handle/123456789/9730
Benadiba, L. (2014). *Otras memorias I: Testimonios para la transformación de la realidad*. Ediciones Maipue.
Berone, L. R. (2020). História em quadrinhos rioplatense e memória histórica: Algumas dificuldades contemporâneas. *9ª Arte (São Paulo), 9*(1), 14–34. https://doi.org/10.11606/issn.2316-9877.v9i1p14-34
Betancor, M., & Ginevra, D. (2012). *Cardal*. Grupo Belerofonte.
Broquetas, M. (2015). Fotografía e identidad. La revista "Mundo uruguayo" en la conformación de un nuevo imaginario nacional en el Uruguay del Centenario. *Artelogie. Recherche sur les arts, le patrimoine et la littérature de l'Amérique latine, 7*, Article 7. https://doi.org/10.4000/artelogie.1060
Caetano, G., & Rilla, J. (1987). *Breve historia de la Dictadura (1973–1985)*. Clahe.
Caetano, G., & Rilla, J. (2005). *Historia contemporánea del Uruguay De la Colonia al siglo XXI* (2da.). Fin de Siglo. www.findesiglo.com.uy/historia-contemporanea-del-uruguay-por-caetano-rilla/
Castro, M. (2019, October 22). Una historia en viñetas que se hace visible. *La diaria*. https://ladiaria.com.uy/cultura/articulo/2019/10/una-historia-en-vinetas-que-se-hace-visible/
Dobrinin, P. (1999). Ángel Umpierrez: Un niño que pronto cumplirá 80 años. *Revista Balazo*. http://balazocomic.blogspot.com/2014/06/balazo-n-1el-regreso-de-la-aventura.html
Galizzi, S. (2021, January 29). *Interview* [Personal communication].
Galizzi, S., & Tolj, E. (2015). *Crónicas del inxilio*. Ninfa Comics.
Hergé (1960). *Tintin au Tibet*. Casterman.
Leguisamo, P. R. (2021, January 21). *Interview* [Personal communication].
Leguisamo, P. R., & Fernández, L. (2015). *Tupamaros, la Fuga 1971*. Loco Rabia y Dragón Comics.
Leguisamo, P. R., Vergara, M., & Di Lorenzo, C. (2013). *Morir por el Che: 1961*. Dragoncomics Editora, Loco Rabia.
Mainero, G., & Costa, J. E. (2012). *La Historieta en el Uruguay. Un viaje en el tiempo 1890–1955: Vol. I*. Fundación Lolita Rubial.
Ostuni, H. (2015). La Historieta Uruguaya. *Revista Latinoamericana De Estudios Sobre La Historieta, 28*.
Peruzzo, N. (2021, February 1). *Interview* [Personal communication].
Peruzzo, N., & Serra, G. (2016). *Rincón de la Bolsa*. Ninfa Comics.
Rodriguez Juele, A. (2011). *La Isla Elefante*. Malaquita Ediciones.
Rodriguez Juele, A. (2020, December 29). *Interview* [Personal communication].

Saibene, M. V. (2020). *Estudio comparativo de la historieta infantil en la obra de Julio E. Suárez y Geoffrey Foladori (Fola), 1938–1942*. Universidad de Montevideo.

Santullo, R. (2021, January 30). *Interview* [Personal communication].

Santullo, R., & Aguirre, M. (2012). *Zitarrosa*. Grupo Belerofonte, Estuario Editora.

Santullo, R., & Bergara, M. (2008). *Los últimos días del Graf Spee*. Grupo Belerofonte.

Santullo, R., & Bergara, M. (2010). *Acto de Guerra*. Grupo Belerofonte.

5
BETWEEN COMICS AND MEMORIES, OTHER STORIES OF BRAZIL

Marilda Lopes Pinheiro Queluz

Introduction

In the last decade, a conservative wave has been hitting several countries around the world. In Brazil, these ideas clung to neoliberal discourses and the expansion of capitalist relations, having devastating effects such as the privatization of public services, unemployment, precarization of working conditions, the destruction of the environment, the invasion of indigenous and quilombola territories, the lack of investment in research, science and education, among others.

With the troubled and tragic turn in the course of Brazilian politics, which resulted in the impeachment[1] of President Dilma Rousseff in 2016, there was a resurgence of extremely conservative and authoritarian thinking, in addition to the increase in poverty, violence, intolerance and prejudices of class, gender, race and ethnicity. Among the proposals of the group that came to power are the defense of nationalism, bourgeois morality, heteronormative family, and Christian values. These people defend retrograde views such as flat-earth and creationism, the polarization of politics, the demonization of gender issues, the disrespect for the constitution and democracy. They incite hatred and attacks on social minorities, the press, intellectuals and artists who criticize the government. They resume authoritarian practices that are very present in the history of this country, such as the myth of racial democracy, patriarchalism, patrimonialism, violent repression and social intolerance (Schwarcz, 2019).

One of the many strategies of these reactionary groups is to erase places of memory, seeking to forget or render invisible diversity, resistance struggles, oppositions and criticisms, traumatic events of the past such as the dictatorship and slavery of black people.

> Collective memory has been an important issue in the struggle for power among social forces. To make themselves the master of memory and

DOI: 10.4324/9781003333296-7

forgetfulness is one of the great preoccupations of the classes, groups, and individuals who have dominated and continue to dominate historical societies. The things forgotten or not mentioned by history reveal these mechanisms for the manipulation of collective memory.

(Le Goff, 1992, p. 54)

On the other hand, in this same conjuncture, it has been possible to observe the appearance of a greater number of artistic works that revisit distant times, confronted by the anxieties of the present. They are poetics that assume a progressive political stance and propose new dialogues with memories, new narratives, emphasizing the agency of common people, giving prominence to marginalized groups, questioning the very making of art and history. It is a cultural production in consonance with the agendas of black movements, feminist movements, LGBTQIA+, indigenous peoples' movements, creating space for disruptive and dissident views. This subject matter appears in the work of many artists, such as Rosana Paulino, Dalton de Paula, Denilson Baniwa, Naine Terena,[2] among others. The interest and concern with those excluded from history and with the reconstruction of their trajectories, their daily lives, their affections and dreams, lived or not fulfilled, contaminated the pages of the comics.[3] In an attempt to understand what could be called *structures of feeling*,[4] in the words of Raymond Williams (2005), our objective is to reflect on the relationships between history and memory woven in contemporary Brazilian comics, considering the way in which comic book artists turn to the past, dive into archives, collections, documents, investigating the visual/material culture to create other perspectives on the experiences lived by ordinary men and women, to represent characters that have been erased or forgotten, and create other narratives about the events. In this regard, this text will analyze two emblematic works, released in 2017: *Sem dó* [*No mercy*], by Luli Penna, published by Todavia and *Angola Janga*, by Marcelo D'Salete, published by Veneta.

Sem Dó is the story of a couple who fell in love in the turbulent São Paulo at the end of the 1920s. The modernization of the city and the changes in behavior are problematized in the representation of the daily life and destiny of two sisters.

Marcelo D'Salete focuses on the daily life of slaves – men and women who fled to Angola Janga ("little Angola" in Bantu Kimbundu language), known as Quilombo of Palmares. Questioning the official documentation about the events of the time period, he builds characters like the leader Zumbi,[5] for example, in a concrete and situated way.

These two graphic novels work with the power of the reconstruction of memory, identities and subjectivities forged in everyday life, with an emphasis on an investigation of written and visual documents, with the intersection of different perspectives, encompassing interdisciplinary knowledge. They propose other narratives from the past, with common people as the main characters. Marcelo D'Salete insists on the representation

Of several other characters who have nothing to do with kings or superheroes. They are people we need to know, to understand this deeper Brazil, who have a lot to teach, both to young people and adults in the country today . . . The history of the African diaspora goes through the trajectory of people who were trafficked, who went through extremely difficult situations, but who managed to establish negotiation and survival strategies. The stories of these people and their descendants needs to be told.[6]

(D'Salete, 2021)

Luli Penna states that, initially, she had a project to make a story about her grandfather and great-uncle, children of a radical anarchist who came to Brazil from Spain, at the end of the 19th century. And then, when she learned the stories of her great-aunts, their sisters, she decided to prioritize these women, placing them as protagonists.

In one of these conversations, I heard the story of their sisters. Then I thought, "No way, I don't want to talk about the famous men in the family (my grandfather and my great-uncle became important architects in the 50s), I want to talk about these two obscure aunts"!

What impressed me most about their story . . . is the difference between the sexual freedom of men and women, brutal then (and today). There is an element in the story that is the ultimate example of this disparity: the device, so to speak, that facilitates men's lives of pleasure is exactly the same that puts an end to women's pleasures. It was exactly when this cousin of my grandparents told me about it that I decided to draw *Sem Dó*.[7]

(Penna, 2017a)

Although in different ways, both use dense research and experimentation in the language of comics as a strategy for struggle, resistance, and poetic and political expression. Luli Penna creates comics without speech bubbles, playing with resources that were used by silent movies to build sequences and dialogues. Appropriating the art deco aesthetic, the artist reinterprets architecture and ornaments to point out feelings, dreams and frustrations experienced by working women, inside or outside the household, facing the problems of a big city, both on the streets and in the domestic environments. Marcelo D'Salete deconstructs the rhythm of the narratives of adventures and heroes, taking advantage of framing and different angles to highlight the daily struggle and resistance of black people enslaved in the quilombos. The representation of the scenarios and the portrayal of the characters, the articulation between landscape, artifacts, bodies and gestures, juxtapose contexts, make the dynamic actions of material and symbolic relations more complex.

The comics work as powerful statements and these, as Bakhtin (2003) defines, reveal the materiality of a communicative situation that depends on the historical context in which it was produced and conveyed, transforming itself with each reading. They can be an important source for reflecting on material culture, as they contribute to other perspectives and approaches to the history of work, the history of technology, the history of everyday life, articulating the interaction processes between people and things, for example.

It is important to treat comic books not as an object, an isolated artifact, but as a social practice, questioning the material conditions of production and consumption, the relations between politics and art (Williams, 2005). The representations present in the comics put into action, with visual and verbal signs, cultural practices that make us understand social processes and power relations in which we are imbricated, and which constitute us.

The context and materiality present in the representations of these two works indicate that it is necessary to know the past in order to transform present society. For black feminists linked to multiple social movements against the wiles of neoliberal capitalist logic, the perspective of intersectionality, considering class, gender, generation, race and ethnicity, "can be seen as a form of critical investigation and praxis"[8] to face the multiple systems of oppression (Collins, 2017, p. 8).

In this sense, these works also help us to problematize stereotypes. *Sem Dó* reveals various types of femininity and masculinity, juxtaposed to the hegemonic models and patterns present in the passage from the 1920s to the 1930s. In addition to gender issues, the graphic novel also questions class asymmetries, generational conflicts and makes a subtle reference to racial issues. *Angola Janga* dismantles the idea of consensus between quilombola groups and leaders, deepening the richness and diversity of paths and thoughts constituted in the practices of the struggle for freedom.

These two graphic novels bring complex representations of individual and collective experiences, adding to the "measurable categories of historical time, the notions of duration [*durée*], of lived time [*temps vécue*], of multiple and relative times, and of subjective or symbolic times. Historical time is rediscovering at a new, very sophisticated level the old time of memory, which is broader than history and supplies it with material"[9] (Le Goff, 1992, p. 20).

Sem Dó

Luciana Artacho Penna, better known as Luli Penna,[10] was born in São Paulo, in 1965. She is an illustrator and cartoonist, graduated in Language and Literature at the University of São Paulo – USP. She did illustrations for the newspaper *Folha de São Paulo*, for the magazines *Casa e Jardim*, *Vogue*, *Revista da Folha*, *Piauí*, in addition to illustrating books and covers.[11] *Sem Dó* is her first graphic novel. In this work, the author makes, in complicity with readers, a love story, a sensitive, delicate and dramatic portrait of the urban experience in São Paulo in the 1920s and 1930s, starring Lola and her sister Pilar. References from movie posters, fashion magazines, newspaper advertisements, radio programs and very few dialogues present the universe of work and household chores as a collection of memories. Characters face social conventions, normative behaviors, standards of beauty, markers of class distinction. Throughout the story, the comics "show the lives of women who suffered the impact of the period on their bodies and choices, and at the same time show us the relationship between the cities and them[12]" (Malcher, 2019, p. 333).

Sem Dó is a romance lived in the dizzying process of modernization marked by the reforms of the streets and avenues, the eclectic architecture, the new technical artifacts, the billboard placed at the movie theater entrance, the advertisements and posters, the shop windows, the movement of pedestrian traffic, cars and trams. As the cover itself suggests, the city is shown not only as a stage for urban transformations, behavior and habits, but as an active character in the plot. The careful layout, scenarios, props and scenes on each page allow us to think about the representations in dialogue with Stuart Hall:

> In part, we give things meaning by how we use them, or integrate them into our everyday practices. . . . In part, we give things meaning by how we *represent* them -the words we use about them, the stories we tell about them, the images of them we produce, the emotions we associate with them, the ways we classify and conceptualize them, the values we place on them.
>
> (Hall, 2003, p. 3)

On the front flap of the book cover, the characters are presented in an almost enigmatic way, synthesizing their importance in the story in very few lines. Dolores is shown in profile, full-length, walking on the sidewalk, in the first square, with the caption "Dolores or Lola – a young maid." The unknown man, "coming from who knows where" is characterized only by his mysterious suitcase, being carried by someone who cannot be seen. Only toward the end of the book do we learn that his name is Sebastião. The definition of Lola's bosses as "a very fine people," already reveals the conflicts and class differences present throughout the story. The images that appear right below the caption "And São Paulo, with its coming and going of hats, trams, streets and rails" summarize the matches and mismatches of this couple, insinuated in the metaphor of the rails in the last panel.

Reading this graphic novel is like flipping through a magazine of the time period, full of photos and illustrations, experiencing nostalgia and enchantment for modern novelties, for technological transformations. Luli Penna highlights the importance of cinema and magazines in her work:

> I collected books about the history of São Paulo, old photo books and postcards. . . . I bought many things, borrowed, consulted many websites, walked around the old center a lot. And I used several frames of silent films. *Limite*,[13] by Mário Peixoto, for example, an absolutely wonderful Brazilian silent film released in 1931, I saw many times. Several panels were copied from there (the retro ones that Lola wears while sewing, her little shoes leaving her house and the very idea of showing a movie within the story were things I copied from *Limite*). . . . I've always liked browsing old magazines, I have

a collection that I inherited from one of the great-aunts on which *Sem Dó* is based.[14]

(Penna, 2017a)

The illustrated magazines from the 1920s helped to establish a new visual culture in Brazil, easing the conflicts between the processes of modernization and the fear of change. The female characters in *Sem Dó* seem fascinated by the world of fashion, cinema and the elites shown by magazines. Movie actresses inspired new ways of dressing, make up, combing, and behaving. Hollywood stars became part of the social imaginary and helped to create the image of modernity. They conveyed an air of undisciplined women:

> They drive, smoke and approach men they want . . . they fall in love and fall out. They choose partners. It is at this moment that the idea of love is combined with that of individualism, associated as never before in modernity. A project that is still ongoing and which gains momentum with the change in the status and the image of women in modern societies, and even with the need for their insertion in the market as a productive force.[15]
>
> (Anchieta, 2019, p. 213)

Consuming these print periodicals was a luxury most of the population could not afford. Therefore, the scene in which Lola gets a huge stack of magazines from her boss and the moments in which these magazines are shared with her mother and sister is significant. The magazines acted as showcases, displaying the news, the products to be consumed and the behaviors to be followed. Between photographs, illustrations and advertisements, the pages drew new paths of the gaze, in a game of seduction, persuasion and information. Through them it was possible to have contact with other places, other cultures.

Sem Dó is a story made up of fragments, dynamic and elusive like the memories of the past. Each part or chapter of the narrative is divided by a page with a black background, with a Philco brand radio and a Duchen cookie box filled with souvenirs, small objects, dried flowers, postcards and photographs. They are thingamabobs that arouse feelings and memories, reiterating Daniel Miller's (2013) idea that artifacts not only represent us but also constitute us, they create us.

The narrative sequence is interspersed with songs, ads and radio news, creating an effect both of a story that starts in the past and leaps into the present, as well as of memories tangled with time. We soon realize, especially from the songs, that this is a time later than the one in which the story is set. We go back and forth in time, immersed in memories, like the character Pilar who, in the end, we discover to be a kind of narrator.

There is a soundtrack from the future (1970s) that is intertwined in this process of recollections, like pauses in the narrative, mingling with Pilar's thinking. The music excerpts are significant in relation to the context of the dictatorship and the plot of the romance. The phrase "we live in the best city of South America" is part of *Baby's* lyrics, composed by Caetano Veloso,[16] in 1969 and can serve as a reference for both Rio de Janeiro and São Paulo. The sweet melody talks about pop culture, cultural industry, mass consumption and North American influence. The word "details" describes the scene of the souvenir box being stirred along with the memories, denotes the romantic mood and marks the pain of nostalgia, and entitles the famous 1971 song by Roberto Carlos.[17] The lyrics of *Que Maravilha*, by Jorge Ben Jor[18] and Toquinho,[19] recorded in 1969, also evoke a love in the midst of big cities, with the passage "Across bank clerks, cars, streets and avenues," listening to "millions of horns blaring incessantly." There is also a reference to *Mal Secreto*, composed by Waly Salomão[20] and Jards Macalé,[21] in 1972, which speaks of the pain of the departure, especially in the phrase "And everything else I play in a verse titled Mal secreto." The chorus "Feeling good was good enough for me" belongs to the composition *Me and Bobby McGee* (1970), best known in the voice of Janis Joplin.[22] It conveys the idea of traveling, of displacement, of being with someone in search of freedom. We also see Lola and Sebastião on one of the strolls they took, and the lyric "just a Latin American boy" refers to a song by Belchior,[23] released in 1976, still during the dictatorship, about a young man that comes from the countryside and suffers from the reality of big metropolises.

The use of black and white, ornaments, elements drawn from photos, fashion, means of transport and art deco architecture enhances the expressiveness of everyday activities. The passage of scenes with many cuts, different framing and angles of view, make the gutter a privileged locus of gaps to be filled by readers. Panels with black backgrounds with white letters for the lines replace the speech bubbles. The drawings were all made in India ink. About the process of creating the book, Luli Penna explains that

> What changed a lot, all the time, on every page, was the sequence of the comics, the framing, etc. If the book has three pages that were laid out the way they were printed, that's a lot. As soon as I finished a page and saw it there, ready, neatly in ink, I cut everything out, moved the comics, reworked, inserted an ad, reassembled it all over again. I can say that the material used was paper, ink and scissors. . . . In this process, the ads were an important part of both the composition of the page and the meaning of the story.[24]
>
> (Penna, 2017a)

The pages invite us to spy, see through the camera, the window of a house, the tram, the train, the bus, the cuts of the zoetrope and the eyes of the characters. One of the tricks to place us in the context of the time is to represent the habit of reading, spying on the newspapers of other passengers, on the train or on the tram, putting us in contact with advertised news, products and services. Among the images of the typewriter, the gramophone, the cassette recorder, the television, the kid gloves and the miniskirt, we learn about the gossip of cinema, the price of coffee, the developmental project of the military period (Trans-Amazonian Highway),[25] the promises of progress brought about by increasing industrialization. The ads tell

Between comics and memories, other stories of Brazil 89

a parallel story, about technical innovations, urban tragedies, fashion, behavior, norms, medicines, health, music and cinema, enabling comparisons between the 1920s and the 1970s.

The traffic, the displacements in the city and between cities mark the reading path and can be considered as metaphors of the rhythm of life of each of these two women. The book begins around the end of the 1920s, highlighting the arrival of the main male character at Estação da Luz, in São Paulo, and ends in the 1970s, with references to the old bus station and Avenida Paulista.

The first scenes show a man, perhaps from the interior of the state of São Paulo, walking along the tracks to the train station, where he prepares himself, and gets ready to take the train to try his hand at life in the capital. Visually, the common need for many Brazilians to "Migrate to prosper, survive" is built (Malcher, 2019, p. 333). The pages dedicated to the waiting and arrival of the train are filled with circles and graphics that suggest movement, smoke and noise (Figure 5.1).

Spatial references are abundant: Bairro do Brás, Santa Helena Building, Praça da Sé and half of the built cathedral, the Luz Station, the old bus station, Paulista Avenue.[26] As Peter Burke (2004) has explained, the imagetic description of cities contained in the arrangements imagined by the artists helps us to understand the relationships between public and private space, the meanings of domestic interiors, the functions of ancient artifacts and the modes of organization from the past. We move, together with the characters, through the world of work and leisure, witnessing the various tactics of these different women to get around the difficulties of everyday life and reinvent ways of giving new meaning, of being in the world.

FIGURE 5.1 Luli Penna. Pages 10–11. *Sem Dó*. 2017b.

90 Marilda Lopes Pinheiro Queluz

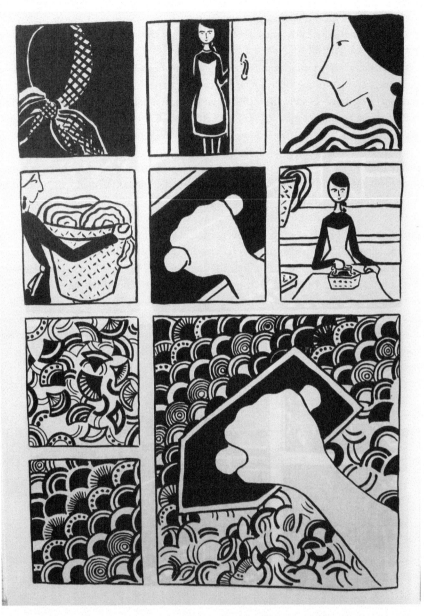

FIGURE 5.2 Luli Penna. Page with scenes of Lola ironing clothes. *Sem Dó*, 2017b.

An important aspect is the different subject positions occupied by these women in the comics. Lola works as a maid for an elite family in São Paulo, helping to pay the house bills. Pilar helps her mother with household chores and is discouraged from working outside the home. Her mother, a housewife, dreams of a good match for her daughters. Lola resists the interest of the boss's son, the future with her cousin who is the driver of her bosses, and throws herself into the adventure of passion for the unknown. The idealization of love and romance clashes against the idea of marriage as the only possible destiny for girls.

The comic book highlights the importance of marriage, which, in this period, was seen as the only institution capable of maintaining social order, as well as promoting and dignifying women in their role as wife, mother and housewife (Maluf and Mott, 1998). The white and bourgeois model of the family was that of legalized marriage, establishing the social position of the woman as belonging to the home and that of the man as the provider of the home.[27] However, there were many other family arrangements and dynamics, from women who were heads of the family due to the abandonment of their partner, separated women, to independent women living free love, contrary to established standards (Soihet, 2006).

Luli Penna's work evokes questions about the daily lives of women at that time, detailing gestures, postures, behaviors, both expected and not socially accepted. Besse (1999) recalls that there was surveillance on women's actions and behavior. In the 1920s, for example, women who were linked to prostitution in public spaces were the target of hygienist campaigns by the Church, the State and doctors with the purpose of regulating and scrutinizing cities, defining the limits of noble, inappropriate, dangerous areas, hierarchizing services and professions. Medical discourses gained strength in the 1920s, by regulating women's bodily and health practices through manuals and reports in magazine newspapers (Besse, 1999).

Sewing and embroidery are valued in the story not only as futile or decorative feminine skills, but they emerge as spaces of desire, the exercise of imagination, freedom and creativity. The female characters immerse themselves in these universes of cloths, fabric cuts, molds, needles, threads, hoops, thimbles, threads and scissors and find pleasure in this solitary activity, the feeling of control over their lives and their creations.

There is a great emphasis on photography, cinema, as a novelty, as a grandiose technical and magical spectacle that creates the illusion of movement. The enchantment of cinema, animation, alludes to moments of pleasure, escape and distance from daily problems.

There are many pages and scenes in which Lola takes a break from work to spin a zoetrope.[28] We are hypnotized by the sequence of cartoons in the protagonist's gestures, following the movements of a boxing match, a gymnast, a dance. We follow these loose bodies, free silhouettes in the alternating rhythm of black and white backgrounds. These are moments of reveries, dreams and freedom, of reinterpretation of everyday life. Luli Penna reveals how this admiration crosses her work:

> The pleasure of drawing a comic and trying to put the characters in motion is a lot like Lola's pleasure of spinning a zoetrope. I think these optical toys that appear in the book, the couple's movie trip and the scene where they're going to take a portrait in Parque da Luz (this moment of image capture)

speak a lot not only of the time but of the whole work of doing a comic book.[29]

(Penna, 2017a)

Throughout the work there are panels and pages that remind us of the Art Deco[30] style, treated at the limit between homage and questioning. The composition of circles, the richness of textures is resumed here in fragments, in abrupt cuts, following the deviations and obstacles that change the characters' trajectories. The beauty and strength of the feelings are reiterated in the expressiveness of the rhythm broken by the contrast of black and white. It suggests a tense and critical re-reading of geometric effects, denouncing how these elements linked to the lifestyle of the São Paulo elite carry values that permeate the routine activities of the poorest people. The architecture's external and internal environments established hierarchies and limits in the use and occupation of spaces. The adornments and decorative elements allow glimpses of class differences and social contradictions behind discourses about progress, scientific and technological efficiency.

Angola Janga

Marcelo D'Salete[31] is a black artist, comic book artist, illustrator and teacher. He was born in São Paulo in 1979. As a teenager, he studied graphic design at the technical college Carlos de Campos. He graduated in Fine Arts from the University of São Paulo (ECA-USP) and completed his Master's in Art History from the same university with the dissertation *A configuração da curadoria de arte afro-brasileira de Emanoel Araujo* [The configuration of Emanoel Araujo's Afro-Brazilian art curatorship], in 2009. Currently, D'Salete also teaches Visual Arts at USP's School of Application. He is the author of several bestselling comics,[32] having recognition within and outside the country.[33] Angola Janga has received many awards and is already considered one of the most important works on this subject matter in Brazil.[34]

Son of an electrician and a nursing assistant, Marcelo D'Salete was raised on the outskirts of the east side of São Paulo and says that it was through literature and rap that he became aware of issues such as the fight against racial discrimination and the black resistance movements.

> I had a lot of influence from graffiti and hip hop from the 1980s to the 1990s. When I was a little older, I took a course on Brazilian History focused on the black population. It was a course with Petrônio Domingues, at USP's Núcleo de Consciência Negra [Black Consciousness Nucleus], in 2004. There I had contact with texts about Palmares . . . My purpose was to escape some archetypes about slavery, to avoid stories that do not deepen these characters and place them only as passive people.[35]

(D'Salete, 2020)

To understand the context of the narrative, it is necessary to know that the Portuguese invasion of Brazil in the 16th century explored the extraction of wood and the production of sugar cane. The sugarcane mill was initially based on forced labor performed by indigenous work force and, later, on the enslavement of Africans and Afro-Brazilians. In 1570, in the region known as Captaincy of Pernambuco, in the northeast of the country, there were 23 sugar mills, and in 1583, there were already 66 sugar mills. At the end of that century, there were already reports of blacks who had fled in that region.

Angola Janga portrays the last decades of the biggest mocambo[36] in Brazilian history: Palmares.[37] The narrative takes place in the 17th century and shows the tactics of enslaved blacks and quilombolas in the processes of resistance against colonial violence. Angola Janga was the region that encompassed Palmares and several other mocambos located near Serra da Barriga, in an area that today belongs to the state of Alagoas, in northeastern Brazil. "The title, once again, is not fortuitous: it indicates the place of Afrodiaspora enunciation of the narrative, as the protagonists are the blacks themselves in search of freedom and autonomy, coming to life, among them, historical personalities such as Zumbi dos Palmares himself, Ganga Zumba and Acotirene[38]" (Custódio, 2018).

Although there are other comics about Quilombo of Palmares,[39] *Angola Janga* stands out for its concern with imagining people's daily lives, personal conflicts, contradictions, affections and networks of social negotiations. The author's research takes into account a "history of interpretations" (Burke, p. 228) about the theme and its characters, seeking to build the point of view of black people. Marcelo D'Salete has investigated, for eleven years, the history of slavery and Brazilian mocambos, including documents and books, interviews and field research, making trips, seeking to know and understand the geography and climate of the place. D'Salete puts into practice the teaching of Le Goff (1996) that the document is not a truth of the past, it is the result of an assembly of the society that produced it according to the relations of forces that held power at the time: "it is necessary to start by dismantling, demolishing this assembly, demounting this construction and analyzing the conditions for the production of documents-monuments[40]" (Le Goff, 1996, p. 548).

The importance of showing comics as the result of dense research appears in the afterword, which contains a vast glossary, theoretical explanations, a chronology of the Palmares war, bibliographical references and maps of quilombola regions and the routes of slave ships in the Atlantic. "But the researcher's work is also visible in the very density of the line, which seeks to reconstruct the African architecture of the mocambos and the dense forests in which the conflicts took place[41]" (Custódio, 2018).

Fiction is used not only to fill in the gaps of history, but to build a less abstract look at the trajectory of these characters, placing them in the materiality of everyday life, in the whirlwind of feelings experienced in the reality of work, in pursuits and in battles. Fiction and history aligned concrete situations of struggle, of love, of suffering and of fear and pain. The characters become more complex insofar as they demonstrate an affection that has always been denied in our official history.

> There are documents mostly from the last decades of the battle. These sources are from soldiers, officers, planters, governors, priests, etc. In short, from people committed to the destruction of Palmares. This work, in turn, intends to conduct the narrative from the perspective of the people of Palmares. In this regard, fiction plays a significant role. It is through it that we can cross walls and access, through poetry and art, those men and women.[42]
>
> (D'Salete, 2017, p. 419)

By juxtaposing several different voices in dialogue, even though they do not have the same power range, D'Salete problematizes colonial stereotypes in relation to not only blacks but also indigenous peoples and mestizos. He questions the role of the Christian church and the prejudices and persecutions of African beliefs and religiosities. At the beginning of each chapter there are one or several quotations from chronicles of the time, which work as a commentary and counterpoint to the graphic narrative, calling into question the oppressors' viewpoint, proposing the perspective of those who were defeated.

The angles and framing highlight the tensions, fears, strength and hope of men and women who fought for freedom. The graphic novel shows how the systematic violence of slavery found resistance in revolts, escapes to the quilombos and even in individual gestures.

> Through graphic narrative strategies and visual perspective changes (high angle and low angle), it becomes possible to show the imbalances in hierarchical relationships in society; at the same time, the same stylistic instruments allow to express the voice of the underlings, their rebellions and daily resistance against the oppressors, showing, for example, close-ups of the protagonists' resolute faces, looks that represent consternation, fear or also reluctance and aversion.[43]
>
> (Wrobel, 2019, pp. 102–103)

It is important to mention that women played an important role in the history of black resistance. Jasmin Wrobel (2019) highlights the construction of complex female protagonists and fighters in the works of Marcelo D'Salete, such as the warrior Aqualtune, mother of Ganga Zumba, maternal grandmother of Zumbi and leader of a force of ten thousand men in the battle of Mbwila, in Angola, in 1665. She was taken prisoner, however, soon managed to flee to Palmares, leading a mocambo that would later receive her name. "Chapter 3, Aqualtune, takes place in the mocambo of the same name, but in the version narrated by D'Salete, the mocambo is named Aqualtune by choice of Acotirene, another warrior-matriarch of Palmares[44]" (Wrobel, 2019, p. 113).

Between comics and memories, other stories of Brazil 95

FIGURE 5.3 Marcelo D'Salete. A sequence that depicts slave ships crossing the Atlantic. *Angola Janga*, 2017, p. 114–116.

Angola Janga is a work that can be read as a historical comic, a realistic or adventure comic, inviting us to review history, sharpening our imaginary of the past. D'Salete's poetic construction combines suspense, romance, extremely dynamic and tense scenes with moments of sublime meditation, reflection. This is the case for the sequence over the Atlantic crossing (Figure 5.3).

According to Gilroy (2012), the slave ship becomes a potent emblem, a living, microcultural and micropolitical system. The trips carried out in the Black Atlantic, great sea or Calunga, in the Kimbundu language, implied the formation and transformation of African matrices and identities, in a transcultural and international movement (Gilroy, 2012). The resistance of African men and women, despite forced exile and violence, took root on Brazilian soil, spreading technological, artistic and philosophical knowledge and practices.

Figure 5.3 shows the connection of this crossing marked in people's memories and bodies. These images also exemplify D'Salete's creative process and the influences that are reinvented in his drawings, highlighting the power of the image over words, the expressive force of black and white, the counterpoints between light and shadow.

> I learned to tell stories from cinema. . . . I learned to draw light and shadow seeing works from Cinema Novo [New Cinema] and Italian neorealism. I paused the film to draw black and white images. . . . I really like black and white works and I got close to artists like (Sergio) Toppi, (Lorenzo) Mattotti, (Alberto) Breccia, Taiyo Matsumoto etc. They were all strong references. I'm fascinated by the infinite possibilities of the play between light and shadow.[45]
>
> (D'Salete, 2020)

The lines and layout of the pages of *Angola Janga* enable us to perceive the diversity of the flora, the different ways of relating to nature. D'Salete builds the interaction and agency of the setting (both in the forest and in the villages), of artifacts, of animals and insects, of symbols, of people and of the marks of ancestors.

In this sense, the book bets on the idea of narrating a plural story in several episodes and from different perspectives. Chronological linearity is broken at every moment by other temporalities: dreams, nature, ancestry, religiosity, omens and imagination. The combination of various temporalities, "time in progress" is reiterated this time of African existence is neither a linear time, nor a simple matter of succession in which each moment is erased, nullifies and replaces all those that preceded it, to the point where a single time exists, simultaneously, within the scope of society. It is not a series, but an interweaving of other present, past and future, each epoch carrying, altering and maintaining all precedents.[46]

(Mbembe, 2018, p. 140)

This intertwining can be seen in the way the symbols of the Asante (Ananse Ntontan[47] – spider's web) and Tchokwe (Sona[48]) cultures appear at various occasions in the plot.

This symbolic manifestation of the visual narrative, in addition to fulfilling a practical function in the story – because the Sona symbols, for example, indicate the escape routes, the safe places of the forest, functioning as a quilombola map, also show the resistance and the permanence of African culture over the centuries.

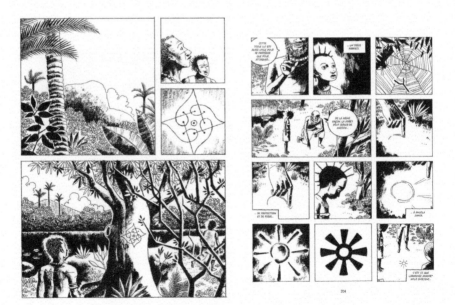

FIGURE 5.4 Marcelo D'Salete. Pages with symbolic manifestations. Angola Janga, 2017. p. 38 and p. 204.

Between comics and memories, other stories of Brazil   97

Symbolic signs create links between African diasporic peoples. As most of the reports about Palmares are from military documents and there are almost no images of the quilombos, D'Salete had to look for other sources of inspiration.

> I needed images thinking about these traditional peoples of Bantu origin in the Angola region, from where most of the enslaved to Brazil came. For that, I looked for photographs, mainly of anthropologists who studied these groups in the beginning of the 20th century. As they were groups whose way of life had not been much affected by civilization, I ended up using them as a reference for these characters. It was also important to see the graphic symbols that are part of these cultures. All this I ended up using to portray their universe.[49]
>
> (D'Salete, 2021)

At the end, there is a game with the present world, with the urban reality of a metropolis. The character Dara finds herself in the middle of the favela and, little by little, he returns to the past.

> Marcelo D'Salete here directly links the history of slavery with the fate of young Afro-Brazilians today. And it is significant that the figure of Dara, Zumbi's daughter, is used to visualize such a relationship, especially since little Dara is also the figure that closes *Angola Janga*: released by Andala, another strong woman in the fiction of the São Paulo comic artist, in the

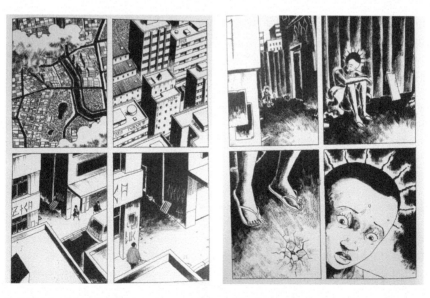

FIGURE 5.5   Marcelo D'Salete. Dara sees the urban future of Brazil. *Angola Janga*. 2017, p. 390–392.

latest vignettes Dara lifts her gaze to the sky, her face full of hope and holding the spear in her arms.[50]

(Wrobel, 2019, p. 116)

The sequence of images, the scenarios and the movement of angles and perspectives lead us to think, on the one hand, that the struggles and teachings of the black movement persist, have a long history and are carried out in daily life in Brazil. On the other hand, it is possible to think that Angola Janga has not ended, it has not been totally destroyed, and that the ancestral dream of freedom and free land persists in the hearts and bodies of Afro-Brazilian people. Through Dara's eyes, we look at the sky, beyond the clouds, farther and farther away, where the stars shine. The infinite universe seems to translate the adinkra symbol on the next page, like the wisdom messages of the black people that are transmitted for many generations.

Considerations

These two works indicate, in the investigation of documents and visualities of the past, how traditional historiography has many silences and that just highlighting this is not enough: "it is necessary to go further: to question the historical documentation about the gaps, to question the forgetfulness, the gaps, the white spaces of history. We must make an inventory of the archives of silence, and make history based on documents and the absence of documents[51]" (Le Goff, 1992, p. 109).

These graphic novels flee from a dichotomous and deterministic view, reinterpreting contexts, showing the contradictions of each period, the tactics and strategies of negotiation, of resistance. These are stories that cover fictional and non-fiction narratives, factual or mythical, micro and macro, written and oral traditions, with a political, economic, cultural and personal character. They are structured in memories that were left aside, on the margin, or forgotten; plural, diverse and inclusive, incomplete, partial, even contradictory (Pedrosa et al., 2018).

Sem Dó is not an openly feminist work, but works with subtleties that question the fixation and naturalization of the social roles of men and women and problematize the sexist, misogynistic and racist precepts of society of the time. It considers the various perspectives of women who worked outside the home and those engaged in domestic work, highlighting the tensions and contradictions arising from gender asymmetries. It draws the daily battles between the dream of romantic love, the idealized future of marriage and the desires and yearnings for autonomy. Luli Penna's investigative process and the construction of a different perspective on women are marked in the musical, literary, advertising and imagetic references scattered throughout the pages. They are clues to be followed, not to unravel the novel, but to arouse reflections and feelings about the different contexts intricate there.

Luli Penna deals with memory and the past as social, active, dynamic constructions, giving people agency, valuing gestures, postures, artifacts as productions of meanings and realities. The photographs and images are appropriated in her work for their technical potentialities, for their hybrid languages, for their expressive force. They function as historical sources (recreated, problematized), objects of affection, starting and arriving points of questioning, emotional triggers and visual stimuli. *Sem Dó* allows for various combinations of images, opening many reading and interpretation possibilities, adding several layers of meanings.

Angola Janga draws on the struggles of black movements to create other stories about how the enslaved men and women resisted colonial oppression, to regain the dignity and autonomy of their lives. It is inserted in a decolonial perspective. D'Salete chooses to address the conflict, inserting family, love and friendship relationships, pacts and alliances, showing how the administration of land and the economy in an alternative way coexisted, negotiated and opposed the hegemonic colonial organization. The scenes from the past dialogue with the present, highlighting how the anti-racist fight persists. "The remnants of many quilombos all over Brazil are still fighting for possessions of their lands. Threatened, but resisting[52]" (D'Salete, 2017, p. 422).

These two works make us think of the contradictions forged in the making of history itself, where the subjectivity of the researcher is involved. Luli Penna and Marcelo D'Salete assume investigative postures that remind us that "History is the subject of a construction whose site is not homogeneous, empty time, but time filled in full by now-time" (Benjamin, 2003, p. 395). Benjamin also states that

> Historical materialism wishes to hold fast that image of the past which unexpectedly appears to the historical subject in a moment of danger. . . . Every age must strive anew to wrest tradition away from the conformism that is working to overpower it. . . . The gift of awakening the sparks of hope in the past is an exclusive privilege of the historian convinced that the dead will also not be safe if the enemy wins. That enemy has not ceased to win.
>
> (Benjamin, 2003, p. 391)

In the current arena of representational disputes, of the history of Brazil as a contested territory, these comics use different graphic and stylistic procedures to question power relations, letting us listen to multiple voices, overlapping temporalities and allowing readers to participate in this resignification process. We are questioned about our political positions, our commitment to a more just and egalitarian, less authoritarian society. Thinking about the past is a way to discuss and transform the future. Stirring in memories and bringing about emotions are acts of resistance and subversion against imposed order.

Notes

1 For Beatriz Vargas Ramos and Luiz Moreira, it was a parliamentary coup since Dilma was not accused of "having committed a crime of corruption, she is not under indictment for misuse of resources, for illicit enrichment, for tax evasion, for keeping accounts abroad, for money laundering, or for participating in a criminal association, or even for receiving bribes and illegal donations," fueling even more controversy over her impeachment (Ramos and Moreira, 2016, p. 57). This period was also known as the neoliberal

right-wing coup or white coup. Michel Temer, the vice president, assumed the presidency of the Republic until the 2018 elections, with the victory of the far-right candidate, Jair Bolsonaro.

2 Rosana Paulino (1967) is a black visual artist whose work questions the violence contained in the images produced about enslaved people, and the position of black women in Brazilian society (www.rosanapaulino.com.br/). Dalton de Paula (1982) is a black visual artist who proposes in his works the recreation and reconstruction of historical and cultural identities, sharing memories and knowledge of enslaved peoples (https://daltonpaula.com/). Denilson Baniwa (1984) is an artist, illustrator and designer, and belongs to the indigenous Baniwa ethnic group. He makes critical interventions in images and documents about the colonization of indigenous territories and the history of white and western art (www.behance.net/denilsonbaniwa). Naine Terena de Jesus is an activist, curator, artist and researcher of the Terena people (www.instagram.com/naine_terena/).

3 *Beco do Rosário* [Rosário Alley] (independent publication, 2015) by Ana Luiza Koehler; *Artistas brasileiras* [Brazilian Artists] (Editora Miguilim, 2018) by Aline Lemos; *A Infância do Brasil* [The Childhood of Brazil] (webcomics, 2015; printed by Avec Editora, 2017), by José Aguiar, among others.

4 The notion of "structures of feeling" developed by Raymond Williams refers to certain sets of aspects that characterize and permeate the various cultural practices of an epoch and their inseparable relationships with other social, political and economic spheres. The idea that certain "creative acts compose, within a historical period, a specific community: a community visible in the structure of feeling and demonstrable, above all, in fundamental choices of form . . . while they correspond very closely to a real social history, of men living in actual and changing social relations, they again often precede the more recognizable changes of formal institution and relationship, which are the more accessible, indeed the more normal, history" (Williams, 2005, p. 16).

5 Zumbi dos Palmares is considered a hero who fought for freedom and a symbol of freedom. Documentation about him is sparse and highly contested. Zumbi would have been born free, in Alagoas, in the year 1655, but was captured and given to a Portuguese missionary priest, being baptized as Francisco. At 15, he would have fled to Palmares. He led many fights against colonial expeditions, being assassinated on November 20, 1695. This date is celebrated as the day of black conscience (Gomes, Lauriano and Schwarcz, 2021).

6 Original text in Portuguese. All the excerpts in Portuguese were translated by this article's author.

7 Original text in Portuguese.

8 Original text in Portuguese.

9 Original text in Portuguese.

10 To learn more about the work of this artist, visit the website www.lulipenna.com.br/.

11 In 2020, she participated in the magazine *Queimada*, published during the quarantine, from May 25 to August 24, 2020, on *Instagram*. Retrieved from: www.instagram.com/_quemada/. Accessed: 20 January 2021.

12 Original text in Portuguese.

13 *Limite* was filmed in 1930 and presented for the first time on May 17, 1931, written and directed by Mário Peixoto (1908–1992), Brazilian filmmaker, screenwriter and writer from Rio de Janeiro.

14 Original text in Portuguese.

15 Original text in Portuguese.

16 Caetano Emanuel Vianna Telles Velloso was born in August 1942, in Santo Amaro da Purificação, a small town close to the capital of Bahia, Salvador. He is an important Brazilian composer, singer, musician and producer who led a musical movement known as *tropicalismo* in the late 1960s that renewed Brazilian popular music. In 1969, he was arrested by the military regime and was exiled in London. To learn more, visit www.caetanoveloso.com.br/.

17 Roberto Carlos Braga (1941) was born in Cachoeiro do Itapemirim, Espírito Santo. He is one of the most famous composers and singers in Brazil and Latin America, being called "King." His career began in the 1960s, influenced by *samba-canção* and *impelled*, was boosted by the rock musical movement *Jovem Guarda*, and followed the path of romantic music. The song "Details" was composed in partnership with Erasmo Esteves (Erasmo Carlos). See www.robertocarlos.com/.
18 Jorge Duílio Lima Meneses is a Brazilian singer, musician and composer, born in 1942 in Rio de Janeiro. He added new elements to samba-rock and to the way of playing music, with features of rock, soul and funk. www.instagram.com/jorgebenjoroficial/?hl=pt-br.
19 Antonio Pecci Filho was born in São Paulo in 1946. He is a Brazilian singer, composer and guitarist. He was a friend and musical partner of the poet Vinicius de Moraes. See www.toquinho.com.br/.
20 Wally Salomão was born in Jequié, Bahia, in 1943 and died in Rio de Janeiro in 2003. He was a Brazilian poet who participated in the tropicalist movement. He was also a representative of the Brazilian counterculture of the 1970s.
21 Jards Anet da Silva was born in 1943, in Rio de Janeiro. He is an actor, singer, musician and composer. His tropicalist aesthetic mixes pop culture, rock and Brazilian popular music. He made soundtracks for national films from the 1960s to the1970s.
22 Fred Foster and Kris Kristofferson wrote this song. The North American singer-songwriter Janis Jyn Joplin (1943–1970), was considered the greatest rock, soul and blues singer of the 1960s, with an unmistakable voice.
23 Antônio Carlos Belchior (1947–2017), born in Sobral, Ceará, was a famous Brazilian singer, composer and musician.
24 Original text in Portuguese.
25 The Trans-Amazon Highway or BR-230 is a federal highway, created during the military dictatorship, in the government of Garrastazu Médici. Unfinished and with many unpaved stretches, it caused a great deal of deforestation and economic damage. It was one of the projects of the Superintendency of Development for the Amazon (SUDAM), created in 1966.
26 Brás is located to the east of the historic center of the city of São Paulo and was known for concentrating many immigrants from the Italian community. The Santa Helena Building was an existing building in Praça da Sé, downtown São Paulo, inaugurated in 1925 and demolished in 1971. With an eclectic architecture with an Art Deco influence, known for the luxury and modernity of its installations, it housed a luxurious cinema-theater. In the 1930s, the building began to attract artists and professionals with lower purchasing power, being the headquarters of the Santa Helena Group, formed by Alfredo Volpi, Rebolo, Clovis Graciano, Mário Zanini, among others. The Luz Station building was inaugurated in 1901. The old bus station was located in the Luz region, downtown São Paulo, and operated from 1961 to 1982. The Sé Cathedral is located in the square of the same name, in the central region. The current building was inaugurated in 1954, with the towers still unfinished, which were only completed at the end of 1969. Paulista Avenue is the main avenue in São Paulo and, during the 1960s and 1970s; it underwent major renovations and landscaping changes, concentrating large and famous office buildings.
27 According to the Brazilian Civil Code from 1916, the woman was subordinate to the male figure (father, husband) and had to ask for authorization to perform any activity outside the domestic sphere. This lasted until 1962, when the Statute of Married Women came into force (Law No. 4.121/62). The State acted as a social regulator, as a brake on the advances sought by certain women, on feminist demands (Maluf and Mott, 1998, pp. 375–376).
28 In 1834, the *daedalum* appeared, a machine created by William George Horner – an English watchmaker. The device was also known as the zoetrope, or wheel of life. Strips with drawings reproduce the successive phases of an action. As the cylinder rotates, the drawings placed within the cuts are visible through the opposite cuts. This apparatus was

quickly marketed together with collections of tapes with drawings that were placed and replaced on the inside face of the cylinder (Lucena Júnior, 2002).
29 Original text in Portuguese.
30 Eclectic architectural and decorative arts style that reached its peak between the 1920s and the 1930s. It is characterized by the use of expensive materials, geometric shapes rounded or zigzag, modernist trends. It became a symbol of luxury, glamour, exuberance, being widespread in cinema and in fashion and decoration magazines.
31 To learn more about the biography and work of this artist, visit www.dsalete.art.br/bio.html.
32 *Noite Luz*, by Via Lettera, in 2008. *Encruzilhada*, published by Leya, in 2011 and by Veneta, in 2016; *Cumbe* (2014), released by Veneta. *Angola Janga* and *Cumbe* together sold more than 200,000 copies in Brazil.
33 *Angola Janga* was also published in France (Çá et Là), Portugal (Editora Polvo), USA (Fantagraphics), Spain (Flow Press), Poland (Timof) and Austria (Bahoe Books).
34 It received the *Grampo Ouro Award* in 2018, the 30th *2018 HQ MIX* trophy in four categories (National Drawer, National Screenwriter, International Highlight and National Special Edition), won the 60th *Jabuti Award* (comics category) and the *Rudolph Dirks Award* 2019 (Best Screenplay).
35 Original text in Portuguese.
36 *Mocambo* (literally a hut) was the name given to the territories of blacks who fled captivity until the 17th century, being replaced later by the term *quilombo*.
37 The Quilombo of Palmares was the largest quilombo that existed in Latin America, built in the region of the current state of Alagoas. It had a population of around 20 thousand inhabitants. Until today it is one of the greatest symbols of the struggle against the colonizers and the resistance of the enslaved in Brazil. During the period of the Dutch invasion of the Northeast (1630–1654), the quilombo registered a significant growth, as the search for escaped slaves decreased and surveillance was weakened, facilitating escapes. Palmares was the target of expeditions organized by the Portuguese and the Dutch. It was destroyed in 1694 and its leader, Zumbi, was killed the following year.
38 Original text in Portuguese.
39 *Zumbi of Palmares*, 1955, by Clóvis Moura and Álvaro de Moya; *Zumbi – the saga of the Palmares*, 2003, by Antonio Krisnas and Allan Alex; *The war of Palmares*, by Carlos Ferreira and Moacir Martins.
40 Original text in Portuguese.
41 Original text in Portuguese.
42 Original text in Portuguese.
43 Original text in Portuguese.
44 Original text in Portuguese.
45 Original text in Portuguese.
46 Original text in Portuguese.
47 Ananse Ntontan: the spider's web, adinkra symbol of wisdom, cleverness, creativity and complexity of life. It is part of a complex set of Asante (Ghana) graphic symbols (D'Salete, 2017, p. 415).
48 "Set of symbols of Tchokwe origin, people who inhabit the northeast of Angola and the regions close to the Democratic Republic of Congo and Zambia. These drawings are formed by dots and sinuous lines made in the sand and accompanied by oral narratives. They are part of the boys' initiation rituals. This drawing represents a place in the forest where fruits and animals abound. The wise old man, when drawing, says: the partridge comes out of the forest, chased by the mukhondo, the sable comes out chased by the lion, and the woman comes out chased by the man" (D'Salete, 2017, p. 418).
49 Original text in Portuguese.
50 Original text in Portuguese.
51 Original text in Portuguese.
52 Original text in Portuguese.

References

Anchieta, I. (2019). *Imagens da mulher no ocidente moderno 3: Stars de Hollywood*. Editora da Universidade de São Paulo.
Bakhtin, M. (2003). *Estética da criação verbal*. Martins Fontes.
Benjamin, W. (2003). "On the concept of history". Eiland, H. & Jennings, M. (eds.). *Walter Benjamin: Selected Writings, Volume 4: On the Concept of History, Writings 1938–1940*. Harvard University Press, pp. 389–400.
Besse, S. K. (1999). *Modernizando a desigualdade: Reestruturação da Ideologia de Gênero no Brasil, 1914–1940*. EDUSP.
Burke, P. (2004). *Testemunha Ocular*. EDUSC.
Collins, P. H. (2017). "Se perdeu na tradução? – feminismo negro, interseccionalidade e política emancipatória". *Parágrafo*, [S.l.], v.5, n.1, pp. 6–17.
Custódio, H. (2018). "Angola Janga: quadrinho e representação histórica". *Literafro*, portal da literatura afro-brasileira, 25 de setembro de 2018. Available in: www.letras.ufmg.br/literafro/resenhas/ficcao/1138-angola-janga-quadrinho-e-representacao-historica Acesso em 20/01/2021.
D'Salete, M. (2017). *Angola Janga: uma história de Palmares*. Veneta.
D'Salete, M. (2020). Interview with Carol Almeida. *Plaf.* Available in: www.revistaogrito.com/plaf-entrevista-com-marcelo-dsalete-2/. Last accessed: 14/09/2022.
D'Salete, M. (2021). Interview with Lia Hama. *ECOA – UOL*. Available in: www.uol.com.br/ecoa/reportagens-especiais/marcelo-dsalete-cultura-banto-tem-presenca-fortissima-na-nossa-linguagem/#cover. Last accessed: 14/09/2022.
Gilroy, P. (2012). *O Atlântico negro*. Editora 34.
Gomes, F., Lauriano, J. & Schwarcz, L. M. (2021). *Enciclopédia Negra*. Companhia das Letras.
Hall, S. (ed.) (2003). *Representation: Cultural Representations and Signifying Practices*. Open University Press.
Le Goff, J. (1992). *History and Memory*. Columbia University Press. Trans. Steven Randall & Elizabeth Claman.
Le Goff, J.(1996). *História e Memória*. Editora da UNICAMP.
Lucena Júnior, A. (2002). *Arte da animação. Técnica e estética através da história*. Editora SENAC São Paulo.
Malcher, M. (2019). "Os (des)encantos do amor romântico na HQ Sem Dó, de Luli Penna". Marino, D. & Machado, L. (eds.) *Mulheres & Quadrinhos*. Script., pp. 333–338.
Maluf, M. & Mott, M. L. (1998). "Recônditos do Mundo Feminino". Sevcenko, N. (ed.). *História da vida privada no Brasil República*, v. 3. Companhia das Letras, pp. 367–421.
Mbembe, A. (2018). "O tempo que se agita". Pedrosa, A., Carneiro, A. & Mesquita, A. (eds.) *Histórias Afro-atlânticas: (vol.2) antologia*. MASP, pp. 125–144.
Miller, D. (2013). *Trecos, troços e coisas: estudos antropológicos sobre a cultura material*. Zahar.
Pedrosa, A. (2018). "*History*, Histórias". Pedrosa, A., Carneiro, A. & Mesquita, A. (eds.) *Histórias afro-atlânticas: [vol.2] antolologia*MASP, pp. 8–11.
Penna, L. (2017a). "Papo com Luli Penna, autora de Sem Dó. Entrevista concedida a Ramon Vitral". *Vitralizado*. Available in: https://vitralizado.com/hq/papo-com-luli-penna-a-autora-de-sem-do-o-que-mais-me-impressionou-foi-a-diferenca-entre-a-liberdade-sexual-dos-homens-e-das-mulheres-brutal-naquela-epoca-e-hoje/. Last accessed: 15/09/2022.
Penna, L.(2017b). *Sem dó*. Todavia.
Vargas Ramos, B. & Moreira, L. (2016). "Ingredientes de um golpe parlamentar". Proner, C. et al. (eds.). *A resistência ao golpe de 2016*. Canal 6, pp. 57–60.
Schwarcz, L.(2019). *Sobre o autoritarismo brasileiro*. Companhia das Letras.

Soihet, R. (2006). "Mulheres pobres e violência no Brasil urbano". Del Priore, M. (ed.). *História das mulheres no Brasil*. Contexto, pp. 362–400.

Williams, Raymond (2005). *Culture and Materialism*. London: Verso Books.

Wrobel, J. (2019). "História(s) redesenhada(s): visualizando analogias entre hoje e o passado – periferias urbanas, resistência negra e vozes femininas na obra de Marcelo D'Salete". *Artcultura*, Uberlândia, v.21, n.39, 99–116. https://doi.org/10.14393/artc-v21-n39-2019-52029

6
BLACK VISUALITIES IN BRAZILIAN COMICS

A historical overview

Ivan Lima Gomes

Introduction

The graphic novel production of the 21st century is characterized by, among other aspects, a deep awareness of its historicity. To say this is to imply the past is mediated in the language of comics in a variety of ways (Witek, 1989). One can see the renewal of these topics alongside the introduction of other forms of dealing with the past through comics: graphic memoirs, or what Hillary Chute has defined as "visual witness" (Chute, 2016); fictional narratives centered around historical facts; or through an explicit engagement with the history of comics, through direct quotation of other comics and exercises of comics genealogy. Moreover, these tendencies work with a largely documented and bibliographical survey, which points out to a hypothesis that writing/drawing comics is a form of writing History (Jablonka, 2014).

I will be presenting a few preliminary notes around the racial visualities in Brazilian comics from a historical perspective. To do that, I will use two case studies in rather distinctive historical contexts as a starting point, so that the rupture and the continuity of operations concerning the black race visibility (or invisibility, if we can put it that way) in the production of comics in Brazil can be highlighted.

One case study discussed here is the graphic novel *Angola Janga*, written and drawn by the Brazilian artist and art school teacher Marcelo D'Salete, and published in 2018. This graphic novel tells the story of the Palmares *quilombo* and the black resistance to slavery during the 17th century of Portuguese colonization in nowadays North-eastern Brazil. Along with *Angola Janga*, we intend to discuss some aspects of the historiographic operation that goes around this graphic novel, seeking to consider its articulation with current debates about racial issues in Brazilian society, the place of comics and its publics in such debates and the roles of media and History as a sort of public history. *Angola Janga* has been celebrated by critics and comics readers and became D'Salete's most relevant work in a moment where racial tensions and inequality are seen as minor problems by conservative governments. Through a case study, the purpose here is to suggest broader theoretical reflection on topics such as historical narrative, remediations of History, media and consumption of history, public history and uses of the past, among other connected issues.

However, to better discuss *Angola Janga* and the comics representation of the Palmares experience, it is important to situate D'Salete's work into a larger history of black characters as depicted in Brazilian comics. It is an already written history (Chinen, 2019), but it is still incomplete and willing to be reviewed. In that sense, to search for comics in Brazilian archives points out several possibilities to rewrite Brazilian comics history. Through another case study (*Bingo, o pequeno jornaleiro*), which was not discussed in Chinen's work and which I found during my PhD research (Lima Gomes, 2018) in several Brazilian archives, I shall further elaborate the issue.

Being a black kid in Brazilian comics: the case of Bingo

Created by Aylton Thomaz, the comic strip *Bingo, o pequeno jornaleiro* [*Bingo, the little paperboy*] substituted for *Piazito*, a kid comic strip (Gordon, 2017), whose main character was a white boy from the Brazilian southern region. *Bingo* was published in the last months of the main action in defense of the local production of comics against the American "cultural imperialism" in the early 1960s, known as CETPA, originally based in the capital city of the Brazilian southern state of Rio Grande do Sul, Porto Alegre. With names like Flavio Colin, Renato Canini and Julio Shimamoto, among others, directly or indirectly involved and the support of politicians like Leonel Brizola and Janio Quadros, the main aim of CETPA was to establish public policies to foster the local production by emphasizing on the harmful influence of comics published in the United States (Lima Gomes, 2018, pp. 35–82).

With a strong caricatural appeal, Bingo was a black kid who sold newspapers and solved crimes. Actually, he is one of very few black protagonists in Brazilian comics. Before that, there had been black characters in Brazilian comics since the first decades of the 20th century: names like Giby, Benjamin and Azeitona are very well recognized among scholars and comics memorialists (Chinen, 2019).[1]

Another example is the comic book called *Gibi*, named after the mascot boy in Roberto Marinho's publication, who would get to be better known than the one previously published by J. Carlos. Sooner, Marinho's creation would aggregate a new meaning to this kind of format of publication; what used to be a synonym for a mischievous boy became the name of this format in Brazil. The visual construction of the character *Gibi* and also a character like *Ebony White*, Eisner's sidekick created for the hero The Spirit, must have been the source of inspiration used by Aylton Thomaz to conceive *Bingo*.

However, *Bingo* is still little recognized by admirers and scholars of this topic, even after being published in big newspapers like *Ultima Hora* and *A Noite* in the first half of the 1960s.

Bingo has a very peculiar history: differently from other CETPA comics, Thomaz's strip was not directly produced by CETPA, but rather was one of the comic strips of the newspaper *A Noite*. It was part of the attractions to relaunch the newspaper, which had been facing financial issues since the mid-1950s. Therefore, it is not a genuine creation of the CETPA studios, which reinforces the fact that none of its group members can remember Thomaz or his work related to the publishing company. It is more likely that Thomaz's strip was distributed by CETPA because it was in agreement with its proposal for nationalizing comics.

Based on *Bingo*'s release, the newspaper seemed to take a stand in the debates about nationalization, giving a larger space for Bingo if compared to other comics published by *A Noite*, like *The Lone Ranger*, *Brick Bradford*, *Beetle Bailey* and other Disney comics. *Bingo* occupied almost half a page of the comics section of the newspaper, and was celebrated as a special national creation for it. After the initial excitement in regard to the comic strip, it started losing ground gradually in the paper until its publishing was interrupted nine months later.[2]

It is possible to point out that *Bingo* had its relevance in the center of CETPA's editorial project, taking into account two characteristics. First, *Bingo* represented the childlike universe, mainly constituted of black characters. Actually, *Bingo* was probably the first Brazilian comic strip with a broad presence of black characters depicting their everyday life in a popular vein.

Even though the graphic image adopted by the strip for the black characters has allowed associations with those blackface representations adopted since the mid-19th century as a funny reduction of the social definition of the black race, it is necessary to be cautious with the establishment of unmediated analogies. *Bingo* pointed toward a different understanding of what had been practiced up to that moment in Brazil when we think about representations of black people in comics. Bingo was the leading character and he was not the support for white characters which were more important than he was. His partner in the adventures was a cousin from the countryside who would get involved in Bingo's daily life, without becoming a sidekick like Robin, Bucky or even Ebony White. Besides, the characters' lines were written in speech bubbles without language misuses or cacophonies that focused on showing grammar mistakes, which was really common among black characters until that moment. Finally, Bingo and his peers' social reality was represented in a way to highlight the sociability and the cultural traditions typical of Rio de Janeiro's lower classes.

The second most remarkable peculiarity of *Bingo* is the urban ambience in the city of Rio de Janeiro, Brazil. *Bingo* reinforced CETPA's speech with another regional reality – Rio de Janeiro's one, which contradicts historiographical attempts to explain the failure of CETPA due to its regional reach (Júnior, 2004, p. 355). This way, *Bingo's* Rio de Janeiro took CETPA, a group from the south of Brazil, into a dialog with another reality.

About the comic strips' plot, the story continues with the news that Bingo's aunt and youngest cousin were moving to his house, which was a reason for his and his mother's joy. All of them were clearly profiled as poor people, as we can assume from the strip shown here: in the first picture, *Bingo* would not stop carrying newspapers, which represented the source for his family's income. Beside him, his cousin Pedrinho would carry a bundle of clothes on his head. Following that, the panel shows a poor community in an idyllic way, with grass and a bird in the foreground.

After a typical family breakfast, Bingo leaves for work and takes his cousin Pedrinho to follow him throughout the city, when the action actually begins in the comic strip. At this point, we can see an explicit reference to the city of Rio de Janeiro: both of them go toward *Barreira do Vasco*, one of the many slums in the city, aboard a fully crowded cable car called *Alegria*, which means *joy* in Portuguese.

Following the hilarious experience regarding the public cable car, the two of them arrive at Barreira do Vasco to meet the community's "gang." With wide knowledge of the art of serenade, they aim at finding an acoustic guitarist called Tuté (a clear reference to Tute, a guitarist who died in 1957 and was responsible for introducing the seven-string acoustic guitar in the *choro*, an instrumental Brazilian popular music genre which originated in 19th-century Rio de Janeiro) – and a local singer. And Bingo also sings. In the following verses, the character exults his origins and the slum where he was born in:

> *I won't leave the favela*
> *Favela of my illusion*
> *All I have belongs to her*
> *And she's in my heart*
> *I won't let my love*
> *Crying with compassion*
> *If I leave the favela,*
> *I'll also leave my guitar.*

Bingo's exaltation of the sociability practiced in the slums became part of a group of massive productions that showed images and representations of the lower classes in newspapers and photos. Briefly, *Bingo*, interacts with a movie like Nelson Pereira dos Santos', *Rio, 40 graus* (1955). It is illustrative, for example, that the first strip published in the newspaper, *A Noite*, was an aerial view of the Sugar Loaf, followed by a description of the Copacabana neighborhood, where you can find nice people and also "smart" people, like pickpockets. The similarity between it and Santos' film is quite clear, as a very similar situation happened in the latter: a series of aerial takes with typical tourist attractions was assembled over an instrumental version of Ze Keti's song *A Voz do Morro*, together with scenes from shanty towns, or *favelas*, as these are known in Brazil, and focusing in the actions of a group of boys.[3] This way, if Santos' movie is usually analyzed from a perspective of Brazilian aesthetics adopting the innovations of Italian neorealist cinema, *Bingo* can be understood in a similar way. By applying aspects of this cinematographic aesthetics to the language of comics, it can be seen as the cornerstone of a national-popular children's culture which was incorporated into an editorial initiative of nationalizing comics.

Other scenarios beyond Rio de Janeiro's "post card" images composed *Bingo*'s urban geography, like the Maracanã stadium, where they go to watch a football game between Flamengo and Vasco da Gama, probably the two most important football teams in the city. Thomaz's strips focused on the supporters' reactions, humorously dealing with the diversified universe of absurd situations that might happen in a football match, such as the crowd, the joy and the rivalry amongst the fans.

Placing Bingo and Pedrinho – black characters living in slums and sympathetic to the ways of life of the lower classes of the region – as supporters for Flamengo, in contrast with those from Vasco, mainly represented by Portuguese descendants, was not a naive choice by Aylton Thomaz. The artist dialogued with an imaginary that linked Flamengo to popular causes, black identity and national identity that was in place between 1945 and 1964 (Soares Coutinho, 2013), having already used such strategy before, in the cover of the magazine *Superman*, published by EBAL.

Back to *Bingo*, the game was left aside after an unscored penalty by "Bellini," Vasco's defense, against one of Flamengo's shooters. The focus turns to the supporters, who go wild and start fighting among each other, which turns out to be a great opportunity for a pickpocket to act. Bingo and Pedrinho intervene and manage, after some struggle, to hold him with police support. As a reward, the victim gives them two thousand cruzeiros, the adopted currency in the country at that time, and they could happily leave to buy some bread for their mothers. End of the story.

If *Bingo* can help us to suggest a historical overview on Brazilian comics of more than a half of the 20th century, now, let's move a few decades later and discuss one major 21st-century Brazilian graphic novel.

Graphic novels in Brazil: Angola Janga and the graphic resistance to slavery

The first decade of the 21st century established *graphic novels* as contemporary narratives to discuss Brazilian history and society. Countless authors, publishers, comic shops and readers arose, eager for issues that are more relevant about topics related to politics, sexual choices and identities. Graphic novels have inspired films and books, as well as having some relevance in literature conferences.

New authors have worked with such narratives to approach topics such as racism and feminism, in a sense of actively intervening in Brazil's society. Most of these are aligned with the fight for historically excluded minorities, which have become the main target of more conservative groups that have lately used political instability to carry out policies of extermination against black people and the poor (see Figures 6.1 and 6.2).

An indicative of this is the brutal murder of the councilor Marielle Franco, from the left-wing party PSOL, and her driver Anderson Gomes in March 2018. After three years the murder remains unsolved, and no answers have been forthcoming regarding who gave the order. Rapidly, her face became a clear synonym of the absurd authoritarianism of Brazilian politics and its plan to suppress minorities. Franco became an icon of this fight, symbolizing the historical and continuous silencing of some identities, as women, black and homosexuals. Comics promptly responded to that and contributed to give Franco a voice and expression, making her a worldwide reference in the defense of a fairer society (see Figure 6.3).

Such works play a sensitive role and allow people to build up, from a historical perspective, "an image of others by giving them a social identity," as argued by Alan Corbin (2005, 19). These "others" disrupt some paradigms found in comics, which stands as a form of expression produced mostly by men, about men and for men, and has superheroes as a narrative genre par excellence.

Together with this debate about genre in Brazilian comics, topics related to the place of black people and the structural development of racism in the country have been a source of interpretation for many Brazilian artists. Works like *Morro da Favela*, by André Diniz, about the reporter and photographer Mauricio Horta, dweller in a famous slum in Rio, the Morro da Providencia. In addition, *Carolina* (2016), a graphic biography by Sirlene Barbosa and João Pinheiro about the black writer Carolina de Jesus, author of *Quarto de Desejo* (1960). Finally, the series *Conto dos Orixás* (2019), by Hugo Canuto, focuses on representing Gods and Entities from Candomblé, the African religion, using the same perspective of superhero comic books, directly inspired by Jack Kirby's work on Marvel Comics during the 1960s.

It is not a surprise that the black resistance to slavery during the colonial period, from the establishment of the "Quilombo dos Palmares," has been turned into comics. After all, it is very likely that it represents a long and multifaceted project of an alternative way of life to the standardized colonial one, sprung from the disobedience of the enslaved black people. In his recent research about black characters in Brazilian comics, Chinen recounts comics produced since the 1950s about Zumbi and Palmares, with a considerable increment in the first years of the 21st century (2019, pp. 229–236).

Among those who erupted in the present scene aligned with the criticism against the maintenance of racist structures in Brazilian society, one of the most internationally celebrated by the public and the specialized critics is certainly Marcelo D'Salete. An artist and graphic illustrator, he is the author of *Angola Janga*, a monumental work that graphically elaborates on a "history of Palmares," as defended in the subheading of the Brazilian edition. It combines bibliographical, documental and iconographical research on topics like the African diaspora and the slavery in the Portuguese America with a dynamic narrative full of symbolisms linked to African-Brazilian culture.

The impact of D'Salete's work can be felt in academic studies – which contrast a lot with the lack of scholarship about a comic strip like *Bingo* or even the comic book *Gibi*, for example. Taking into account the fact that Angola Janga was published about two years ago, it is remarkable that it already presents considerable academic critical baggage around itself. In general, these works highlight the relevance of D'Salete's work in relation to the visibility of black slavery in Brazil, comparing it to present days. Excerpts of works like *Angola Janga* and *Cumbe* (2014) – a work prior to *Angola Janga* but with the same interest in approaching topics linked to the colonial slavery – are available in academic journals (D'Salete, 2018b, pp. 70–72). Interviews with D'Salete conducted by researchers are also available in English and Portuguese (Jesus and D'Salete, 2018, pp. 56–69; Lima Gomes and D'Salete, 2019, pp. 117–124). Recent research in History teaching, focusing on creating a comic book to represent the feminine resistance to slavery during the 19th century, inspired by primary sources, finds inspiration in his work (Veloso, 2018), which clearly signposts the richness of the exchange of History written in and outside Academia.

Here, I would like to highlight three studies to understand the possibilities behind comics studies of Black narratives of History as represented in Brazilian comics. Firstly, the German researcher Jasmin Wrobel emphasizes the homology in 17th century's Palmares and present-day Sao Paulo in topics like violence, racism, death, and the main role of black men and women in rewriting their own stories of life. Wrobel is able to notice an "inverted timeline" between D'Salete's first works, situated in the urban outskirts of big cities, and more recent ones – like *Cumbe* and *Angola Janga* – which try to show slavery during Brazil's colonial era (Wrobel, 2019, p. 101–102).

D'Salete seems to confirm the author's comprehension by clearly recognizing the social place of his work in a context with aggravated social conflicts and the growth of a conservative agenda that intends to silence the black voices that try to address the racial issue in Brazil:

> Let me put it this way: the size, the dimension of such endeavour was gradually formed through time. Little by little, I noticed that there was something to explore, through comics, when it comes to the fight against violence during colonial times. A counter narrative, opposing the concept of racial and social harmony as our background, which remains until today. Now that we have a fierce presidential election, this debate is even more important. Such discourse tries to nullify intense conflicts against a colonial and centralizing project. Resistance ruled by marginalized black and indigenous populations. I was slowly realizing the dimension of the book in this environment. Many times, while talking to other people, new ideas and possibilities of understanding these pictures and stories arise. Therefore, the idea of the book is to present these characters in a more human and fully complex way.
> (Lima Gomes and D'Salete, 2019, pp. 119–120, translated by me)

A second study focuses on the critical views of Flavio Gomes, a Brazilian historian specialized in slavery and black resistance in Portuguese America.[4] He discusses D'Salete's comics as "original experiments" which update the debate about the *quilombos*'s experience to the 21st-century reader by prioritizing Africanism

112 Ivan Lima Gomes

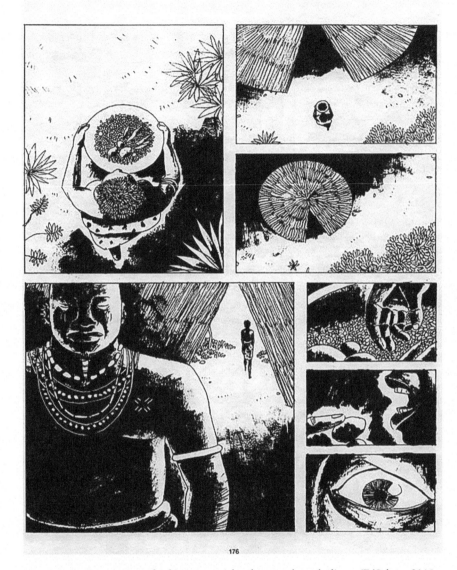

FIGURE 6.4 Recreation of Africa: material culture and symbolisms (D'Salete, 2018a, 176).

in them. Since these refugee's communities also worked as a recreation of Africa, they were represented with a "perspective of a cosmos that linked spirits, forests, memories and ancestors." (dos Santos Gomes and D'Salete, 2020, p. 162)

While talking specifically about *Angola Janga*, Gomes points out that it is A History of Palmares, instead of defining it as The Definite History of Palmares. This and the use of the expression "Angola Janga" ("Small Angola") to represent the

Quilombo dos Palmares, as some of its first inhabitants did – in contrast to the word "Palmares," which D'Salete almost never uses, Gomes suggests that the work implies the possibility of several Palmares – in the past and in the present, we may add (dos Santos Gomes and D'Salete, 2020, p. 163). He also reinforces that there is a choice for a non-linear historical approach, in contrast to a narrative focus on the origin, the rise and the downfall of black resistance.

Despite not directly discussing *Angola Janga*, the interpretation of the researcher Nohora Arrieta Fernández regarding *Cumbe* suggests interesting reflections of D'Salete's works. Fernández analysis is based on concepts like "opaqueness," "detour" and "marronage," elaborated by the Martinican philosopher Édouard Glissant. From these, she understands that the stories in *Cumbe* operate on a narrative logic which is ambiguous and escaping, trying to compose "a new archive, a counter argument which faces founding narratives about the black subjectivity established in Brazil with works like *Casa Grande e Senzala* (1933), written by the sociologist Gilberto Freyre" (Arrieta Fernández, 2019, p. 142, translated by me).

Hence, his attention to focusing on black visibility while drawing, is also present in *Angola Janga*: it operates as an ambiguous and dark struggle with the traumatic experience of colonization, in contrast with a whole series of former representations of "silenced slavery" which Fernández associates with Freyre.

Conclusion – paths to follow

May 13 is a historical date associated with the fight of black movements, as it represents the Abolition of Slavery, which occurred in 1888. The Palmares Foundation, officially committed to the "preservation of cultural, social and economic values derived from black influence in constituting Brazilian society" published in May 13, 2020 the following quotes on its official web site: "Zumbi: hero of the black consciousness enslaved by the left-wing."[5]

It intends to deconstruct the image of *Zumbi*, one of the main leaders of Quilombo dos Palmares and a symbol of black resistance, which had been claimed, until these days, by the fight against racism and prejudice. The messages posted on the site of Fundação Palmares add up to countless others sad expressions of prejudice and disrespect to African-Brazilian populations uttered by the current government. It is possible to surmise that updating in a critical way the narrative of Quilombo dos Palmares, aka, Angola Janga, is to take part in the safeguard of tolerance and racial equality. It means, above all, opposing authoritarianism. It therefore reinforces the political relevance of D'Salete's work.

Part of the relevance of D'Salete's work is his effort to suggest a deep reconsideration of Brazilian historiography, not only in terms of topics and issues at first neglected in academic research on slavery, but in a way close to what the French historian Ivan Jablonka suggested as the "third continent," where the narrative potentialities of history and fiction join forces to develop an affective and effective way of narrating the past: an emotional and affectionate understanding of the past is necessary to lead to a record of History – and of a history of historiography as a critic of historicity (Araújo, 2013, pp. 34–44) – which sees the past as a sphere of possibilities that suggest challenges to present times. As a result of the Portuguese process of colonization and its domination project upon African bodies, Palmares is a place/continent full of histories to be told. This also leads to another combination from the perspective of History as a discipline and its public relevance to discuss the experience of colonialism embodied in the trajectories of black men and women, which goes along with the public extent of historical knowledge and the importance of Angola Janga in mediating these discussions.

To think in terms of other histories must also apply to Brazilian comics history as a whole. In other terms, it means that it's important to move beyond linear narratives that reinforce entrepreneurial and successful trajectories mostly developed by white men. As D'Salete teaches us, it's important to visit the archives and to let it introduce new doubts to our current research. That's what happened to me when I first met *Bingo*. On the one hand, it maintains several of the stereotypical representations of black people presented in comics' history; however, its plot doesn't support discrimination or other controversial topics historically related to b lack characters in comics during the first decades of the 20th century. In fact, *Bingo* invites the reader to meet the everyday life of a poor Brazilian kid. And it also invites comics scholars to engage and research, on a deeper level, further Brazilian comics, in order to forge a Black tradition of comics in Brazil. By the way, we must remember that in Brazil it's still common to call comic books *gibis*. It's time to assume all of its consequences.

As a final conclusion, I would like to bring here a quote from Achille Mbembe's *Critique of the Black Reason*, as it is a suggestive interpretation of the crisis we live in the present time:

> But who among us can doubt that the moment has finally arrived for us to begin-from-ourselves? While Europe goes astray, overtaken by the malaise of not knowing where it is within and with the world, is it not time to lay the foundation for something absolutely new? To do so, will we have to forget Blackness? Or perhaps, on the contrary, must we hold on to its false power, its luminous, fluid, and crystalline character – that strange subject, slippery, serial, and plastic, always masked, firmly camped on both sides of the mirror, constantly skirting the edge of the frame? And if, by chance, in the midst of this torment, Blackness survives those who invented it, and if all of subaltern humanity becomes Black in a reversal to which only history knows the secret, what risks would a Becoming-Black-of-the-World pose to the promise of liberty and universal equality for which the term "Black" has stood throughout the modern period?
>
> (Mbembe, 2007, p. 7)

I am quite aware that Mbembe does not refer exactly to comics when he suggests the relevance of Blackness in contrast to the "false power" of "that strange subject, slippery, serial, and plastic, always masked." But this sounds suggestive enough to allow thinking of Blackness in Brazilian comics as a critique of several operations of invisibilization that still work nowadays, which delegate the potency of Black visual culture in comics, in Mbembe's term, to "the edge of the frame." Now maybe it's time to move beyond this frame.

Notes

1 A collection of J. Carlos' *Giby* was edited by Cardoso (2013).
2 A NOITE. Rio de Janeiro, 27 set. 1961, p. 8.
3 The opening scene can be seen here: www.youtube.com/watch?v=byIljMWslVI.
4 For a more descriptive and engaged review of the political and educational uses of Angola Janga, cf. Batista, 2018, pp. 305–312.
5 GOBBI, Nelson. No 13 de maio, Fundação Palmares publica artigos questionando Zumbi e o movimento negro e gera reação. *O Globo*, May 13, 2020. https://oglobo.globo.com/cultura/no-13-de-maio-fundacao-palmares-publica-artigos-questionando-zumbi-o-movimento-negro-gera-reacao-24424927.

Cited works

Araújo, V. L. (2013). "História da historiografia como analítica da historicidade". *História da Historiografia*, v. 6, n. 12, pp. 34–44.
Arrieta Fernández, N. (2019). "'Lo que contiene esa oscuridad': estéticas de la ambigüedad en la novela gráfica *Cumbe* de Marcelo D'Salete". *Mitologías Hoy*, v. 20. Universidad Autónoma de Barcelona, pp. 141–164.
Barbosa, S. & Pinheiro, J. (2016). *Carolina*. Veneta.
Batista, K. (2018). "Resenha do livro D'SALETE, Marcelo. *Angola Janga: uma história de Palmares*". *Caderno de Pesquisa do CDHIS*, v. 31, n. 2, pp. 305–312.
Canuto, H. (2019). *Contos dos orixás*. Ébórá Comics Group/Editora Independente.
Cardoso, A. E. (2013). *Memórias d'O Tico-Tico: Juquinha, Giby e Miss Shocking*. Editora do Senado Federal.
Chinen, N. (2019). *O negro nos quadrinhos do Brasil*. Peirópolis.
Chute, H. (2016). *Disaster drawn: visual witness, comics, and documentary form*. The Belknap Press of Harvard University Press.
Corbin, A. & Vidal, L. (2005). "Alain Corbin o prazer do historiador". *Revista Brasileira de História*, v. 25, n. 49, pp. 11–31.
Cury, C. (2018). "Tirinha Marielle Franco". Available in: www.teoeominimundo.com.br/2018/11/19/tirinha-marielle-franco. Last accessed: 15/09/2022.
dos Santos Gomes, F. & D'Salete, M. (2020). "Cumbe". *The American Historical Review*, v. 125, n. 1, pp. 160–164. https://doi.org/10.1093/ahr/rhz1314
D'Salete, M. (2014). *Cumbe*. Veneta.
D'Salete, M. (2018a). *Angola Janga*. Veneta.
D'Salete, M. (2018b). "From Cumbe". *Callaloo*, v. 41, n. 1, pp. 70–72.
Gordon, I. *Kid comic strips: a genre across four countries*. New York: Palgrave Macmillan, 2017.
Jablonka, I. Histoire et bande dessinée. *La vie des idées*. 18 nov. 2014. https://laviedesidees.fr/Histoire-et-bande-dessinee.html
Jesus, C. M. de. *Quarto de despejo: diário de uma favelada*. Rio de Janeiro: Francisco Alves, 1960.
Jesus, M. G. de; D'Salete, M. Interview with Marcelo D'Salete. *Callaloo*, v. 41, n. 1, 2018, pp. 56–69.

Júnior, G. *A Guerra dos gibis: a formação do mercado editorial brasileiro e a censura aos quadrinhos (1933–1964)*. São Paulo: Companhia das Letras, 2004.

Lima Gomes, I. (2018). *Os novos homens do amanhã: projetos e disputas em torno dos quadrinhos na América Latina*. Prismas.

Lima Gomes, I. & D'Salete, M. (2019). "Imaginando uma outra história da resistência negra: entrevista com Marcelo D'Salete". *ArtCultura*, v. 21, n. 39, pp. 117–124.

Mbembe, A. *Critique of black reason*. Translated by Laurent Dubois. Durham, NC and London: Duke University Press, 2007.

Nelson Pereira dos Santos. Rio 40 graus [opening scene], 1955, 1h40min. www.youtube.com/watch?v=byIljMWslVI

Renata Nolasco. September 19, 2018. https://politicashq.tumblr.com/post/178244484261/por-renata-nolasco

Sá, L. (1933). *Réco-Réco, Bolão e Azeitona*. Coleção Biblioteca d'O Tico-Tico. Rio de Janeiro: Editora O Malho, 1933.

Soares Coutinho, R. (2013). *Um Flamengo grande, um Brasil maior: o Clube de Regatas do Flamengo e o imaginário político nacionalista popular (1930–1955)*. Tese (Doutorado em História) – Departamento de História, Universidade Federal Fluminense Niterói.

Sophia, M. A. 2018. https://politicashq.tumblr.com/post/178178179260/por-sophia-martinez-andreazza

Superman. Brazilian edition by Editora Brasil-América Limitada (EBAL), Rio de Janeiro, 1955. http://guiaebal.com/superman01.html

Veloso, R. M. *Imagens de uma escrava rebelde: quadrinhos, raça e gênero no ensino de História*. Dissertação. Mestrado Profissional em Ensino de História, IFCH, Unicamp, 2018.

Witek, J. *Comic books as history: the narrative of Jack Johnson, Art Spiegelman, and Harvey Pekar*. Jackson, MI: University Press of Mississippi, 1989.

Wrobel, J. (2019). "História(s) redesenhada(s): visualizando analogias entre hoje e o passado – periferias urbanas, resistência negra e vozes femininas na obra de Marcelo D'Salete". *Artcultura*, Uberlândia, v. 21, n. 39, pp. 99–116. https://doi.org/10.14393/artc-v21-n39-2019-52029

7
AND YOU WILL COME MARCHING WITH ME[1]

The Chilean comics after the social mobilization

Hugo Hinojosa Lobos

One of the most striking and relevant elements that we could appreciate, after the "social outburst" produced in October 2019, was the relevance acquired by graphics (in its various manifestations), embodied not only on the walls of the cities through posters, billboards, graffities and other visual expressions but also in digital media and social networks, where webcomics, illustrations, collages, among others, served as some of the most powerful proposals to convey the message raised by the population in their demands. This is clearly not a novelty in the history of Chile, but it acquires relevance to the extent that it becomes part of a visual archive essential for understanding the different concerns, ideas and emotions that were behind each citizen committed to the protest. However, one of the most significant components of this graphic hatching, beyond its testimonial value, is that it was able to make even more perceptible the usual communion between the collective action of the demonstration and its search for channels of visibility in images.

This leads us directly to a reconsideration of the ways in which the great Chilean social movements have been represented. In this sense, the role occupied by Chilean graphics since the 2019 protests comes to be one more paradigmatic example of the communicative potential of visuality, not only in the transmission of a given message but also in its settlement within the population. It is for this reason that this text wants to give account of other interesting cases in their work of graphic recovery of collective memory, particularly focused on some of the most important social mobilizations developed in Chile. Specifically, my interest lies in approaching the field of comics as a relevant space of visuality, and to show the ways in which it has managed to approach the historical social processes that took place in the country. To this end, several examples of contemporary Chilean comics will be presented, which have taken, partially or totally, the protests and collective demands as a theme. The same, can be seen as distinctive examples of a gaze where a discourse that crosses the historiographic with the individual and collective

DOI: 10.4324/9781003333296-9

memory is articulated, to end by addressing the last great mobilization of the country: the social outbreak of October 2019.

Social mobilization in contemporary Chilean comics

Despite its more than 100 years of development, comics in Chile have not addressed with much profusion the social manifestations produced throughout its history. Beyond the approaches from political satire in graphic humor magazines such as *Topaze* (1931–1970; 1989–1996), comic strips occupied, during the first stage of its history, a space more closely associated with childhood and youth, avoiding more complex issues or those that demanded clearer ideological positions. Assuming its role as a mass entertainment product, linked mainly to the press or magazines located in newsstands, comics focused on adventure, action and humor, rather than on looking at its own reality. In spite of the above, already in such iconic works as "von Pilsener" (1906–1907), we find small references and, in this way, demonstrations appear as a backdrop to deal with humorous situations, although from a festive context, as shown in one of his strips published in *Zig Zag* magazine, in issue 74 of July 15, 1906.

With the passing of the 20th century and the expansion of the readership of comic strips (mainly in humor and picaresque magazines for adults), the medium allowed itself to begin exploring new thematic possibilities. It was already at the end of the 1960s, with the processes of political polarization, that social movements and the specific demands of the most disadvantaged population began to emerge in various publications, such as *La Firme* (1971–1973) of the state publishing house Quimantú. An example of this politicization of the contents can be found, for example, on the cover of issue 34 of *La Chiva* (1968–1970), where the inhabitants of the fictitious shanty town Lo Chamullo literally squatter the cover, in a gesture that we could consider not only political but also metatextual.

With the entry of the dictatorship and the cultural blackout that ensued, it became much more complex to address these issues, due to the processes of silencing and persecution established by the regime. The role of graphics as a representation of protest acquired codified forms, as was the case of *Cauce* magazine in its No. 22 (1984) where, in view of the ordinance imposed by the DINACOS (Division of Social Communication), they decided to leave blank the spaces assigned to the images, accentuating the value of the visual as a message through its absence, and marking an iconic gesture of protest against censorship. The same magazine, in response to the so-called "bando n°19," points out: "why do you censor the most direct contact between the reading public and the truth, which is the image without intermediaries? The voice of the images is the one that now the regime in its desperation tries to silence" (p. 26). Paradoxically, the regulation imposed by the state organism intended to neutralize any reference to the protests that took place during September 4 and 5 of the same year, but it only made it more evident.

Another interesting example from the same period is the iconic Margarita, a graphic humor section created by Gus [Gustavo Donoso], which was published in the newspaper *Fortín Mapocho* between 1984 and 1991. In it, it was common to find encrypted messages directed against the regime, such as the famous "Y va a caer" (And it will fall), which readers could infer by completing the drawing of a cow (a pun on the Spanish word *vaca*), and thus creatively circumvent the information gag.

For its part, comics assumed a counterculture role, through the various magazines and fanzines that emerged since 1983, approximately, but even when its discourse was conditioned by an ideological imprint of opposition, its contents were more directed to the provocation of the regime than to its denunciation. Violence, sex, as well as dystopian scenarios were recurring themes in most of the stories published, as if trying to break with that tradition that existed prior to the seventies, much more linked to the children's world. In this sense, the social manifestations continued to see the street as the central axis of its actions.

On the other hand, various sites of cultural resistance, such as the Matucana 19 shed (and its magazine), were epicenters of the artistic activity of the time, where comics and their authors were also housed. Thus, while the people in the streets directly confronted the regime, through the increasingly recurrent demonstrations and protests, comics became a space of irreverence and transgression as a way of showing the oppression, not only social and economic but also cultural, of the dictatorship.

With the return to democracy and its transition process during the 1990s, Chilean comics remained outside the processes of social manifestation, with only a few exceptional cases, such as *Chancho Cero: el libro* (2002) by Pedro Peirano, a humorous comic strip originally published in the supplement "Zona de contacto" of the newspaper *El Mercurio*. In one of its episodes, the students at the fictitious Lobotomy School demonstrate in public, seeking public approval. The author approaches this incident with a satirical tone, revealing the indifference of the people to the demands of the young, as well as explicitly depicting the excessive repression of the police.

After this, it would not be until the end of the 2000s that he would again take interest in local productions. It was probably after the so-called "Penguin Revolution"[2] carried out by high school students in 2006 that the social fabric of protest began to be reconfigured. Likewise, the Chilean comic strip emerges with force and the level of production begins to grow exponentially. Within this new creative impulse, the place of the historical graphic narrative assumes a relevant place. It will be in these works where the cartoons and pages will become spaces for mediation between historical reality and the possibility of its rewriting and reflection, making visible that-other-that marches, denouncing the indolence of power, the fear and horror of repression, or the strength of the collective, among other topics.

But it is the question not only about the comic as a medium for historical discourse, but also about memory, and how in these texts operates a device for the recovery of a collective identity, a history that feels its own, but that has been silenced by official history. As Jorge Manzi et al. (2003) point out:

> The idea that memory has a social character finds one of its antecedents in Bartlett (1932), who proposed that it is essentially constructive, and not reproductive, which means that it is not stable, but a recreation of the past. Such recreations have a collective dimension, because when remembering events of everyday life, the importance of social factors is intensified, being often the social institutions and cultural characteristics of the groups, the ones that determine in a central way the forms of memory.
>
> (p. 178)

In a certain way, the authors of these works operate as spokespersons of a discourse with a strong ideological matrix and which, in most cases, arises from a need to rewrite or re-imagine (understood as the process of constructing new images) certain conflictive or traumatic events in Chile's history. For example, in the field of literature aimed at young people, we will find works such as *Al sur de la Alameda. Diario de una toma* (2014), by Lola Larra and Vicente Reinamontes, in which the personal annotations of a student mobilized in 2006 are intertwined with the graphic story that Reinamontes constructs, allowing the crossing between the personal perspective with the collective process. Now, the clash between a discourse from history and another articulated from memory will be even more relevant in the way in which the national comics themselves articulate their narratives.

In this perspective, in the complex process of historical reconstruction there is also an exercise of mediation of history, a crusade in turn for memory. This is where the place of the image within a historical reading from visuality acquires a new value or meaning within the community. Therefore, the exercise of the current Chilean historical graphic narrative aims to position itself as a counter-discourse or, at least, a reappropriation of certain episodes of local history, articulating images that, many times, from the perspective of an official discourse, are seen as a threat to the permanence and persistence of society, particularly when it is configured from what is determined by power and, therefore, must move forward without alterations.

Situated in a position of defiance of the established, the various social movements come to constitute that space of destabilization of the status quo, and the usual response to those discourses is their eradication and subsequent silencing within the "official" history. Therefore, as I have pointed out before: "forgotten, and even denied, by citizens, these episodes usually circulate as a sort of 'imaginary of the margin'" (Hinojosa 2018, 58), which tries to emerge in the public discussion. Therein lies the relevance of these current comics, given that, through them, it is possible to put the silenced discourses into a graphic form.

Precisely, one of the first current examples we can find was created to expose the arguments behind the protest. "¿Por qué nos movilizamos?" (*Why do we mobilize?* 2011) is a short four-page story, written and drawn by Gaspar Ortega, in which the author explains the reasons that pushed thousands of young people to demonstrate in the streets and take over their own educational institutions, in what is known as the second Penguin Revolution. With a simple graphic style, his objective was to approach in a friendlier way to the sectors of the population that did not understand the reasons why the students were protesting (Figure 7.1).

FIGURE 7.1 Gaspar Ortega, "Por qué nos movilizamos" (*Why do we mobilize?* 2011).

Another interesting point of view on the same conflict in 2011 was provided by the renowned national cartoonist Marcela Trujillo (Maliki), who in her work *El diario íntimo de Maliki 4 ojos"* (2011) gives us the view of the spectator of the marches. Empowered by the autobiographical tone of the work, we can reconstruct some of the distinctive elements of these marches, such as the posters, the urban artistic interventions, as well as the festive tone that accompanied the slogans.

For his part, cartoonist Vicente Cociña gives an account of how 2011 was a particularly effervescent year in social mobilization. In a cartoon called "Cicletada de protesta," published in April of the same year, the author presents a demonstration encouraged by the adherents to the cycling movement. In it we can see that, despite being a different type of protest than the previous examples, the slogans and concerns are transversal: criticism of the State and the legacy left by the dictatorship; the atmosphere of community and joy that moves the participants, and the animosity against the police and certain political sectors.

Before concluding this first review, I would like to comment briefly on the case of *El viudo*. Set in Santiago in the 1950s, the title comprises a series of comics of the noir novel genre, created by the scriptwriter Gonzalo Oyanedel, accompanied by a large team of cartoonists and inkers. Particularly noteworthy is the author's concern for integrating real data and events into the fiction. Indeed, it will be in the volume *La cueca del manco* (2014) where Oyanedel refers to the so-called "Battle of Santiago," produced in early April 1957, due to increases in the cost of public transport. Both the vignettes and the text give an account of the violence of the demonstrations as well as the serious consequences to the city. Considering the events of October 2019, it is striking that some episodes of Chilean history present the same causes – as well as the same results – hence its importance in returning to them.

Chilean graphic novels and social mobilization

In the case of contemporary Chilean graphic novels, we can also find some relevant examples, particularly those that try to reconstitute certain historical processes, and that read citizen movements from the comics. In this way, since 2013, interesting works are beginning to take shape. For example, given the commemoration of the 40th anniversary of the coup, a series of cultural approaches to this dark episode of our history, as well as to its consequences, are originating. The new impulse of the authorial production of comics in Chile allowed the emergence of several graphic novels that dealt with this episode. Now, the very particular and demanding conditions surrounding the creation of a comic book did not allow these works to be published during the same year. This is how in 2014 *El golpe: el pueblo 1970–1973* by Nicolás Cruz and Quique Palomo, was published. It's a graphic novel that addresses the arrival to power of the UP (Unidad Popular[3]) until the interruption of its mandate due to the coup. Even though social mobilization appears briefly during its reconstruction of Salvador Allende's campaign as presidential candidate, it is much more interesting to observe the beginning of the work, which starts with the student demonstrations of 2011 (Figure 7.2).

On the page, we can find the current congresswoman Camila Vallejos, as representative of the FECH (Federation of Students of the University of Chile), while in the central vignette the police dissuade the university students with water cannons. This particular historical episode will be the trigger for the actions of the work, when one of the students is arrested by Carabineros (Chilean police), which will revive the historical trauma of her parents, once young people during the seventies.

The same year, another graphic novel was published, although now focused on the process of the dictatorship itself. *Historias Clandestinas* (2014), by siblings Sol and Ariel Rojas Lizana, tells us, in the form of a testimonial work, the experience they lived as children when hiding political dissidents with their family. In this work, social mobilization is presented in its different variants. The contrast of the text is produced by opposing the initial images, which show the different demonstrations in favor of the future Allende government, and then, in the course of the work, exposing the protests that took place in the midst of the dictatorship in an attempt to recover democracy, or the search for the disappeared detainees. Later, at the end of the graphic novel, the demonstrations call for the search for justice, after sixteen years of military regime.

FIGURE 7.2 Nicolás Cruz y Quique Palomo, *El golpe: el pueblo 1970–1973*.
Source: Pehuén Editores.

In 2015, *Los años de Allende* was published. It remains as one of the graphic novels with the greatest editorial impact, not only in the country, but also abroad, with numerous translations to date. Written by Carlos Reyes and drawn by Rodrigo Elgueta, it presents the path that the Allende government went through from its genesis, from the perspective of a North American journalist. Committed to its documentary approach, at the moment of presenting the mobilizations in favor of Allende, we can not only observe images of the demonstrators to visually reconstruct that moment, but also, through the text, better understand the context behind them. In this way, unlike the more autobiographical perspectives, the approach to the historical fact pretends to be a mimetic reconstruction of it, assuming a certain documentary intention or reconstituted archive, which contrasts with the fictional narrative that crosses the story.

Finally, two graphic novels that directly address social movements as a theme. The first one *Santa María, 1907 (la marcha ha comenzado)* by Pedro Prado. Published in 2015, the work is part of a larger project that is not yet finished. Based on the novel *Santa María de las flores negras* by Hernán Rivera Letelier, the text partially reconstructs the historical event, addressing only the march of the workers and their families from the saltpeter offices to the city of Iquique, the product of claims for better wages. The second part -not yet published- plans to directly address the bloody incident of the Santa María Massacre, where hundreds of workers were murdered inside the school where they were housed, on December 21, 1907.

This graphic novel proposes a peculiar procedure, in which its author decides to move away from the way of approaching the historical episode marked by some previous references, such as the renowned Cantata de Santa María (1969), written by Luis Advis and set to music by Quilapayún, one of the emblematic groups of the new Chilean song. To this end, Prado prefers to avoid the model of a worker's epic, focusing his narrative on human relations, emphasizing the hope of the men and women of the Pampas involved in this historical event and, in this way, being able to accentuate what will be the future tragedy, of which they are not even aware.

On the other hand, we have *Lota, 1960. La huelga larga del carbón*, which manages to establish different ways of mediating the same social historical phenomenon. Published in 2014, with script by Alexis Figueroa and illustrations by Claudio Romo, Ibi Díaz, Elisa Echeverría, Vicente Plaza, Fabián Rivas and Francisco Muñoz, this graphic novel is made up of six stories that reconstitute the strike carried out by the coal miners in Lota during 1960, which was interrupted by the historic earthquake that affected Chile the same year. Thus, the work is constituted as a testimonial frieze, an accumulation of memories that takes advantage of the paradoxical condition of fragment and unity of the comic in order to constitute a coherent story.

Finally, in the constitution of an imagery of historical facts, the consideration of the social destiny of the images must always be present, how they are inserted in society and construct realities in the face of the events of history (even future and possible realities). But these images come from individuals, and what they are through their memories, and that allows to articulate a discourse that the graphic novel appropriates. In this regard, Trabado (2013) states that:

> The performance of memory as a generator of the graphic narrative entails a dismantling of the narrative. Memory does not adjust to the conditioning logics of the story and its causal principles. The memory exploits the fragmentary character and is organized around a sort of photographic album in which the different moments are agglomerated as visual flashes.
>
> (p. 23)

It is there where, as Didi Huberman (2014) puts it, the game between the construction of a commonplace versus the awareness of a place of the commonplace is established, a repositioning of the fact that has been silenced and is now unveiled through the images. In this way, in each of the stories presented in this work, a new perspective is always open to us in order to understand that, in this specific case, social movements are much more than improvements in people's living conditions and are not reduced only to political harangues. These deeds refer to communities, dreams, families, memories and hopes (possible as well as broken). For example, when their authors decide to tell a story set in the past, they also project how the desires of a past generation of workers can be truncated in the future, and therein lies the challenge of recovering memory.

Chilean comics and the social outburst

But the readings of historical processes in Chilean comics are not only to the past, but also act from the contingency. Indeed, the social outburst of 2019 also implied in parallel an important graphic outburst, pushed by the need – in real time – to tell what was happening in the country. Pasted on walls or widely disseminated on social networks, hundreds of images and vignettes operated as a graphic correlate of what was happening in the streets and homes of the Chilean people, functioning as the visual chronicle of one of the most important social events of the last decades in the country. Now, in order to understand the graphic production of this historical event, it would be necessary to consider it in three more or less defined moments, which we will briefly review later.

A first moment will be the very effervescence of the social "outburst" of October 2019. It all began with a rather minor incident in appearance. On October 6, there would be a new increase in the price of public transportation in the city of Santiago, based on the recommendation of a so-called "panel of experts." The population's annoyance was not long in coming, but it would be the high school students who would take the lead. Thus, a massive evasion of the Santiago subway was called. The government's response was direct, and instead of calming tempers, it decided to toughen sanctions against evaders. The conflictive climate reached its boiling point on Friday, October 18, when, as a result of the different disorders and demonstrations, it was decided to close several stations of the capital's subway system.

Late at night, the situation got completely out of control when a series of arson attacks ended up destroying some stations, and the protest took to the streets (while images of the president eating pizza at a family meal in a restaurant were broadcast). The government decided to file charges under the State Security Law, and on Saturday, October 19, the president declared a state of emergency in the city of Santiago and decreed a curfew. The levels of violence had not been seen in decades in the country, and demonstrations began to take place all over the country. On the other hand, police brutality as well as military presence was a permanent feature during the last weeks of October. In this context of social chaos, and with a country mobilized against the government, artists used all available means to show their position on the conflict. Given that the serious events were happening day by day, every minute, local production was mainly focused on illustration, given the time required to produce a comic, time which was not available at the moment. Likewise, the most direct space for diffusion in this first phase was social networks, such as Facebook or Instagram, which were used by cartoonists to display their slogans in support of the mobilization.

We have the case of cartoonist Estefani with E, who on October 17 echoed the slogan "evade, don't pay, another way to fight," in homage to the students who initiated the protests. Production went in crescendo after October 19. The president's statements at a press conference on October 20 only served to further inflame tempers. "We are at war against a powerful, implacable enemy, who respects nothing and no one, who is willing to use violence and crime without any limits," were the words issued by the president, which were interpreted by a large part of the population as a declaration of war on the citizens (aggravated by the presence of the military in the streets, which brought back the memory of the horrors of the dictatorship), and the graphic response was not long in coming. Prominent national comic artists published their allusive works in their own networks. We have the proposals of Claudio Romo (October 24 and 26), with allusions to protest slogans, such as "Chile woke up," or statements of the first lady[4]; Felix Vega (October 23), who intervenes the national flag with bullets and changes the star for the peso sign; or Marko Torres (October 30), where the beloved character of Ogú (from the *Mampato* series) beats the police. There is also the case of Martín Cáceres, who on October 27 published an illustration where iconic characters of Chilean comics, such as Mawa, El Manque, von Pilsener, Mampato, among others, replicate the phrase "We are not at war."

In the case of female authors, we have cases such as Rebeca Peña (October 21), who responds to criticism about the non-peaceful form of the protest, or the prominent Marcela Trujillo, aka Maliki (October 31), who, taking advantage of the Halloween celebration, portrays the president and the minister of the interior as famous horror movie characters.

In addition to the slogans and slogans of the demonstrations, a topic that will become recurrent will be the representation as heroes of various characters that emerged in the middle of the marches, such as the black dog "Matapacos" ("cop killer dog," whose image reached the subway cars in New York City); Pareman; the sensual Spiderman; Aunt Pikachu, among others, as well as the main center of the protest, Plaza Italia, now renamed Plaza de la Dignidad (Dignity Square). An example of this is the work of colorist Carlos Badilla, who in collaboration with other artists, such as Alex Reyes or Nicolás Verdejo, gave life to powerful images in an aesthetic very close to the superhero comic book. Representative of this will be the illustration published on November 7 by Marsupial, which Badilla will color on November 9.

In a second stage, with the passing of the weeks, it is possible to distinguish the elaboration of more extensive and elaborated publications, and where the comic begins to have more presence in the discourse of the events. A first approach is the work of the editor and illustrator Francisca Cárcamo (Panchulei), currently based in Barcelona, who published in November "Carta abierta a mis amigxs artistas: el arte como arma de lucha y resistencia" (Open letter to my artist friends: art as a weapon of struggle and resistance, 2019). In this short comic-fanzine, the author exposes her own personal experience as a protester, which has marked her perception of what has happened in the country, to then make a call to her colleagues to take a more active and politically committed position. In September of the same year, Cárcamo had already exposed her experience in the streets, taking the renamed "Plaza de la Dignidad" as the axis of a short story published in the British newspaper *The Guardian*. "This conflicted place made me who I am," which became a graphic foreshadowing of what would happen just a few weeks later.

The image as activism and denunciation will account for a turn in the production of comics where it now becomes a direct part of social mobilization. Such is the case of *Que no pare la revolución* (2019) by Guido "Kid" Salinas and Sebastián Castro, a duo known for their comic book series based on the Arauco War called *Los guardianes del sur* (*The guardians of the south*). Using the superhero genre aesthetics (also present in their other works), the authors develop a narrative where the different characters that became referents of the marches, such as the dog "Matapacos" or "Pareman," become the heroes against repression (see Figure 7.3). The comic was originally distributed for free on its digital platform, but is currently sold to raise funds to help low-income families, both during the period of mobilizations and in the current COVID-19 contingency.

A last example to consider is the comic *Pesadillas y ensoñaciones en estado de Rebeldía* (*Nightmares and daydreams in a state of Rebellion*, 2019), by Ibi and Marz, two young authors from Concepción. Conceived from a residency of fanzine artists at Estudio Mafia (Buenos Aires), the comic presents us with a 24-page story that, as in the case of Panchulei, proposes a reading from the distance of the facts, that is motivated by the anxiety to become part of the mobilization. In the words of the creators, as published in the digital publication's page, "we put our nightmares and reveries on social despair and political-corporate brutality," showing that there are many comic artists today who understand the value of graphics as a political weapon (see Figure 7.4).

We can identify the third stage of this process around the outburst, as the one that has come to account for everything produced during the weeks and months following the October protests. An example of this was the renowned *Brígida* magazine, a publication that only edits female comic authors and illustrators, which made a call for a special issue on the outburst in November 2019. Finally, issue number 7 (see Figure 7.5) was launched in February 2020 at the Museum of Memory and Human Rights, with a great number of artists and public attending.

Another striking sample is the case of the Colectivo Cacerola, who have made a series of anthologies of comics about the outbreak, called *The Chilean Way*, which to date already has published four issues.[5] As their Instagram page indicates, "we turn into comics the pot-pan contingency of our territory in resistance. We draw so as not to forget." Alluding to the gesture of hitting a pot or pan as a form of protest, the comic also resonates visually with its message of denunciation. Although no new volumes were published, at the end of 2020 the first volume was published in English in Canada, by Credible Threat Press under the title *The Chilean way 1. A comic anthology about the Chilean social crisis*.

Meanwhile, another of the first compilation volumes was *Chile despertó* (*Chile woke up*), a project promoted by Germán Valenzuela, founder and editor of publishing house Ariete, which between October and December 2019 digitally published 11 issues through an open call, where a diversity of artists, amateurs and professionals, could make known their critical stance, but also served as a space to publicize figures and data of the events that were occurring in the country.[6]

Finally, the last compilation effort around the social outburst was carried out by Nauta Colecciones. Launched in late 2020, *18.10. Visual Reflection of the Social Outburst in Chile* (2020), is a volume that through an open call held between October 29 and November 10, 2019, managed to gather more than 500 works, which were then reviewed by a team of artists and editors who selected the ones that ended up being included in the publication, and which also has texts in Spanish, English and French. The work can be accessed by purchasing it directly from the publisher's website in digital format.

Conclusion

As we could see, Chile suffered the most important social outburst in the last 30 years, after Pinochet's military dictatorship, causing thousands of people to mobilize in the streets of the country. What began as a simple response to the increase in subway fares, mutated into collective demands that had been contained for years. For its part, the government reacted by hardening its response, and with the military taking to the streets, social traumas were revived, but at the same time, it led to a feeling that varied from rage to hope. Even when the soldiers were taken off the streets, police repression increased, with hundreds of wounded, complaints of excessive aggression and torture, as well as deaths and a sad record of people with eye loss.

In this context of violence and social mobilization, comics and illustration played a central role as a means of denunciation, of in situ narrative, and also of rebellion. Multiple authors constantly shared, both on social networks and in the streets, works that functioned as the real-time reconstruction of the memory of a process that changed the face of the country. Figures of the street, such as the famous dog "Matapacos," curious protesters and the day-to-day life of the protest, took shape in drawings. But the slogan raised in those days of "it's not 30 pesos, but 30 years," also dialogues with graphic works that previously commented on a history of abuses and truncated social changes.

In this sense, this article is intended to serve as a contextual analysis of the mobilization from a graphic perspective, exploring at the same time a trajectory already traced in previous years in the world of Chilean comics. With a current political process where a new constitution is being debated (overcoming the one made under the Pinochet dictatorship), it is undeniable that looking at the comic as a historical document and testimony of a collective memory is becoming increasingly relevant. As it has happened in other moments of our history, comics have echoed every social process, and if mobilization takes place again, cartoonists will also be there to give an account of what happened, because we already know that images have a fundamental value for memory, that which is projected not only on paper but also on the streets, posters and walls.

Notes

1. The title is part of the lyrics of "El pueblo unido" (The people united), a song performed by the Chilean group Quilapayún. Recorded and released in the 1970s, it is one of the country's most famous protest songs, and one of the references of the so-called "Nueva canción chilena (The New Chilean Song).
2. The term *penguin* refers to the similarity between the traditional clothing of high school students in Chile and the physical appearance of these birds.
3. Unidad Popular (Popular Unity) is the name of the political coalition that led Salvador Allende to victory in the 1971 presidential elections.
4. On October 21, an audio of the First Lady, Cecilia Morel, was leaked, in which she states, "we are going to have to reduce our privileges and share with others," and calls the demonstrations a "foreign, alien invasion."
5. Some of the volumes can be found at www.flipsnack.com/cacerola/.
6. The 11 issues of the collection can be reviewed at https://issuu.com/chiledesperto.

Bibliography

Graphic works

Cárcamo, F. (2019a, September). "This conflicted place made me who I am". *The Guardian*. Retrieved from: www.theguardian.com/cities/2019/sep/13/this-conflicted-place-made-me-who-i-am-santiago-a-cartoon. Last accessed: 15/09/2022.

Cárcamo, F. (2019b, November). *Carta abierta a mis amigxs artistas: el arte como arma de lucha y resistencia*. Retrieved from: https://issuu.com/panchulei/docs/carta_abierta_panchulei_espa_ol_baja. Last accessed: 15/09/2022.

Castro, S. y Salinas, G. (2019). *Que no pare la revolución*. Nük Cómics.
Cociña, V. (2011, abr.). *Cicletada de protesta*. Retrieved from: www.vicentejose.cl/?p=184. Last accessed: 15/09/2022.
Cruz, N. y Palomo, Q. (2014). *El golpe: el pueblo 1970–1973*. Pehuén Editores.
Figueroa, A., Díaz, I., Echeverría, E., Plaza, V., Rivas, F., Romo, C., Mallea, C. & Muñoz, F. (2014). *Lota, 1960. La huelga larga del carbón*. LOM Ediciones.
Ibi & Marz. (2019). *Pesadillas y ensoñaciones en estado de Rebeldía*. Retrieved from: https://issuu.com/edicionesbababooks/docs/estadodrebeldia
Larra, L. & Reinamontes, V. (2014). *Al sur de la Alameda*. Santiago: Ediciones Ekaré Sur.
Lustig. (1906). "Von Pilsener, un alemán en Chile". *Revista Zig Zag* N° 74 (July 15, 1906). Retrieved from: www.memoriachilena.gob.cl/archivos2/pdfs/MC0052561.pdf
Ortega, G. (2011). *¿Por qué nos movilizamos?* Retrieved from: http://quilpencils.blogspot.com/2011/06/un-comic-por-que-nos-movilizamos.html
Oyanedel, G., Márquez, J. & Campos, R. (2014). *El viudo: la cueca del manco*. Dogitia Productora.
Prado, P. (2014). *Santa María 1907. La marcha ha comenzado*. LOM Ediciones.
Reyes, C. & Elgueta, R. (2015). *Los años de Allende*. Hueders.
Rojas Lizana, A. & Rojas Lizana, S. (2014). *Historias clandestinas*. LOM Ediciones.
Salinas, G. & Castro, S. (2019). *Los Guardianes del Sur*. Nük Cómics!
Trujillo, M. (2011). *El diario íntimo de Maliki 4 ojos*. RIL Editores.
Vivanco, A., Hervi, Palomo, J. & Vivanco, J. (2011). Portada La Chiva, número 34. *La Chiva ¡y qué jue!* Feroces Editores.

Reference works

Didi Huberman, G. (2014). "Repartos de comunidades". *Pueblos expuestos, pueblos figurantes*, pp. 95–146. Manantial.
Hinojosa, H. (2018). "Una memoria ilustrada: problemas de la narrativa gráfica histórica contemporánea en Chile". *CuCo, Cuadernos de Cómic*, n° 11, pp. 52–80. Retrieved from: https://doi.org/10.37536/cuco.2018.11.1199. Last accessed: 15/09/2022.
Manzi, J., Helsper, E., Ruiz, S., Krause, M. & Kronmüller, E. (2003). "El pasado que nos pesa: la memoria colectiva del 11 de septiembre de 1973". *Revista de Ciencia Política*, v. XXIII, pp. 177–214. Pontificia Universidad Católica de Chile.
Trabado, J. M. (2013). "La novela gráfica en el laberinto de los formatos del cómic". Trabado, J. M. (ed.). *La novela gráfica. Poéticas y modelos narrativos*, pp. 11–61. Arco/Libros.
V.V.A.A. (1984). "El miedo a la verdad: bando n°19 censura voz de la imagen". *Cauce*, Año I, n. 22., p. 27. Retrieved from: https://issuu.com/josevergara/docs/cauce-22. Last accessed: 15/09/2022.

Intertextuality and iconic images 131

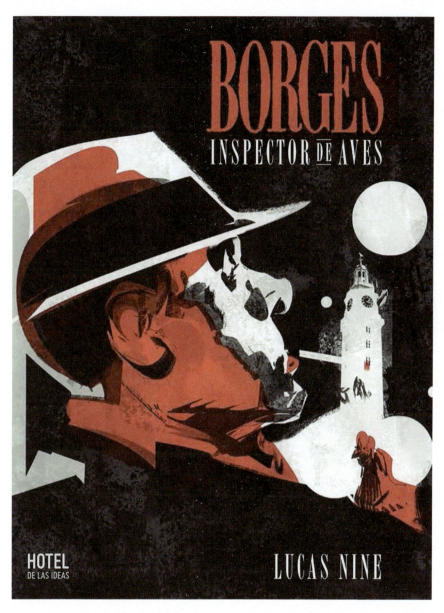

FIGURE 1.1 Cover of the 2017 Hotel de las Ideas edition of *Borges, inspector de aves*. All images are reproduced with authorization from the author, Lucas Nine.

FIGURE 2.1   On the left: Cover of Los Agachados, with the photograph taken by Armando Lenin Salgado. On the right: the drawing of *Grito de Victoria* is based on the same image.

Historical graphic novels in Uruguay 2000–2020 133

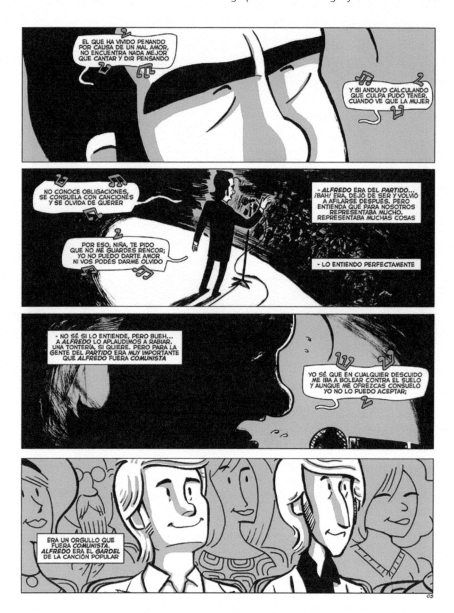

FIGURE 4.2 Santullo, R., & Aguirre, M. (2012). *Zitarrosa*. Grupo Belerofonte, Estuario Editora.

FIGURE 4.3 Leguisamo, P. R., & Fernández, L. (2015). *Tupamaros, la Fuga 1971*. Loco Rabia y Dragón Comics.

FIGURE 4.4   Peruzzo, N., & Serra, G. (2016). *Rincón de la Bolsa*. Ninfa Comics.

FIGURE 6.1 (Left): Sophia Martinez Andreazza, published in September 17, 2018.
Source: https://politicashq.tumblr.com/post/178178179260/por-sophia-martinez-andreazza

Black visualities in Brazilian comics 137

FIGURE 6.2   (Right): Renata Nolasco, published in September 19, 2018.
Source: https://politicashq.tumblr.com/post/178244484261/por-renata-nolasco

FIGURE 6.3 Caetano Cury, 2018.

Source: www.teoeominimundo.com.br/2018/11/19/tirinha-marielle-franco

FIGURE 7.3 Guido "Kid" Salinas and Sebastián Castro, *Los Guardianes del Sur* (2019).
Source: Nük Comics!

FIGURE 7.4 Ibi and Marz, *Pesadillas y ensoñaciones en estado de Rebeldía* (2019).
Source: Baba Books/Estudio Mafia.

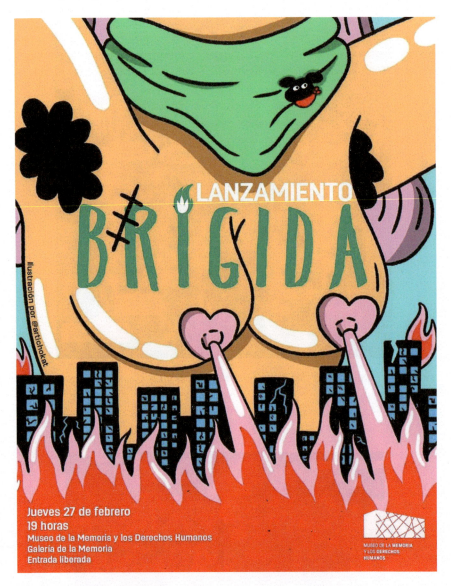

FIGURE 7.5 @artichokat [María Gazale Carinao], *Brígida* N. 7 (2020).

Source: Revista Brígida.

FIGURE 9.2 Panchulei (2020 [2019]): "La matria y la cacerola," in: *ManosManifiesto*. Barcelona: self-published [fanzine], p. 25.

FIGURE 9.3 Baldachin from Tost (c. 1220), Museu Nacional d'Art de Catalunya. https://commons.wikimedia.org/wiki/File:Baldachin_from_Tost_-_Google_Art_Project.jpg (last accessed 20 June 2021).

Resisting imposed lines 143

FIGURE 9.4 Panchulei (2020 [2019]): "La matria y el canino," in: *ManosManifiesto*. Barcelona: self-published [fanzine], p. 26.

FIGURE 9.5 Antependium from the Chapel of Sant Quirc de Durro (mid-twelfth century), Museu Nacional d'Art de Catalunya. https://commons.wikimedia.org/wiki/File:Frontal_d%27altar_de_Durro.jpg (last accessed 20 June 2021).

FIGURE 12.3 Edo Brenes: "Garçon," in: *Poder Trans* (2018), pp. 76–77.

Pervertion through funny comics **145**

FIGURE 13.1 Characters from *El Sr. y la Sra. Rispo* (2009). *El Sr. y la Sra. Rispo* blog (29/10/2009).

146 Rodrigo O. Ottonello

FIGURE 13.4 Diego Parés, *El Sr. y la Sra. Rispo*. Illustration posted on Diego Parés' official Facebook site (2013).

PART II
Genre and sexual dissidence

8
APPROACHES TO REMEMBER THE BODIES IN TWO LATIN AMERICAN COMICS

"Notas al Pie" by Nacha Vollenweider and "Las Sinventuras de Jaime Pardo" by Vicho Plaza

Jorge Sánchez

Memory

Since the 1980s, the theme and the problem of presenting past events in a comic has been gaining relevance in the West. Particularly in the United States, with the Comix movement led by Crumb, the figure of the author is placed as a privileged witness of social events, working with daily routine experiences that are related to current social problems in the context of production. Crumb's gaze, both in the aforementioned events and in the gesture of looking at the past, has the power to fit with a conception of teleological time that does not affect him as a witness. For instance, in his classic work "A Short History of America," each tier is divided into three numbered panels, in which the same place is shown during different years. The first vignettes draw a landscape dominated by nature and then, little by little, it is replaced by the prototypical image of a city: electricity, houses, businesses. The work ends with a brief writing, located on the left side of the last panel, which reads: "what next?!!"

In that comic, Crumb takes to the extreme his usual gaze of the witness, in which he staged his own body narrating or participating in current events. Additionally, in this case the body is invisibilized, empowering its way of contemplating, and leaving just the deictic of the writing. It is assumed inside the idea of a story, even if it is brief, that the structure is sequential, logical, transparent and waiting for a future.

This type of witness' gaze appears in a group of comics that has become paradigmatic, generally referred in theoretical texts that reflect on memory in graphic narratives (Witek, 1989; El Refaire, 2012; Chute, 2016; de Arriba, 2019).[1] For instance, in her study about testimonial comics, Hilary Chute groups three works that she assumes as representative of the canon: "I Saw it" by Keiji Nakasawa,

DOI: 10.4324/9781003333296-11

"Maus" by Art Spiegelman, and "Palestine" by Joe Sacco. These comics, according to the author, are intended to be a testimonial look at the acts of violence that "driven by the necessities of re-seeing the war in acts of witness, comics proposes an ethics of looking and reading intent on defamiliarizing standard or received images of history while yet aiming to communicate and circulate" (2016: 31). However, that act of defamiliarizing in "I Saw it" and "Palestine" does not concern the body, because it is positioned as a privileged materiality that does not experience violence, protected by the temporal logics of historical duration.

Regarding that topic, only "Maus" problematizes the violence of recalling that affects the body. In this graphic novel, the main character wishes to recount his father's war memories. When the stories are presented, the characters become animalized: mice, pigs, dogs, cats, etc. Those characters distance themselves from the body of the witness, that is to say, the father. In fact, and during the first volume, the patriarch appears as a human. However, during the second volume, it is made evident how the narrator sees himself with a mask and surrounded by corpses. This visual metaphor can be read from the affliction of memories in the body of the witness, who becomes precarious facing past events.

When we think about Latin American comics, most of the critical approaches insist on highlighting productions that present these kinds of privileged witnesses (Fernández, 2016; Neco, 2016; Hinojosa, 2018; Catalá Carrasco et al., 2019) defending the idea of the potential of comics to show "social, cultural, and political processes that have helped to define the region" (Catalá Carrasco et al., 2019: 7), especially the "historical" one of representing silenced images by the hegemonic narrative. "The comic, in its status as a visual and sequential medium and assuming its role as part of the cultural marginalization has included, from its language, those historical discourses that have also been excluded" (Hinojosa, 2018: 60) in which the authors are able to recover a collective identity, reconstituting key events for a community (64). The given examples in these theoretical reflections involve comics in which the characters would possess the ability and power of showing and narrating past events. Moreover, in one of the few books that refer exclusively to the topic of memory in Latin American works, "Comics and Memory in Latin-America" (Catalá Carrasco et al., 2017), the selected works only included those that stand out as a narrative that "shows" facts ignored by the official historiography, with witnessing/protagonist bodies that are adapted to a chronological rationality and that also have the ability to remember transparently.

In these critical studies, the included comics are positioned as models of the Latin American territory, encapsulating them in a reading that conceives memory as a display. That is to say, as a representation of facts, bodies and truths. A corporal stability of the witness and the characters of the comics.

However, there are works that allow a reading that problematizes the idea of a successful witness and the notion of time as a classic narration.[2] Related to this, we will consider Ricoeur's reflection about fictional narration. He states that it is an action in which there is no intention of connecting to a time without aporias or giving a globalizing response. In these works, the aforementioned contradictions are exhibited by the sake of showing them. Therefore, these narrations do not omit or become disassociated from the practical world or lived time, but rather "redirect the gaze towards the features of the experience that 'invents', that is to say, that discovers and creates at the same time" (Ricoeur, 2004 (b): 492). Thus, it demands going beyond the features of everyday experience, generating a fictitious experience of time.

In this regard, and from the comic theory, Smolderen (2014), Pintor (2017) or Groensteen (2007) make clear a sensitive presentation of time as a kind of unstable flow that affects (itself) throughout the comic. Smolderen highlights Töpffer as one of the founders of the comics. His reading about this artist reveals the criticism of the conception of time in the context of industrial progress, using and exploring the same images that the hegemonic discourse offers. Thus, the theorist does not encapsulate an apparent tubular and sequential sense of Töpffer's production with a transparent meaningful adjustment, but rather as a critique of that mechanical way of looking. In addition, Smolderen demonstrates how the emerging comic of the 19th century did not respond to the idea of progressive sequential narration, but rather introduced a disruption in the way of narrating actions through the absurdity of the encapsulation/measurement of time, freeing it from the nascent technologies of temporal parametrization, together with the incitement to a multivectorial perspective of images.

A tension is produced, existing since the birth of the comic, between a series of static and separated panels. Sometimes the relationship is not evident, with a seemingly regular and transparent narrative displacement. Pintor (2017) qualifies this fact as a dialectical relationship between continuity and discontinuity, which in comics is reflected in the generation of methods "to give up the strategies that create continuity" (10), placing the traditional conceptions of time in crisis (transparent sequential narratives). For instance, when referring to Tardi's work, he states that the "presentation of History as an object of a structure whose place is not constituted by a homogeneous and empty time, but by an absolute one: the time now" (11–12).

Pintor reinforces the idea of discontinuity, understanding it as an escape to a particular flow of time. That phenomenon would happen due to deceleration strategies, which are sorts of explicit defamiliarization or obfuscation in the narration of the comic. For instance, through stripping off the code (defined by Pintor as code transvestism) or stylistic heterogeneity (what Smolderen conceives as polygraphic).

What is particular about the explained topics is that, in general, when the historical or memory comic is studied, it is interpreted from a classic narratological scheme, imposing on the reading a hegemonic idea of time. However, there is a constellation of works that goes unnoticed in a large extent of the theoretical approaches about comics and memory, which present a persistence in the act of remembering but with witnesses who assume the failure in representing past events. Works as "1973" by Ricardo Fuentealba (2017); "Sátira Latina" ["Latin Satire"] by Mariana Paraizo (2015); "Las Sinaventuras de Jaime Pardo," by Vicho Plaza (2013); and Nacha Vollenweider's "Notas al Pie," exemplify ways of mediating memories differently from exemplary works. In the following sections I will discuss the last two, under the light of the question: How does this discontinuous time affect the presented bodies, turning them into precarious witnesses?

Like a bandoneon in Sternschanze: "Notas al pie" and the migrant body

> Footnotes should not be too long. Otherwise, the researcher might reconsider the value and the relevance of the information.
>
> (APA Style)

Nacha Vollenweider was born in 1983 in Río Cuarto, Argentina. Her first productions were published by the independent house Llanto de Mudo Ediciones. Also, she has contributed to magazines such as *Clítoris*, *Fierro* and *Altamira*.

"Notas al Pie" is one of her most renowned works. It is presented as an autobiographical memory comic. The main character narrates her childhood, youth and present in a life where migration left a mark. Those stories and intensities are woven/migrate with those of her relatives. All of this, under an additional narration: the past dictatorial violence and the contemporary aggressions, staged in the discrimination against migrants, gender options beyond heteronormativity and narratives that hide the past violence against the bodies.

In this way, a comic built with several overlapping narratives generates an open textual fabric, in tension and always in a making. Thus, this work follows a particular narrative form: an editing machine in which rather than reversing narrative/visual orders, it presents them from simultaneity. On the one hand the title "Notas al Pie" alludes to the narrative method of the comic strip, which is assembled by narratives that make a kind of zoom, through footnotes, to aspects of what would be a main story. And, at the same time, it inverts a minor and accessory text (footnotes), causing a break in the dichotomy between the primary narration and the minor one, opting for the possibility of having simultaneous narratives that occur in a community, making the political act of activating images/narrations in the footnotes as a necessary flow that dismantles the hegemony of the official voices/images. In this case every order falls into pieces, and the "minor" is updated as an escape from the hegemony.

The readings highlight how the main character subverts aspects of gender and sexuality (Saxe, 2019), the discourse about migration (Filion, 2020) or memory (Turnes, 2017), always with the common denominator of a detour from official visual logic. In that regard, I will focus on the way of presenting the body as a discourse that does not manage in being represented, since it escapes at every moment, or it is just found in the certainty of an oblivion.

The body that circulates, or how a map is not necessary to travel

In this comic, full of narratives that refer to discourses of violence, the body moves, appears, disappears, gets confused, hides and seeks. After all, it migrates. The first tier presents a space divided by three panels, which is a conventional page layout (Peeters, 2003: 52). In general, this layout aims to produce an effect of a causal

Approaches to remember the bodies in two Latin American comics 153

FIGURE 8.1 Nacha Vollenweider. The migrant body. *Notas al Pie* (2017).

progressive advance. In this particular case, this structure is broken due to that effect, presenting a space that is apparently static and monovector, since the grid loads it with duration when transforming it into three panels. But mostly it is filled up with temporal intensities while being crossed by the body of the protagonist, turning it into a multi-vector effect.

From the beginning of the narration, this work shows a migrant body. The succession of images that follows the first tier, in which Nacha is already on the train, causes a display of instants that are being activated in the memory of the main character. I insist that this is not a causal story, or in other words, it is not only available to be read from causality. On the contrary, it is a random memory that migrates, escaping to any previously imposed order. The protagonist moves physically on the train while sightseeing. Simultaneously, she activates images of photographs of her grandfather, of landscapes of her past and of the recent history of Argentina and Germany, objects that migrate from her childhood to her current life. Those vignettes function as kinds of postcards, most of them without reference to the place where they come from. Also, to move from one to the other you have to look at the gutter marked by the author's written narration. In this way, the reading gaze is made tense to go across simultaneity, to activate mobile senses that do not contain all the information. To put it in another way, the images and texts do not function as a transparent referential travel diary, but rather reflect the migrant journey/memory of the protagonist as a complex assembly machine marked by violence and freed by its escapes from that violence.

At this same point, the panels are presented as a kind of order that is deterritorialized by images of memory and bodies. This implies a sort of questioning or examination of both the comic language and the language of the migrating body. Here, the idea of the vignettes as a transparent order, a resource which prevails in superhero comics but without experimental page designs (such as a rhetorical one), is shattered. The conventional use of the page is stripped from the meaning of the sequential order. It does not rely on the cause-effect, and it escapes from common sense, proposing a new map to migrate. This fact is related to another form that wishes to order the spaces and bodies that pass through it: the chequerboard scheme (*damero*).

Both the first page and the last page refer to this urban scheme, set up by the Spaniards in most of Latin-American cities: order of the space, order of the bodies, the arrival of modernity and of capitalism. The wink, of course, is not only in what is said in the text but also in the comic itself and its structure, in the way of telling a story and in the way of going through it while reading it. A return to the language of the comic itself reconfigurates the gesture of memory and the territorial order of the bodies.

The simultaneity and the rearrangement of the narration[3] are appreciated when the protagonist observes the shape of the Spanish colonial grid on the upholstery of the train seats. The narrator clarifies that this type of order of spaces/bodies did not occur in Germany, a territory not guided by any architectural plan, but a barbaric opposition to civilization that is inferred from the official history cited by the narrator. Of particular interest is the crisis of the control of the bodies that the migrant protagonist begins to visualize in Germany. First, when commenting about the diversity of bodies that she finds on the train, showing on two pages various corporealities that are seated in the chairs upholstered with figures similar to Spanish squares, forms that function as a kind of visual marks close to the skin. Second, when Nacha gets off the train, and contrasting with the appeal of the no-gridiron plan that would exist in Germany, it is observed how two policemen detain an afro-migrant, based on an administrative ordinance.

This action reveals an update of the violence regarding the classification of the migrant bodies in Germany, appearing repeatedly through the comic. We have bodies persecuted by the invaders in Argentina during the colony; the disappearance of bodies during the Argentine dictatorship; the search for the bodies by the grandmothers of Plaza de Mayo; the illegality of migrant bodies in Germany; or the loneliness in the lesbian relationship that the protagonist has. This political gesture is assembled with Nelly Richard's position about art: "in the arts, it is not enough to stage images of the past. It is necessary to ensure that the past dialogues with the present, producing some kind of shock. It is not enough to commemorate. You have to re-energize the memory, to start a conversation with an unconformable present." The gesture of going back and remembering that migrant body will always be a penultimate gaze, since as we explained, the body will always escape.

The body as an unknown

Benoit Peeters argues that a state of metamorphosis predominates in the comic: "Nothing is stable. Everything is capable of metamorphosis, including the most peaceful objects, and the most reassuring images" (1998: 35). Space, time and bodies are presented in the continuous flow of change.

In this graphic novel, and in addition to the simultaneity of time, a metamorphic body occurs that escapes or articulates with objects, photographs, animals, insisting on showing/narrating a testimony that sidesteps the written mark. By this way, sorts of records/files are generated, about the corporealities that migrate, disappear or are so abused that they abandon the space.

I will focus on the first metamorphosis, in which the objects act as the absent body. I am talking about a body that is no longer in the house, generally shown with nods to panels in which group photographs are drawn. In the sequence where the dictator Videla appears at a press conference, he is presented cutting the protagonist's narration about her childhood memories and her disappeared uncle. Three panels in which the dictator explains the notion of "disappeared" as an incognito:

These panels finish with a house. Inside that place, and in the following pages, a set of objects expresses memory, a kind of metonymy of the disappeared. The body is not there and its forgetting/memory happens in the object, which allows the narration the ability to migrate.

"Every object in your house tells a story" is said in the comic, showing the traveling objects that Nacha's grandmother treasures. Each one of them is marked by a

FIGURE 8.2 Nacha Vollenweider. "Every object in your house tells a story." *Notas al Pie* (2017).

journey that apparently never ends, and that insists on the verification of oblivion. Red threads link stories and bodies, despite the gutter of time. Thus, cardboard coasters, passports, miniatures, dwarf figures, *ekekos*, bottles and *mates* are exposed as the expression of the incognito that the hegemonic power aims to locate into the unnamable or attempts to camouflage as the tapestry of a train chair. They are mobile objects that mark journeys that have not yet ended. They tag an oblivion in which the gaze of a precarious witness is sustained, a gaze that is articulated with what Sergio Rojas comments: "the crisis of the dominant narrative matrix of history as a meaning-producing economy brings with it the *insubordination of the past*" (249). Also, in this situation the figure and the body of the witness changes, since it locates itself in defeat. "The witness has lost both the narrative of his own life (that was taken from him because of the circumstances in which he found himself when everyday life was shaken) and the account of the event itself, always 'altered' by the emotional thickness of his own mnemic intimacy" (252). Time and body are activated by memory gestures that only confirm the absence, deformity or unlimited change.

To finish this section, I insist on conceiving memory as paths which, returning to the gridiron plan, are not commanded by pre-established transits, not even by the time mandate. In "Notas al Pie," the bodies and their metamorphoses effectively go across the line/route of the train but, at the same time, they travel through the deterritorialization itself of the idea of travel, memory and body, as a bandoneon in Sternschanze, or as Pablo Turnes states: "Notas al Pie is the testimony turned into a story about how to give oneself a proper voice through the voice (and images) of others that constitute us, even if we do not suspect it" (2017).

"Las Sinaventuras de Jaime Pardo" by Vicho Plaza: forgetting the body as a memory versus the figurative representation of the body as history

Vicho Plaza began his work as a cartoonist and scriptwriter of comics during the eighties. He contributed to recognized magazines such as *Trauko* and *Bandido*. Also, he has several printed and online publications, from which his character "El Gato Vicente" [Vincent the Cat] stands out, an alter ego that appears as a marginal drawing that observes the Chilean progression.

His work has been described as disturbing (Reyes, 2018); risky (Jorge Quien, 2014) and eccentric (Montealegre, 2020). In addition, even though he has authored several comics, specialized criticism has ignored him.

"Las Sinaventuras de Jaime Pardo" narrates the incidents of Jaime Pardo during his childhood in the seventies. Although it is not explicitly an autobiographical writing, a memory exercise is presented regarding the context of those years and the problem of looking at the past and facing oblivion. That was the same historical period in which the author was a teenager and began to learn about design and printing in high school.

This is not an adventure

When reflecting about the relationship between memory and body that is presented in the comic, a key aspect is to think about the word "adventure." Its Latin root is *adventūra*, which means "what is going to come": what will happen. This origin can be articulated with the use of the adjectival mode of "adventure," which is utilized to describe a certain type of cinema that is structured as a series of linked actions characterized by its effects of tension and emotion, that is to say, by what "is going to come." Also, in this arrangement the hero of the account has the ability to produce actions that have an effect on the central plot of the story.

Taking into account those reflections, the title is significant. On the one hand, and under a superficial analysis, the comic could be easily considered as just the narration of a set of memories about the protagonist's childhood during the 1970s in Chile, including typical childhood "adventures," as in Marcela Paz's *Papelucho*. We are talking about situations in which the main character has problems with his family, school and friends. In other words, classifying this work as a regular adventure comic. However, and starting with the term "sinaventuras" ["no-adventures"], this work presents a tension regarding the traditional sequential narration, since the speaker has no omniscient power to be able to remember everything. Furthermore, the narrator is set out from the failure of memory. This is connected to one of his cartoons in which he compares the joy of Mampato and Ogu (characters from the comic *Mampato* by Themo Lobos) with its characters.

About this tension the protagonist, Jaime Pardo, tries to remember his childhood, but from the first plates he is already aware that he is not able to do it precisely, regarding not only facts (which will contribute to build a memory account) but also places, names and images.

In the first speech bubble of the comic, Jaime Pardo says: "this must be his house," referring to the possible home of his childhood's teacher. The conditional nature of the memory concerning the address moves to doubt, something that Jaime Pardo will maintain throughout the text. The question is not "how to remember?" nor if it can be remembered. The question is how to get closer to a past that is known to be incomplete, full of forgetfulness and ambiguities.

The contrast with the aforementioned acceptance is the historical discourse of teleological logic that insists on confiscating both the truth about a past and the way of narrating it. The evident opposition could be seen as the clash between history and memory. This is staged in the next tier, in which Jaime Pardo meets his former teacher "Mr. López" and a dialogue is generated. In that conversation Mr. López, as an enlightening historical address, positions himself as the speech of truth, precise in his memory: "mm, now that I see you, I start to remember you . . . Jaime Pardo, from Escuela 18." Also, the teacher corrects information about Jaime Pardo: "you were not in the fifth grade, but in the eighth. I'm sure." Additionally, he is eternal: "heh, heh. Sure! I look as I did in 1975." But above all, challenging: "Are you coming to draw me? I'm saying this because you still can't reach my figure, right?"

Facing the last question, the protagonist not only assumes his inability to sketch a sole, complete and permanent figure, but also he is the fictional Vicente Plaza unable to achieve a drawing. The fact that the main character and the creator could work as counterparts underlines the gesture of memory captured by the comic, because there is a subjectivization of the explicit reality. The lack of ability is not related to drawing, but to not being able to draw in a figurative way. As Deleuze (1984) states, the figurative follows a narrative logic of semantic transparency and here, in the analyzed comic, an escape from the figurative form is made evident.

However, the protagonist's acceptance of the lack of capacity for figurative representation by not finding the exact figure, nor the precision of the data, means to conceive forgetting as a constitutive part of remembrance. The bodies are seen as sketches, always imprecise, always fluctuating, always unsure whether they are progressing or not. It seems that the body is always escaping the framing of history and capturing the uncertainty of the memory.

On the bottom tier we can see the tension between story and memory on a visual level. This tightness prevails throughout the entire comic, among the panels' rigid structure and its contents. Even if the construction of the page follows a conventional use (Peeters, 2003), the interesting thing about this arrangement is that it produces, in general, a sense of progression based on a set of facts encapsulated in the panels (p. 53). This is similar to the idea of historical discourse. As Cuartango states, this discourse is characterized by: "the flattening of time, its conversion into a series of similar instants, can be seen as a consequence of the supremacy of reason that considers everything as calculable, usable and disqualified" (2002: 202). In this

Approaches to remember the bodies in two Latin American comics 159

FIGURE 8.3 Vicente Plaza. Bodies as sketches. *Las Sinaventuras de Jaime Pardo* (2013).

way, there is a possible link between the arrangement of the panels and the historical narrative order.

There is a contrast between this arrangement and the drawings that are accepted as poor figurative representations of a memory. They are incomplete, badly executed illustrations, even when they are apparently simple. In the lower tier, the protagonist approaches the teacher and looks at him. But, as it is seen in panels 3 and 4, it is impossible for him to make a face based on the drawn lines. In this way, the effect of meaning is produced by the iconic solidarity[4] between the page organization and its drawings, a clash between a temporary organization of the page that follows a sequentiality that moves forward versus the drawings that, as the teacher states in the last panel: "as in so many things, I don't know if we are advancing" (p. 13).[5]

Deleuze's concept of "Figure" is appropriate to think about this drawing described as imperfect by the teacher. The philosopher's proposal is based on his

FIGURE 8.4 Vicente Plaza. Poor figurative representations of memory. *Las Sinaventuras de Jaime Pardo* (2013).

interpretation of Bacon's paintings, in which the painter avoids figurative and abstract representations, both related to the narrative and to the intellect, in order to get to the Figure. This is characterized by representing the body, so to speak, "bodying," escaping configurative, structured and definitive discourses, breaking with the object – subject dichotomy. Therefore, it could be thought that the comic presents incomplete, spasmodic[6] bodies that fell into oblivion, "bodying" in/from memory, assuming the spasm of obscurity and being in a permanent metamorphosis (Peeters, 2003: 35).

In contrast to canonical works about memory, the bodies in "Las Sinventuras" metamorphose at every moment. Also, they are assumed to be unstable, since they are conscious of being expressed from a narrative based on oblivion, that is to say, the work of memory exercises the lack of information. In other words, incompleteness appears as a condition to recall. This idea of memory is associated with the reading of current Chilean art made by Rojas, in which memory: "does not proceed by following causal strings, describing processes or selecting the precedents that allow us to understand an era. On the contrary, memory operates by apprehending a time that was subjectivized in an atmosphere of immanence" (2015: 236). Considering this, it is observed how the main character subjectivizes his representation, affected by the absence of memory, ergo, by the lack, by the oblivion that establishes his own representation.

A possible conclusion or a Shower of Oblivions

In Chapter 5 of "Las Sinaventuras de Jaime Pardo," as in "Notas al Pie," the body transits to objectification. This is known as "Shower of Oblivions." "Now an adult, the protagonist is surprisingly visited by Mr. López, who is metamorphically represented as a human body and as a chair. Throughout the chapter, they engage in an apparent dialogue monopolized by the teacher, who recounts his life justifying certain actions, until he explains his death. At the end of the chapter, Jaime leaves the chair/teacher in a repair shop, also finishing the story.

In the aforementioned dialogue, the calls and precepts of the teacher are meaningful, especially when he affirms to Jaime: "do you always get complicated by images?" Similarly, when he asks "what do you think, Pardo? What is the history for?" Pardo does not answer, but his face gets distorted. In front of memory, the image responds by revealing the oblivion. If the word can disappear or cannot be, the image must always be manifested, appearing. In fact, let's think that even a "blank" panel is an image. Under the requirement of the appearance in the comic, the answer is generated under the notion of outbreak, deformation or mutation. Those are ways to show the oblivion, the scarcity, the truncated gaze of a witness.

In this situation, it can be argued that image and history are the axes of the whole comic, under the question if history can be fixed in an image that manages to represent it. Then, if this would have some utility/meaning. Primarily in the last chapter, the image of Mr. López's metamorphic body shows that visual stability would be found in a kind of objectification: the chair. The spasmodic body has no historical image, at least figuratively, that is to say, a body with the following features: stable, measurable, able to be narrated, charged and present in the events that the story tells. If the chair is affected, it is repaired. That furniture as an instrument is stable, in contrast to the body and its unfixed and elusive image, which is absent from the events that history assumes as past.

This aforementioned visual metaphor reinforces the idea of generating an image that can be manipulated in a useful object but, at the same time, derives in the idea that it does not show a memory, a memory data. The chair is nothing more than that: it is empty of all historical narration or emotiveness. It is just one more drop in a shower of oblivions.

Thus, the cartoon seems to tell us that the possibility of remembering is what allows us to approach a spasmodic body. Furthermore, it is a kind of condition. Otherwise, chairs are seen occupying predetermined spaces. At the end of the story, the protagonist assumes that oblivion is not an inability to have a memory, but it plays a role in that practice, which allows to represent the body as a figure and not a figuration. The bodies that are affected by this "Shower of Oblivions" are disclosed in their constituent incompleteness, in their necessary forgetfulness while memory is exercised.

Thus, in both comics the bodies escape from a mode of remembering that wants to impose a certain kind of memory politics. A relationship of power in which there would be privileged means to make patent past sensations, subjects, events and violence, clearly and differently. In their visual strategies, Nacha and Vicho capture page structures and panel sequences that, in general, are related to the causality and linearity of the events. But both artists use them in the estrangement of the memory sequence itself. There are simultaneity, temporary breaks, narrative hiatuses, in which the bodies travel.

These bodies jump between panels, move or explode outside the limit established by corporal matter. They are chairs, paintings, houses. Or they are disfigured into animals or monstrosities. That metamorphosis or corporal variation is due to the impossibility of fulfilling the mission of remembering or of the way in which this act is hegemonically commanded: transparently, following a sequence and including the exhibition of the memory. In both works the bodies are not easily shown according to this norm, but rather explode to connote oblivion.

Sergio Rojas states that, in the arts, the modern body takes a chance in the presentation, which he conceives as:

> That instant in which the constitutive difference of representation, the difference between the represented and the representation (between the order of the signified and the order of the signifier) is put into question and, with that, the hierarchy that is constitutive to the meaning of the world is put into question too.
>
> (2018: 153)

Additionally, Rojas affirms that the body is "what cannot fully emerge in the representation" (151), since it "only comes into presence as an alteration of the representation, as an alteration of its established rhetoric" (152). Considering this, one might think that both Nacha and Vicho, in a different sense from the consumerist logic that represents the body, have produced works that expose the problem of "how to represent the unrepresentable without suppressing the otherness." This is because, in the analyzed comics, the body in relation with the memory does not express as a matter that assumes a transcendental meaning, but as an impossible, as a crack that puts on trial the discourses that want to fall into it.

Notes

1 In these theoretical texts, neither examples nor analysis of Latin American comics are included, generalizing analysis criteria and conclusions into universal theses.

2 We recur to Ricoeur's conception of classic narration. He describes it as that transparent and teleological sequence between events, associated with the historical discourse that hides the aporias of time itself "by virtue of its insertion into the great chronology of the universe" (Galardi, 2011: 114). In other words, it gets round, in its own representation condition, the nonlinear features of time.

3 Ricoeur, differing from the proposal of Jakobson, restricts the descriptive language in its referential capacities, since it would not have the ability to refer to certain aspects of reality. Its own mechanisms or forms are a limitation to name a set of phenomena. On the other hand, poetic discourse would have that referential capacity by bringing "to language aspects, qualities, and values of reality that lack access to language that is directly descriptive and that can be spoken only by means of the complex interplay between the metaphorical utterance and the rule-governed transgression" (2004b: p. 33).

Ricoeur names this operation as a metaphorical reference, a conceptual gesture that broadens the textual strategies that describe, point to or refer to reality, thereby expanding what we can understand as reality. Metaphorical reference is a synthesis of the heterogeneity that produces "new logical species by predictive assimilation" (p. 32). It is this synthesis of the varied that makes Ricoeur relate the metaphor with the narrative, since in both a synthesis is exercised that produces a modification on the daily uses of language. If in the metaphor "innovation lies in the producing of a new semantic pertinence by means of an impertinent attribution" (p. 31), in the narrative the semantic innovation "lies in the invention of a plot" that reshapes the usual idea about time, generally reduced to a historical timeline or to dead-end aporias. Then, the narrative discourse would have the ability to refer to an apparent irreducibility such as time.

4 Concept developed by Groensteen, defined as a group of interdependent images that are plastically and semantically articulated.

5 A similar use can be found in Alan Moore's "Watchmen," This work follows a classic panel structure, not only aiming for the sequential effect but also to present global page designs that have particular aesthetic goals.

6 While analyzing Bacon's "heads," Deleuze states that: "It is not I who attempt to escape from my body, it is the body that attempts to escape from itself by means . . . in short, a spasm" (1984: 11).

Bibliography

Bubenik, M. (2019). "Producción independiente de historietas en Córdoba. Un análisis sociológico de la trayectoria de Llanto de Mudo Ediciones (2008–2015)." Trabajo Final para optar al grado académico de Licenciatura en Comunicación Social, Universidad Nacional de Córdoba (inédita). Disponible en Repositorio Digital Universitario.

Castillo, M. (2010). Sobre la rememoración y la política: tensiones entre W. Benjamin y P. Ricoeur. III Seminario internacional políticas de la memoria. Recordando a Walter Benjamin. Justicia, Historia y Verdad. Escrituras de la Memoria. Tiempo de la historia-tiempo de la justicia. La revolución copernicana en la historiografía y el primado de lo político. Buenos Aires, Argentina.

Catalá Carrasco, J. L., Drinot, P. & Scorer, J. (2017). *Comics and Memory in Latin America*. University of Pittsburgh Press.

Catalá Carrasco, J. L., Drinot, P. & Scorer, J. (2019). *Cómics y memoria en América Latina*. Cátedra.

Chute, H. (2013). "Comic as literature? Reading graphic narrative". En *Journal of the Modern Language Association of America*, Vol. 123, N° 2 (2008), pp. 452–465.

Chute, H. (2016). *Disaster Drawn. Visual witness, comics, and documentary form*. The Belknap Press of Harvard University Press.

Cuartango, R. (2002). *La destrucción de la idea de futuro*. En *Cruz, Manuel. Hacia dónde va el pasado. El porvenir de la memoria en el mundo contemporáneo*. Paidos.
de Arriba, D. F. (ed.) (2019). *Memoria y Viñetas. La memoria histórica en el aula a través del cómic*. Desfiladero Ediciones.
Deleuze, G. (1984). *Francis Bacon. Lógica de la sensación*. Arena.
Diéguez, I.; Farías, M.; Insunza, I.; Saavedra, L. (comp.). (2017). *Poéticas del dolor. Hacer del trabajo de muerte un trabajo de mirada*. Oxímoron.
Eisner, W. (1996). *El cómic y el arte secuencial*. Norma Editorial.
El Refaire, E. (2012). *Autobiographical comics. Life writing in pictures*. The University Press of Mississippi.
Fernández, L. (2016). "La historieta como relato de un trauma social en América Latina: los casos *Historietas por la Identidad* (Argentina) y *Acto de Guerra* (Uruguay)". *Miguel Hernández Communication Journal*, N° 7, pp. 191–215. Universidad Nacional de Córdoba.
Filion, L. (2020). "L'usage des stéréotypes nationaux et ethniques et la structuration des dialogues interculturels dans *Fußnoten* de Nacha Vollenweider et *Im Land der Frühaufsteher* de Paula Bulling". En *Seminar: A Journal of Germanic Studies*, Vol. 56, No. 3–4. https://doi.org/10.3138/seminar.56.3-4.06
Fuentealba, R. (2017). *1973*. Pehuén.
Galardi, P. (2011). "La reconfiguración del tiempo en la narración historiográfica según Paul Ricoeur". *Estudios de Historia moderna y contemporánea de México*. N. 41 (enero-junio). Instituto de Investigaciones Históricas-UNAM.
Groensteen, T. (2007). *The system of comics*. University Press of Mississippi.
Hinojosa, H. (2018). "Una memoria ilustrada: problemas de la narrativa gráfica histórica contemporánea en Chile". *CuCo, Cuadernos de cómic*, N° 11, pp. 52–80. Retrieved from: https://doi.org/10.37536/cuco.2018.11.1199. Last accessed: 15/09/2022.
Jorge Quien. (2014). "Desajuste de un terráqueo". *En Ergocómic*, 23 de enero. http://ergo-comics.cl/wp/2014/01/23/jorge-quien-habla-sobre-las-sinaventuras-de-jaime-pardo/
LaCapra, D. (2009). *Historia y memoria después de Auschwitz*. Prometeo Libros.
McCloud, S. (2014). *Entender el cómic. El arte invisible*. Astiberri.
Montealegre, J. (2020). "Cuaderno de viaje a Chiapa" de Vicente Plaza: la cocinería de un artista. En *El Desconcierto*. www.eldesconcierto.cl/tipos-moviles/2020/01/05/cuaderno-de-viaje-a-chiapa-de-vicente-plaza-la-cocineria-de-un-artista.html
Neco, J. (2016). "História e evolução do gênero biográfico nos quadrinhos". *Enquadrando o real*. Vergueiro, W., Ramos, P. & Chinen, N. (eds.), pp. 10–77. Editora Criativo.
Paraizo, M. (2015). *Sátira Latina*. Selo Piqui.
Peeters, B. (2003). *Lire la bande dessinée*. París: Flammarion.
Pintor, I. (2017). *Figuras del cómic: Forma, tiempo y narración secuencial*. Universitat de València.
Plaza, V. (2013). *Las Sinaventuras de Jaime Pardo*. RIL Ediciones.
Reyes, C. (2018). "De la historieta a la novela gráficaActas del II Seminario Internacional" ¿*Qué leer, cómo leer?. Lecturas de juventud*, pp. 399–406. Ministerio de Educación-República de Chile.
Ricoeur, P. (2004). *Tiempo y Narración 1*. Siglo XXI Editores.
Ricoeur, P. (2004b). *Tiempo y Narración 2. Configuración del tiempo en el relato de ficción*. Siglo XXI Editores.
Rojas, S. (2015). "Profunda Superficie: Memoria de lo cotidiano en la literatura chilena". *Revista chilena de literatura*, N° 89, pp. 231–256. Universidad de Chile.
Rojas, S. (2018). "El cuerpo moderno y la ruina del signo". *"Las obras y sus relatos II."* Ediciones Departamento de Artes Visuales.
Sánchez, C. (2005). *Escenas del cuerpo escindido. Ensayos cruzados de literatura, filosofía y arte*. Cuarto Propio.

Saxe, F. (2020). "Hacia un cuerpo marica: una reflexión situada sobre investigación, memoria queer/cuir, infancia sexo- disidente y trols". *En Aletheia*, Vol. 10, N° 19. Universidad Nacional de la Plata.

Smolderen, T. (2014). *The origins of comics: from William Hogarth to Winsor McCay*. University Press of Mississippi.

Todorov, T. (2002). *Memoria del mal, tentación del bien*. Ediciones Península.

Traverso, E. (2012). *La historia como campo de batalla. Interpretar las violencias del siglo XX*. Fondo de Cultura Económica.

Turnes, P. (2017). "Dibujos pese a todo. Sobre 'notas al pie' de Nacha Vollenweider". *Revista Kamandi*. Retrieved from: www.revistakamandi.com/2017/08/21/dibujos-pese-a-todo-sobre-notas-al-pie-de-nacha-vollenweider/. Last accessed: 15/09/2022.

Urzúa, M. (2017). "Cartografía de una memoria: *Space Invaders* de Nona Fernández o el pasado narrado en clave de juego". *En Cuadernos de Literatura*, pp. 302–318. Editorial Pontificia Universidad Javeriana. https://doi.org/10.11144/Javeriana.cl21-42.cmsi. Last accessed: 16/09/2022.

Vollenweider, N. (2017). *Notas al Pie*. Maten al Mensajero.

Witek, J. (1989). *Comic books as history: The narrative art of Jack Jackson, Art Spiegelman, and Harvey Pekar*. University Press of Mississippi.

Wrobel, J. (2021). Entrelazamientos de memoria(s) entre Hamburgo y Argentina: la representación de la ausencia forzada en *Notas al Pie*, de Nacha Vollenweider. *Decir desaparecido(s) II. Análisis transculturales de la desaparición forzada*. Lit Verlag.

9

RESISTING IMPOSED LINES

(Feminine) territoriality in the work of Chilean comics artist Panchulei

Jasmin Wrobel

Introduction

In the last two decades, graphic narratives have become an important artistic space of feminist resistance in Latin America. Although the comics scene remains dominated by male artists and readers, women[1] are increasingly using the medium to de- and reframe hegemonic and heteronormative social structures, challenging lines[2] imposed not only by their male peers but also by colonial and "Western" art traditions. The examination of (neo)colonial relations, (neo)extractivism, and reproductive rights in Latin America is, moreover, taking place in a region whose history and geographic toponomy is marked by allegorical "feminization," and, at the same time, in a medium in which women's bodies have historically been subjected to the (White)[3] male gaze. Despite, or rather, precisely *because* of this, the graphic language of comics with its hybrid and multimodal nature becomes a critical, but also ironic and playful way to subvert hegemonic visual and textual traditions, which in turn helps to explain why it has become such a highly effective tool for a wide range of political movements.[4]

Against this backdrop of a (globally) growing market for comics created by women – a phenomenon that the Spanish scholar Ana Merino has referred to as "feminine territoriality" (Merino, 2008; 2017, pp. 113–133) – the following article builds on Merino's notion of a "conquest" of space and visibility within a male-dominated art scene to investigate how Latin American female comics artists challenge the hegemonic, mostly male/heteronormative gaze in their representations, break down patriarchal and (neo)colonial structures, and symbolically and explicitly cross imposed lines, especially within the context of current protest movements.

Of particular interest in this regard is the Chilean comics artist Panchulei (1987), whose work reflects this double sense of "feminine territoriality." On the one hand, Panchulei can be considered an important transnational networker, who actively

DOI: 10.4324/9781003333296-12

advocates for greater visibility for female comics creators. On the other hand, she is concerned – especially in her most recent work – with the decolonial and feminist potential of comics, placing women characters at the center of her graphic activism. In order to reflect on the connection between territoriality, corporeality and visibility not only on the pictorial level but also on the level of production, I begin with two introductory observations, or rather *gazes*, before examining Merino's notion of "feminine territoriality" more closely. The final part of this article makes use of this concept to discuss Panchulei's *Matria* series (2019/2020), which is characterized by a combination of visual protest codes and transmedial dialogue.

The colonial gaze

In his 1507 map of the world, the German cartographer Martin Waldseemüller assigned the latinized name "America" to the land masses that had been "discovered" in the West in honor of Amerigo Vespucci. In his letter *Mundus Novus* (1502/1503), Vespucci had been the first to point out that the "New World" was probably a separate continent. One of the best-known pictorial representations of the "encounter" between the supposed "Old World" and the "New World" is Theodoor Galle's engraving *America*, completed between 1590 and 1600, and based on an earlier drawing by the Flemish painter Jan van der Straet (Stradanus). It is the first of 19 plates included in Stradanus's series *Nova Reperta*.

I do not intend to discuss the engraving in any great detail here,[5] but would like to highlight at least some of the key attributes of the figures depicted in the complex allegorical image, and the dichotomies they represent (see also Wrobel, 2021, pp. 65–66). In the foreground to the right, we see a fully clothed Amerigo Vespucci girded with a sword and holding an astrolabe and a banner emblazoned with a cross. Vespucci is standing in front of a female figure, who is naked except for a feathered headdress and a loincloth that identify her as an Indigenous woman. The woman appears to be rising from her hammock and looks up at Vespucci with an astonished expression, while holding out her hand toward him in an inviting or obedient manner. The accompanying legend reads: "Americen Americus retexit – Semel vocavit inde semper excitam" ["Amerigo (re)discovered America; he called her once, and from then on she was awake forever"].[6]

The female figure's nudity serves as an allegory of the whole continent: not only does it allude to her supposed "purity" (in the sense of a scarcity of attributes of her own), but it also exposes her to the voyeuristic gaze of the "conquering White man," whose supposed superiority is made evident not only by the insignia he carries, but also by his position (he is shown standing, looking down at "America") and by his name (which becomes hers). The violent conquest, colonization, and designation of the female *cuerpo-continente* that lies at the heart of this image – Michel de Certeau referred to the latter as an "*écriture conquérante* [que] va utiliser le Nouveau Monde comme une page blanche (sauvage) où écrire le vouloir occidental" (de Certeau, 1993, p. 3)[7] – has resonated throughout history and continues to do so in contemporary debates.

A blank(ed-out) gaze – gazing at a void

In 2016, the list of nominees published by the Festival International de la Bande Dessinée d'Angoulême, the largest and most prominent comics festival in Europe, was met with outrage: the thirty nominees for the Grand Prix were all men. In response, the French feminist group *BD Égalité – Collectif des créatrices de bande dessinée contre le sexisme* published an image that quickly became an emblem of this outcry of indignation.

Drawn by Jul Maroh, the author of the graphic novel *Le bleu est une couleur chaude* (2010; *Blue Is the Warmest Color*, 2013), the image shows Olive Oyl, the tall, slender girlfriend of Popeye the sailor, flexing her biceps and smoking a pipe in the manner of her more famous companion. A cloud of smoke, which rises from Olive's pipe in place of a speech bubble, contains the exclamation "We Do It Too!" Clearly, this is a visual quote not only of Elzie Crisler Segar's cartoon character, but also of the iconic poster created by J. Howard Miller for the Westinghouse Electric Company in 1943, which shows a female factory worker proudly displaying her muscular arm and insisting "We Can Do It!" – associated with the figure of Rosie the Riveter ever since its "rediscovery" in the 1980s, this image has been co-opted for a variety of political causes, including feminism.[8]

In the case of Maroh's image, "We Do It Too!" is, at first glance, an overt reference to the Angoulême Festival's lack of recognition of the work of female comics artists. However, it can also be read as a critique of the way women have been represented throughout the history of comics; a medium that has been dominated not only by male artists, but also by the male gaze to which women's bodies have been subjected (Wrobel, 2020, pp. 17–19). One particularly telling detail is that Olive's face is represented without its moving parts (eyes, eyebrows, forehead wrinkles, mouth, etc.), that is, without the features and facial expressions that characterize an individual: hers is a blank(ed-out) gaze, while the viewer in turn gazes at a void. That said, there remains room for a variety of interpretations. On the one hand, the character whom we have come to know as a comical version of the "damsel in distress" is still "legible" as Olive by way of her clothes, hair, and posture (which in fact mimics Popeye's). On the other hand, as a *pars pro toto* figure, she represents the multitude of female comics artists whose faces (and identities) are eclipsed by the oversized male forearm and the clenched fist. While this motif evokes associations with (male) violence, the very same arm is raised militantly toward the viewer as a symbol of the unbroken "fighting spirit" displayed by female comics artists in their struggle for visibility and acknowledgement. Fittingly, instead of Popeye's anchor tattoo, Olive's forearm is adorned with a swallow – perhaps in reference to the proverb "Une hirondelle ne fait pas le printemps" ["One swallow does not make a spring"].[9]

"Feminine territoriality" in Latin American comics

As noted earlier, the growing role of female authors has turned comics, which since their emergence in the 19th century constituted "un espacio que pareciera ser hasta muy poco un 'territorio masculino'"[10] (Borges et al., 2018, sp), into a privileged medium with which to question, criticize, and subvert hegemonic and patriarchal structures. The term "feminine territoriality" as coined by the Spanish comics scholar Ana Merino refers, on a more general level, to the creation of new spaces or "territories" for women's comics and their greater visibility in formats like the (autobiographical) graphic novel. It also marks the North American Underground Comix as a decisive precursor for the construction and consolidation of this global phenomenon (2017, p. 114). In another contribution to the field, Merino speaks of an "eje femenino americano [que] se ha consolidado gracias a la trayectoria histórica de grandes autoras que construyeron y construyen discursos estéticos y narrativos comprometidos con su propia identidad" (2016, p. 36)[11] in reference to the inspirational impetus that the (partly) autobiographical and often taboo-breaking works of North American authors[12] have had on artists such as Maliki (1969, Chile) and Powerpaola (1977, Colombia/Ecuador).

Scholars and creators Gabriela Borges, Katherine Supnem, Maira Mayola, and Mariela Acevedo have also traced the emergence of a "feminine territoriality"[13] in Latin American comics art, and have thereby helped to promote an awareness of the field's own genealogy, historicity, and interconnectivity.[14] Drawing on Brazil, Mexico, Chile and Argentina as case studies, they have given a "face" (or, rather, "faces") to female comics artists from the early 20th century to the present. To my knowledge, their work constitutes the first broader investigation of female comics production in Latin America from a transnational perspective. In their conclusion, they introduce a conceptual metaphor that places an even greater emphasis on diversity and interconnectivity, namely "biodiversity":

> Y aunque es cierto que revistas de autoras y espacios de activismo feminista son recientes en el campo *historietil* cuando forjamos genealogía y unimos las trayectorias, esfuerzos y propuestas sí podemos delinear una historia colectiva. . . . A veces cuando pensamos en autoras de historieta latinoamericana se nos ocurre solo uno o con suerte dos nombres. Es como el árbol que tapa el bosque. Hemos intentado, en este artículo no caer en este error, en lugar de trepar al árbol nos hemos internado en la espesura y descubierto algunas flores, plantas carnívoras y hasta yuyitos medicinales para la panza y el corazón. Les invitamos a descubrir esta biodiversidad de autoras y a seguir forjando una genealogía que permita incluirnos en la historia oficial de la historieta latinoamericana.
>
> (Borges et al., 2018, sp.)[15]

When it comes to the production side of things, the concept of "feminine territoriality" as I understand it in dialogue with Merino and Borges et al. refers not only to "conquest" or "occupation" but also – and perhaps more importantly – to the active creation of spaces and platforms for the development, exhibition, and interconnection of female comics artists' works. Far from being preoccupied with putting themselves in the center of a space that they do not wish to be invaded by others, these authors seek to create inclusive spaces that are often conceived as intersectional from the get-go. This "territorial," yet simultaneously inclusive and intersectional approach is highlighted, for example, in the recently published catalog *Coordenadas gráficas. Cuarenta historietas de autoras de España, Argentina, Chile y Costa Rica* (2020). In the editors' introduction, programmatically titled "Mapear el territorio, construir genealogías" ["Mapping the territory, constructing genealogies"], they emphasize:

> Esta cartografía que estamos construyendo incluye autoras, historias, tiempos, relatos, contados desde la autobiografía a la ficción, en blanco y negro o en colores, con viñetas o utilizando toda la página. Diferentes formatos, desde diferentes países, con diferentes perspectivas, que comparten un mismo contexto y una historia en común, como mujeres y personas de la comunidad LGBT+. En este territorio en construcción se pueden superponer otros pliegos, marcar distintas trayectorias, entablar diálogos, generaciones y experiencias narradas y dibujadas, en una genealogía inconclusa y abierta. . . . Quienes realizamos la selección de materiales nos quedamos con las ganas de seguir mapeando y situando algunas de las historias en este atlas abierto. En efecto, en cada país de los que respondieron a la convocatoria se ha avanzado en distintos grados en la construcción de genealogías. Algunas investigaciones van más adelante, otros recién están empezando a descubrir nombres y obras, siguiendo indicios y pistas, tal cual como cuando explorando un territorio se van dibujando los mapas en la creación de cartografías.
> (McCausland et al., 2020, p. 11)[16]

With the emergence of inclusive spaces such as comic magazines – for example *Tribuna Femenina Comix* (Chile, 2009–2014), *Clítoris* (Argentina, 2010–2018), or *Brígida* (Chile, since 2018) – and feminist collectives like *Tetas Tristes Cómics* (Chile) or the international group *Chicks on Comics* (with Powerpaola as one of its founding members), themes related to gender, sexual and/or racial discrimination and violence, (sexual) self-determination, (de-stereotyped) body image(s), heteronormativity and (neo)colonial relations have been increasingly explored in Latin American graphic narratives authored by women.[17] As I would like to argue, the concept of "feminine territoriality" can thus be applied not only to the significant shift in the (Latin American) comics production but also on a representative, discursive level, as artists confront the hegemonic (colonial, patriarchal, heteronormative) gaze and its accompanying (super)structures. One especially crucial element of this critical engagement is the authors' use of the space of the panel to deterritorialize the female body. Particularly noteworthy in this context is the transmedial dialogue that is created between works of Western "high" culture with all its colonial associations and so-called "popular" culture, in the course of which imposed (territorial and artistic) lines are symbolically and explicitly crossed.

Powerpaola's well-known graphic memoir *Virus tropical* (2011) is a case in point. Here we find several splash pages that are inspired by, or based on, complex

Resisting imposed lines 171

transmedial references and entanglements. The one for the chapter "La adolescencia" (Figure 9.1),[18] for example, depicts the protagonist Paola departing from Quito to the Colombian city of Cali as a teenager: both cities are represented in the image.

FIGURE 9.1 Powerpaola (2013 [2011]): *Virus tropical*. Barcelona: Mondadori, p. 91.

In a manner that is quite typical for the coming-of-age genre, Paola experiences her first menstruation and the usual turbulences associated with adolescence on top of her move from Ecuador to Colombia. The scene that we encounter in Figure 9.1 is inspired by at least three images: a 16th-century engraving from Herodotus' *Histories* that shows the rape of Io by the Phoenicians[19]; the abduction of Ann Darrow by King Kong as pictured in Cooper's and Schoedsack's iconic movie; and a panel from Canadian Julie Doucet's graphic short story "Heavy Flow" (reprinted in 1993). While the first two scenes, one from an Early Modern edition of an ancient author and one from a 1933 monster adventure movie, show the capture of a mostly passive woman, Paola is propelled to the next chapter of the book (and of her life) by means of her own menstrual flows, or in other words, by her own corporeality. At the same time, she is shown holding a blonde Barbie doll in her hand. Closely resembling the way King Kong holds Ann Darrow, this posture gestures toward the feelings of monstrosity that come with adolescence, but it also symbolizes a young woman being confronted with Western beauty standards. Powerpaola's transmedial response includes another visual quote, which (re)connects her splash page to North American (Post-)Underground aesthetics: Paola's torrential menstrual flows, pouring unstoppably through her panties, are reminiscent of a one-page panel in Doucet's "Heavy Flow" that shows her avatar as a monstrous version of herself, stomping through downtown Montréal, flooding the streets with menstrual blood and snatching up (male) passers-by on her rampage through the city.[20] This image of "undisciplined corpography" derives much of its power from the association of (female) body fluids with drawing ink: both Julie and Paola monstrously dominate the space of the page, "overflowing" the lines predefined and enforced by hegemonic (and misogynist) art traditions.

In the following section, I will discuss how similar forms of transmedial dialogue are created in the most recent work of Chilean comics artist Panchulei, and how they help to create a visual code of protest and resistance by symbolically and explicitly crossing imposed lines and boundaries.

Panchulei: graphic activism and feminine territoriality

Francisca Cárcamo Rojas,[21] better known as Panchulei, is a comics artist, editor, and illustrator from Santiago de Chile. After moving to Barcelona in the autumn of 2018, Panchulei entered a new chapter of her creative career. Along with the migratory experience, which proved challenging enough in and of itself, she experienced two simultaneous waves of protests in October 2019. From up close, she witnessed the protests that took place between October 14 and November 20 in the wake of the sentencing of the leaders of the Catalan independence movement. From further afield (at least physically), she was profoundly impacted by the *estallido social* (literally: "social outburst") in Chile; a series of massive demonstrations that originally erupted in response to a raise in the Santiago Metro's subway fare, but then quickly evolved into a full-fledged protest movement against social inequality and rampant corruption. The violence that ensued led to the death of dozens of civilians, while thousands suffered severe injuries as a result of globally condemned police brutality. A particularly high number of eye injuries occurred due to the extensive use of rubber bullets by the Chilean security forces (Montes, 2019). This experience was a doubly traumatic one for Panchulei, as the protests reawakened family memories of the military dictatorship, while being so far away from the unfolding events meant that she was unable to give direct support to her family and friends, and could not participate in the emerging resistance movement in situ.

> Ese fin de semana la urgencia de los días comenzaron [sic] a pesar como el reloj de una bomba a punto de explotar. Llamo a algunos ilustradores, teníamos que hacer algo. Gráficas apuradas, textos en grande, la simpatía de traer al presente los estilos de los antiguos maestros del arte de resistencia, las burlas al eurocentrismo, las historietas entre lo digital, la tinta, acuarelas, óleos y serigrafía me ensuciaban las manos, en lo que en esos momentos sentía que era una necesidad de primer orden. Once mil kilómetros me distanciaban, pero yo no podía estar ajena a todo lo que estaba sucediendo en esos momentos.
> (Panchulei, 2020, p. 4)[22]

In the highly politicized environment of Catalonia, Panchulei soon found allies who joined her and Barcelona's Chilean community in their efforts. The "collective body" of the protest, which took place in pre-pandemic times, was thus formed from participants in two different movements joined together in reciprocal solidarity. On this occasion, as the author herself points out, "[l]a hiperconectividad que muchas veces criticamos . . . nos sirvió como escudo frente a la prensa oficial" (9),[23] and also made it possible to participate in the protests *in* Chile, albeit from afar.[24]

Among the visual codes and (counter-)archives of protest and resistance used and/or created by Panchulei in her works related to the *estallido social*, a series of four images seems particularly pertinent to the present context, especially with regard to the concept of "feminine territoriality": "La matria y la cacerola" (2019), "La matria y el canino" (2019), "La matria y la resistencia" (2020), and "Apruebo" (2020). Each occupying a single page,[25] the four images have been published on Panchulei's social media profiles and her website, in the form of limited-edition posters (approximately 50), as well as in the (so far only digitally published) fanzine *ManosManifiesto* (2020), alongside other material. Inspired by four works of art that the author saw in the Museu Nacional d'Art de Catalunya, which contains one of the most important collections of Romanesque art in the world, the series engages with the upheavals in form of a complex, multifaceted and multi-layered visual protest that connects various political movements and forms of resistance. Here I wish to look more closely at two of the images, "La matria y la cacerola" and "La matria y el canino."

"La matria y la cacerola" ["The Matria and the Pan"] (see Figure 9.2) is a "reinterpretation" (in Panchulei's own words, 28) of the Baldachin from Tost (see Figure 9.3), a Romanesque tempera painting originally in the Church of Sant

Martí de Tost in Catalonia (c. 1220), which shows Christ in Majesty surrounded by a mandorla and a tetramorph featuring the symbols of the four evangelists (Matthew, Mark, Luke, and John), each of whom is identified with a label bearing the respective name. Christ holds a book inscribed with the words, "Ego sum lux mundi" ["I am the Light of the World"], while his right hand is raised in a gesture of benediction. In Panchulei's drawing, we see a female figure assuming the place of the "Christian Savior" (the following statement by the artist refers to the series in general, not only to this specific image):

> Las cambié [las figuras centrales en las imágenes] por una mujer que podría ser yo o cualquier mujer latinoamericana. Piel morena, ojos rasgados, pañoleta verde para recordar nuestras luchas actuales, el perro *Negro Matapacos* y un sin número de elementos alusivos a nuestra lucha, imágenes que se están impregnando en nuestra cultura popular con una velocidad y orgullo que nunca antes había visto y que pensaba que no vería.
>
> (p. 28)[26]

In her right hand, the woman is holding a pan in reference to the resistance culture of *cacerolazos* – a form of popular protest that consists of a group of people making noise by banging on pots, pans, and other cooking utensils. She is also wearing the *pañoleta verde*, a green bandana that has become the emblem of the yearlong protests for the right of women to a legal, medically assisted, and free abortion in Argentina; a political struggle that has not only spread all over Latin America but also inspired emancipatory movements around the world, turning the *pañoleta* into an instantly recognizable icon of transnational feminism.[27] The image appears to allude to Christ's dictum, "Ego sum lux mundi" (followed by "Whoever follows me will never walk in darkness, but will have the light of life" in John 8:12), albeit with significant modifications. For example, in the center of the night sky in the background, the octagonal Guñelve star that is featured on the ancestral Mapuche flag – a symbol of Venus – serves as an aureole for the seated female figure, who, in Panchulei's recreation of the Romanesque painting, assumes the role of protector and preserver of the lands we know as "Chile" today. There are also references to the contemporary Chilean Mapuche flag,[28] such as the sun and the moon that are to be seen in the night sky, and the woman's sleeves and train, which follow the flag's color scheme. Next to the pan and the wooden spoon in her hands, an open book symbolizing education to her left, and a bottle of water with bicarbonate and a sliced lemon (to counter the effects of tear gas) to her right, allude to the violent political struggle that played out on Chile's streets. The captions in the mandorla can be translated as "there cannot be peace without justice. All the bullets will be returned" in an evident reversal of the Christian moral imperative of forgiveness. The evangelists are likewise replaced by the symbols and tools of resistance: alongside musical instruments (music also played a crucial role during the military dictatorship in Chile) and paint (the presence of which is, of course, highly self-referential), the dog Negro Matapacos appears on the bottom left.

The Chilean stray – his epithet means "black cop killer" – who appears in almost all of Panchulei's works of this nature became famous for his participation in the 2011 student protests in Santiago de Chile.[29] Apart from his black fur, another conspicuous feature was the red bandana that he wore tied around his neck. Although Negro Matapacos died in 2017, his image became an emblem of resistance against police brutality in the 2019 and 2020 protests in Chile and beyond – for example, stickers with his image appeared during the 2019 New York City subway protests in Downtown Brooklyn (Anania, 2019). In the drawing being discussed here, he carries a sign with the acronym ACAB, as does the Pikachu figure on the bottom right, the latter being a reference to the inflatable costume that was worn by Giovanna Grandón as she danced through the streets during "La marcha más grande de Chile" ["The biggest march of Chile"] on October 25, 2019, going viral as Tía Pikachu [Aunt Pikachu] when she took a telegenic stumble over the curb and fell down.[30] The figures of Negro Matapacos and Tía Pikachu have since made major inroads into comics culture: they form part of the "Chilean Avengers," a group of symbolic figures that played a prominent role on the streets and in social networks during the protests (Arros, 2019).

"La matria y el canino" ["The Matria and the Dog"] (see Figure 9.4) was likewise inspired by a Romanesque work of art, an antependium originally in the Chapel of Sant Quirc de Durro (see Figure 9.5).

At the center of the tempera painting, we see the early Christian martyrs Cyricus and Julitta, depicted in the manner of a Madonna and Child. Their names are written to the left and right of the surrounding mandorla, respectively, while their martyrdoms play out around them in another tetramorph. The antependium is surrounded by a frame decorated with geometric patterns.

The central figure of Panchulei's reinterpretation is, once again, a woman with a green bandana and Negro Matapacos by her side. Here Julitta is replaced by a feminist activist who holds a rock in her hand, ready to put the slogan of "La matria y la cacerola" ("All bullets will be returned," see above) into action, while the image's own caption exclaims: "Guys, this is on, resist no matter how." Again, various scenes of protest and resistance surround the central female figure. In the lower right corner, for example, an elderly woman *tomando once* ["having afternoon tea"] with a little bottle of water with bicarbonate next to her represents Olga Inés Echeverría Monarde from the Chilean city of Valparaíso who sat at a table in the middle of the streets on November 18, 2019, in a gesture of protest against low pensions, with video footage of the incident creating a buzz on the Internet.[31] It is noteworthy that Panchulei chose to show two instantly recognizable female figures involved in the protests in both of her reinterpretations, Echeverría Monarde in this example and Tía Pikachu in "La matria y la cacerola." Meanwhile, the mandorla is surrounded by references to extraterrestrials; an ironic allusion to what Cecilia Morel, wife of Chile's ex-president Sebastián Piñera, said about the demonstrators, who resembled, according to her, "an alien invasion" (BBC News Mundo, 2019). Framing the whole image, as well as the individual panels, is a blood-red liquid, while the eyeballs around the outer edges recall the many eye injuries caused by the police's rubber bullets.

The visual code of protest created by Panchulei is constructed from global (ACAB) and local (Negro Matapacos, Mapuche iconography, etc.) references, and is characterized by a transtemporal dimension that brings Romanesque Christian paintings (i.e., the rejected or at least increasingly challenged colonial "substrate," or to put it differently, the former, violently imposed superstrate) into dialogue with phenomena that have gone viral during the recent protests. At the same time, she (re)connects these protests to the ongoing (global) feminist movement regarding reproductive rights. Last but not least, the specific artistic approach and apparent (im)materiality of Panchulei's reinterpretations create a marked contrast to the 12th- and 13th-century Romanesque paintings, whose authority and supposed superiority as artworks seem to be confirmed not only by their age and (quite literally) crafts*man*ship,[32] but even more so by the fact that they have been preserved, archived, and exhibited in a museum of international stature. Panchulei's images, on the other hand, have been drawn digitally and have, at least at first glance, a much more ephemeral character. At the same time, this apparent volatility also gave them more visibility by making them adaptable to different media ranging from online spaces to printed posters and fanzines, where they could be published in conjunction with other works that visualized (and archived) the protest codes of the Chilean protests in 2019/2020.

In one final point, I would like to briefly comment on the titles of the image series, and thereby connect them to the central topic of this article as outlined at the beginning. The term "Matria" has been adopted by recent feminist[33] and Indigenous movements in Latin America as a counter-concept to "Patria"/Fatherland and "Madre Patria," which refers to the (neo)colonial "motherland" of Spain. In response to the colonial trope of figurative feminization of lands and territories, which was accompanied by an exoticization and eroticization of the Amerindian woman,[34] the "Matria" that is envisioned here focuses on women as the social fabric, the very pillars and leaders of their communities. In Panchulei's *Matria* series, actively resisting female figures replace Christ in Majesty and the Christian martyr Julitta, respectively. Even if the artist makes use of fundamental pictorial building blocks or "frames" of Romanesque paintings, such as the tetramorph and the mandorla, she transforms them into structural elements of her own graphic language, disturbing and transgressing the iconographic "demarcation lines" of Christianity and Western Culture. In the process, the templates and patterns that were imposed on the supposedly "(wild) blank page on which to write the Western will" (de Certeau, 1993, p. 3) in the course of colonialism are irreverently painted over.

(In)Conclusion – *Un territorio en construcción*

Panchulei's feminist and decolonial[35] work – and especially her *Matria* series, which links the recent protests in Chile to a provocative reinterpretation of Romanesque Christian paintings – shows that comics art with its multimodal language, its hybrid character, and its location between different semiotic systems has (or rather:

continues to have) significant subversive potential in that it can destabilize and de-sacralize hegemonic structures, iconographies, and dominant visual archives. Precisely because the medium has historically been dominated by male creators and readers (who are, for the most part, cisgender, heterosexual, and White), it is important to highlight that this subversive potential can be applied to the ex- and re-appropriation of this supposedly "male territory," and can in the process help to disturb and dismantle its lines of demarcation.

I would like to conclude by pointing out how some of Panchulei's most recent works make other female creators in the field visible in the spirit of "una sororidad que va más allá de las fronteras,"[36] as McCausland et al. (2020, p. 10) put it. Together with Catalan creator and editor Montserrat Terrones, Panchulei initiated the project *Mujeres entre viñetas* [*Women Between Panels*] in 2020.[37] On their website, they portray female comics artists from all over the world, each being honored with a one-page comic that highlights the most important works and moments of her career. In so doing, they create a continuously growing alternative archive that serves to fill the gaps – and quite literally shows the faces – of those who have often been forgotten and left out of (official) comics history. This is also the aim of the recently published catalog *Mujeres chilenas en la historieta* (Lavín et al., 2021), a portrayal of 56 Chilean comics artists available in Spanish, French, English, and Korean. Again, this project is a collaborative effort between artists and scholars which showcases the interconnectivity between women and the multiple roles that they assume in comics production. Without wanting to idealize or romanticize a scene that, as a market, remains highly competitive, the sheer amount of collaborative, collective, and decidedly inclusive work being done by creators, researchers, and gatekeepers is nothing short of striking. The "territory" of women's comics in Latin America is very much "under construction" (McCausland et al., 2020, p. 11) – and there are a lot of helping hands.[38]

Notes

1 My usage of the term explicitly includes all persons who identify with the female gender.
2 With Tim Ingold, I understand the "imposition of lines" as a modus operandi of colonialism: "Colonialism, then, is not the imposition of linearity upon a non-linear world, but the imposition of one kind of line on another. It proceeds first by converting the paths along which life is lived into boundaries in which it is contained, and then by joining up these now enclosed communities, each confined to one spot, into vertically integrated assemblies" (2007, pp. 2–3). This idea was further explored in relation to the graphic language of comics in the framework of the international conference "Crisis Lines: Coloniality, Modernity, Comics" organized by Haya Alfarhan and Dominic Davies at City, University of London, on 9 and 10 June 2021 (www.city.ac.uk/news-and-events/events/2021/06/crisis-lines-coloniality-modernity-comics/_nocache; last accessed 20 June 2021). A previous version of this article was presented on this occasion.
3 In this article, I will capitalize all racial as well as ethnic identity markers including 'White,' following, among others, Ann Thuý Nguyễn's and Maya Pendleton's (2020) recommendation: "To not name 'White' as a race is, in fact, an anti-Black act which frames Whiteness as both neutral and the standard. . . . We believe that it is important to call attention to White as a race as a way to understand and give voice to how Whiteness

functions in our social and political institutions and our communities. . . . While we condemn those who capitalize 'W' for the sake of evoking violence, we intentionally capitalize 'White' in part to invite people, and ourselves, to think deeply about the ways Whiteness survives – and is supported both explicitly and implicitly."

4 This article is part of a monograph with the working title "Body/Images – Foreign/Gazes: (Feminine) Territoriality and Corpography in Latin American Graphic Narratives," an ongoing project which is being funded by the Deutsche Forschungsgemeinschaft (DFG, German Research Foundation) under Germany's Excellence Strategy in the context of the Cluster of Excellence "Temporal Communities: Doing Literature in a Global Perspective" – EXC 2020 – Project ID 390608380.

5 Both the engraving and the original drawing have been studied and discussed extensively by scholars from the fields of art history and post/decolonial studies. See, for example, Rabasa, 1993, pp. 23–48; Schmidt-Linsenhoff, 1998; Jáuregui, 2008 [2005], pp. 59–60.

6 It is quite intriguing (especially for comics scholars) that Stradanus's original drawing does not feature this legend. Instead, the word "America" is placed within the image itself, spelled backwards "as if uttered by Vespucci" (Rabasa, 1993, p. 23).

7 "[C]onquering writing [that] will use the New World as a (wild) blank page on which to write the Western will." All translations in this article, unless stated otherwise, are my own.

8 Feminists found in the image a form of self-empowering representation, in that it unites all women in the struggle against gender inequality, a reinterpretation of the poster's original goal of boosting worker morale in the armaments industry.

9 See also Hugo Hinojosa's essay "Comiqueras: El panorama de las autoras de historietas en Chile" (2018), where he uses the example of the 2016 Angoulême Festival to illustrate the global scale of the structural discrimination against women creators in the field.

10 "[A] space that seemed to be until very recently a 'male territory.'"

11 "[A]n American feminine axis [that] has consolidated itself thanks to the historic trajectory of great authors who have built and continue to build aesthetic and narrative discourses committed to their own identity."

12 See, for example, Sina, 2020, for an analysis of the instrumentalization of obscenity and taboo breaking in Aline Kominsky-Crumb's works.

13 Borges et al. do not use Merino's concept explicitly, but speak, as quoted earlier, of (former) "masculine territories" in relation to comics in general and, for example, to the Argentinean comics magazine *Fierro* in particular.

14 In this context, see also the dossier "Mulheres, Humor e Cultura de Massa," edited by Cintia Lima Crescêncio, Mara Burkart, and Maria da Conceição Francisca Pires (in *Tempo & Argumento*, 2020), and the exhibition catalogs *Presentes: autoras de tebeo de ayer y hoy* (Berrocal et al., 2016), *Nosotras contamos: un recorrido por la obra de autoras de historieta y humor gráfico de ayer y hoy* (Acevedo 2019) and *Coordenadas gráficas. Cuarenta historietas de autoras de España, Argentina, Chile y Costa Rica* (2020).

15 "And even if it is true that women's magazines and spaces of feminist activism are recent phenomena in the comics field, when we forge genealogy and bring together trajectories, efforts, and proposals we can outline a collective history. . . . Sometimes when we think of female Latin American comic authors, only one or luckily two names come to mind. It is like not seeing the forest for the trees. In this article, we have tried not to make this mistake – instead of climbing the tree, we have gone into the thicket and discovered some flowers, carnivorous plants, and even medicinal herbs for the belly and the heart. We invite you to discover this biodiversity of female authors and to continue forging a genealogy that will allow us to be included in the official history of Latin American comics."

16 "This cartography we are building includes authors, stories, times, tales, told from autobiography to fiction, in black and white or in color, with panels or using the whole page – different formats, from different countries, with different perspectives, that share the same context and a common history, as women and people from the LGBT+ community. In this territory under construction, other layers can be superimposed, different trajectories can be marked, dialogues, generations, and experiences can be narrated and

drawn, in an unfinished and open genealogy. . . . Those of us who made the selection of materials are left with the desire to continue mapping and locating some of the stories in this open atlas. Indeed, in each of the countries that responded to the call for papers, progress in the construction of genealogies has been made to varying degrees. Some investigations are forging further ahead, others are just beginning to discover names and works, following hints and clues, just as when exploring a territory, maps are being drawn in the creation of cartographies."

17 The panorama of publication platforms, magazines, festivals, artists' collectives, and academic events with a specific focus on Latin American female comics artists is, of course, much broader and, above all, steadily growing (see Borges et al., 2018, and footnote 14 of this chapter).

18 For a detailed analysis of this splash page, see Wrobel, 2020, pp. 29–31, 2021, pp. 75–77. For a more general discussion of *Virus tropical*, see Gómez Gutiérrez, 2015; Andrade Ecchio, 2019, pp. 24–26; Wrobel, 2022.

19 The correspondent woodcut from the first French edition of the first Latin translation of Herodotus' *Histories* (1510) can be found here: https://camillesourget.com/en-607-rare-books-first-edition-precious-books-herodotus-herodote-herodoti-halicarnassei-thurii-historie-parentis--the-first-french-edition-of-.html (last accessed 20 June 2021). I would like to thank Paola Gaviria (Powerpaola) for this reference and for kindly allowing me to reproduce the splash page in this article. I am also very grateful to my former student, Oxana Dubova, who interviewed the author in connection with a seminar I taught in 2015 ("Comics and Graphic Novels in Brazil and Hispanic America," Freie Universität Berlin).

20 As Frederik Byrn Køhlert astutely observes in his analysis of "Heavy Flow," "[t]he grotesque vision of unruly femininity reaches its peak in a page-size panel showing Julie as a growling King Kong-like version of herself rampaging among the skyscrapers, menstrual fluids cascading from her loins and with her clothing unable to contain her breasts. . . . Excessive and corporeally undisciplined in every way, including also her unshaved legs, unwashed hair, and unpedicured feet, Julie is the male nightmare of loss of control over the female body" (2019, p. 34).

21 I am very grateful to Panchulei for her openness towards my enquiries, her generous explanations, and also for the kind permission to reproduce her images in this article.

22 "That weekend, the urgency of the days began to weigh like the time fuse on a bomb about to explode. I call some illustrators, we had to do something. Rushed sketches, large texts, the sympathy of bringing to the present the styles of the old masters of resistance art, the mockery of Eurocentrism, comics in digital and ink, in watercolors, oils and silkscreen printing made my hands dirty, in what I felt at that moment was a necessity of the first order. Eleven thousand kilometers separated me [from Chile], but I could not be oblivious to all that was happening at the time."

23 "The hyperconnectivity which we often criticize . . . served us as a shield against the official press."

24 As a side note, it is interesting to think about how and to what extent the "collective body" that is so important for protest culture in general, and for *feminist* protest culture in particular, can – under conditions of the COVID-19 pandemic – in some way be substituted by a "digital collective body" that is formed, for example, on social media platforms. The *marea verde* or "green wave" of Argentinean women fighting for the right to abortion, whose protest resonated throughout the internet and spawned similar movements in many other countries, is a case in point.

25 Panchulei's *Matria* series is proof of the versatility of comics as an art form: here, the images do not depict a series of events in sequential panels – rather, they function as individual, yet interconnected compositions.

26 "I exchanged them [the central figures in the images] for a woman who could be me or any other Latin American woman. Brown skin, slant eyes, a green scarf to recall our current struggles, the dog *Negro Matapacos*, and a myriad of elements alluding to our

struggle, images that are permeating our popular culture with a speed and pride that I had never seen before and that I never thought I would see."
27 The *marea verde* has achieved its goal: on January 14, 2021, President Alberto Fernández signed into law a bill that legalizes abortion on demand up to the 14th week of pregnancy.
28 The Wenufoye ["The Heaven's Winter's Bark"] flag was conceived in 1991, after a call for designs by the Chilean Mapuche organization *Aukiñ Wallmapu Ngulam*. The references to Mapuche culture and iconography in Panchulei's work can be explained by their role in (contemporary) Indigenous political resistance movements in Chile and Argentina. Historically, the Mapuche successfully resisted Spanish colonization for over 300 years and maintained an independent state from the mid-16th century until 1883.
29 The dog famously marched with the rioters and defended them from the *pacos*, a derogatory term for the Carabineros, Chile's national police force.
30 Video footage of Tía Pikachu can be found here: www.youtube.com/watch?v=EkHGVWx1bfQ (last accessed 20 June 2021). Social activist Giovanna Grandón has recently been elected as a representative of the 12th District for the Chilean Constitutional Convention of 2021.
31 The footage can be found here: www.gamba.cl/2019/11/video-abuelita-de-valparaiso-se-puso-a-tomar-te-en-medio-de-la-calle-como-protesta/ (last accessed 20 June 2021).
32 As evinced, for example, by the longevity of the tempera used as a painting medium.
33 One example of this is the political collective *MuMaLá, Mujeres de la Matria Latinoamericana*.
34 Another example of this would be the chronicles of the conquistadors, who claimed to have seen sirens or Amazons on their travels, with the latter having an immediate effect on the naming of one of the region's most prominent topographical features.
35 In this context, see especially her ongoing and interactive project *El otro archivo*, www.elotroarchivo.com (last accessed 20 June 2021), and her recently published fanzine *El mundo fue pensado por unos pocos* (2021), which includes "[f]our essays about the outlying [sic] world. Concepts such as decolonialism, feminism and immigration form the central elements of a story that gives an alternative view of Western thought imposed on the Abya Yala (which means mature land or land of vital blood and is synonymous with America)" (quote originally in English, cited from *Mujeres chilenas en la historieta*, 2021, p. 93).
36 "[A] sisterhood that goes beyond borders."
37 https://mujeresentrevinetas.com/2021/05/18/ana-miralles/ (last accessed 20 June 2021).
38 I am very grateful to the editors, Lauri Fernández, Amadeo Gandolfo, and Pablo Turnes, for their attentive reading of my manuscript and their many helpful comments. I would also like to thank Martin Bleisteiner and Gabriella Szalay for their meticulous editing of this text. As a German scholar in the field of Latin American (literary) studies, I have increasingly worked on graphic narratives from the continent in recent years, with a special focus on the representation of social inequalities, memory discourses, and the presence and visibility of female comics artists. In so doing, I have benefited greatly from collaborations with colleagues from Latin America and Europe, many of whom are referenced in this article. However, I would like to particularly highlight the Latin American research network *RING. Red de investigadoras e investigadores de narrativa gráfica* (https://ringlatinoamerica.wordpress.com/; last accessed 20 June 2021) and the Leverhulme-funded project *Comics and the Latin American City: Framing Urban Communities* (2016–2019; https://comicsandthelatinamericancity.wordpress.com/; last accessed 20 June 2021) and express my gratitude toward their coordinators, Hugo Hinojosa and Javiera Irribarren (*RING*) and James Scorer (*Comics and the Latin American City*), for their unflagging support and the many fruitful exchanges.

Works cited

Acevedo, M. A. (ed.) (2019): *Nosotras contamos: un recorrido por la obra de autoras de historieta y humor gráfico de ayer y hoy* (Exhibition Catalog). Buenos Aires: Mariela Alejandra Acevedo.

Anania, B. (2019): "The Cop-Attacking Chilean Dog Who Became a Worldwide Symbol of Protest," in: *Hyperallergic*. https://hyperallergic.com/526687/negro-matapacos-chilean-protest-dog/ (last accessed 20 June 2021).

Andrade Ecchio, C. (2019): "Narrativa visual producida por mujeres en Latinoamérica: el autocómic como espacio de cuestionamiento y denuncia," in: *Universum. Revista de Humanidades y Ciencias Sociales*, Vol. 34, No. 2, pp. 17–40.

Arros, F. (2019): "'Avengers chilenos': las figuras de las manifestaciones agrupadas por Twitter," in: *La Tercera*, 6 November. www.latercera.com/mouse/avengers-chilenos-twitter-manifestaciones/ (last accessed 20 June 2021).

BBC News Mundo (2019): "Protestas en Chile: la controversia después de que la primera dama Cecilia Morel comparase las manifestaciones con 'una invasión alienígena,'" in: *BBC News*, 23 October. www.bbc.com/mundo/noticias-america-latina-50152903 (last accessed 20 June 2021).

Berrocal. C., McCausland, E. & Colectivo de Autoras de Cómic (2016): *Presentes: autoras de tebeo de ayer y hoy*. Exhibition Catalog. Madrid: AECID.

Borges, G., Supnem, K., Mayola, M. & Acevedo, M. (2018): "Historieta feminista en América Latina: Autoras de Argentina, Chile, Brasil y México," in: *Revista Tebeosfera*, 6. www.tebeosfera.com/documentos/historieta_feminista_en_america_latina_autoras_de_argentina_chile_brasil_y_mexico.html (last accessed 20 June 2021).

Certeau, M. de (1993 [1975]): *L'écriture de l'histoire*. Paris: Gallimard.

Coordenadas gráficas. Cuarenta historietas de autoras de España, Argentina, Chile y Costa Rica (2020): Exhibition Catalog, org. Elisa McCausland, Mariela Acevedo, Paloma Domínguez Jería, Isabel Molina, Iris Lam. Madrid: AECID.

Doucet, J. (1993): *Lève ta jambe, mon poisson est mort!* Montreal: Drawn and Quarterly.

Gómez Gutiérrez, F. (2015): "*Virus tropical*: presencia y relevancia del personaje autobiográfico femenino en la novela gráfica colombiana," in: *Iberoamericana*, Vol. 15, No. 57, pp. 85–102.

Hinojosa, H. (2018): "Comiqueras: El panorama de las autoras de historieta en Chile," in: *ergocomics*. http://ergocomics.cl/wp/2018/04/24/comiqueras-el-panorama-de-las-autoras-de-historieta-en-chile/ (last accessed 20 June 2021).

Ingold, T. (2007): *Lines: A Brief History*. London/New York: Routledge.

Jáuregui, C. A. (2008 [2005]): *Canibalia. Canibalismo, calibanismo, antropofagia cultural y consumo en América Latina*. Madrid/Frankfurt am Main: Iberoamericana/Vervuert.

Køhlert, F. B. (2019): *Serial Selves: Identity and Representation in Autobiographical Comics*. New Brunswick: Rutgers University Press.

Lavín, V., Aguayo, M. E. & Cárcamo, F. (2021): *Mujeres chilenas en la historieta*. Catalog. Santiago de Chile: VLP Agency.

Lima Crescêncio, C., Burkart, M., Pires, M. da C. F. (eds.) (2020): "Dossiê – Mulheres, Humor e Cultura de Massa," in: *Tempo & Argumento*, Vol. 12, No. 31.

McCausland, E., Acevedo, M., Domínguez Jería, P., Molina, I. & Lam, I. (2020): "Mapear el territorio, construir genealogías," in: *Coordenadas gráficas. Cuarenta historietas de autoras de España, Argentina, Chile y Costa Rica*. Exhibition Catalog, org. Elisa McCausland, Mariela Acevedo, Paloma Domínguez Jería, Isabel Molina, Iris Lam. Madrid: AECID, pp. 10–11.

Merino, A. (2008). "Feminine Territoriality: Reflections on the Impact of the Underground and Post-Underground," in: *International Journal of Comic Art*, Vol. 10, No. 2, pp. 70–88.

Merino, A. (2016): "El eje femenino americano y la consolidación de sus miradas," in: *Presentes: autoras de tebeo de ayer y hoy*. Exhibition Catalog, org. Carla Berrocal, Elisa McCausland, Colectivo de Autoras de Cómic. Madrid: AECID, pp. 24–36.

Merino, A. (2017): *Diez ensayos para pensar el cómic*. [León]: Servicio de Publicaciones de la Universidad de León/EOLAS.

Montes, R. (2019): "La polícia de Chile suspende el uso de perdigones tras herir a mil personas," in: *El País*, 21 November. https://elpais.com/internacional/2019/11/20/america/1574270472_273528.html (last accessed 20 June 2021).

Nguyễn, A. T. & Pendleton, M. (2020): "Recognizing Race in Language: Why We Capitalize 'Black' and 'White,'" in: *Center for the Study of Social Policy.* https://cssp.org/2020/03/recognizing-race-in-language-why-we-capitalize-black-and-white/ (last accessed 20 June 2021).

Panchulei (2020): *ManosManifiesto*. Barcelona: self-published [fanzine].

Powerpaola (2013 [2011]): *Virus Tropical*. Barcelona: Mondadori.

Rabasa, J. (1993): *Inventing America: Spanish Historiography and the Formation of Eurocentrism*. Norman, OK and London: University of Oklahoma Press.

Schmidt-Linsenhoff, V. (1998): "Amerigo erfindet Amerika. Zu Jan van der Straets Kupferstichfolge 'Nova Reperta,'" in: Heide Wunder/Gisela Engel (eds.): *Geschlechtsperspektiven: Forschungen zur Frühen Neuzeit*. Königstein/Taunus: Helmer, pp. 372–394.

Sina, V. (2020): "'The Good, the Bad, and the Ugly'. Obszönität und Tabubruch in den Comics von Aline Kominsky-Crumb," in: *Closure. Kieler e-Journal für Comicforschung*, Vol. #6.5, pp. 99–122.

Wrobel, J. (2020): "Tinta(s) femenina(s): la recuperación del cuerpo en la narrativa gráfica española y latinoamericana," in: Berit Callsen/Angelika Groß (eds.): *Cuerpos en oposición, cuerpos en composición. Representaciones de corporalidad en la literatura y cultura hispánicas actuales*. Madrid/Frankfurt am Main: Iberoamericana/Vervuert, pp. 17–44.

Wrobel, J. (2021): "Körper/Blicke und Selbst(be)zeichnungen bei Pagu, Laerte und Powerpaola," in: *Closure. Kieler e-Journal für Comicforschung*, Vol. #7.5, pp. 64–81.

Wrobel, J. (2022): "Latin America's *Tinta Femenina* and Its Place in Graphic 'World Literature,'" in: James Hodapp (ed.): *Graphic Novels and Comics as World Literature*. London: Bloomsbury, pp. 33–53.

10
BOLIVIAN COMICS AND THE SUBALTERNITY

Marcela Murillo

Twentieth-century depictions of the Chola maternal bond

The maternal facet of the Chola has been presented literally in two opposite versions in the 20th century. In the popular theater, the Chola is presented positively as a loving and forgiving mother while the nationalist novel presents her in a shameful and disdainful light. In both genres the mother represents the indigenous culture, but only in popular theater she affirms and ultimately celebrates her indigeneity.

The dissent in the representation of the Chola mother is caused by the adherence of the novel, as a literary genre, to the nationalist project that promoted miscegenation as an ideological discourse; the *mestizaje*. The Bolivian sociologist Ximena Soruco Sologuren (2012), indicates that the nationalist project is embodied in the novel through the romantic union between the acculturated mestiza and the Creole. The condition for this union is the total rejection and detachment of the mestizo from her Cholas roots. The filial break between the Chola mother and the mestizo daughter is understood as the denial of their Cholo home. However, the popular theater does not adhere to this ideology and calls for the return and affirmation of the Chola identity. The popular plays by Raúl Salmón and Juan Barrera benevolently present the Chola-mother. The theatrical plays *Me avergüenzan tus pollera*s (1998), *Joven, rica y plebeya* (1949) and *La birlocha de la esquina* (1945) illustrate this good mother depiction.

The three aforementioned plays narrate a similar plot: the daughter of a Chola who refuses to continue dressing as her Chola mother. This rejection is not only a sartorial choice, but a cultural one. The Chola dress is the most visually distinctive aspect of her identity, her dismissal incurs the abandonment of the daily performance as a Chola. In all plays, the daughters opted for a westernized look, which materializes their desire to pertain to a non-Chola and hegemonic femininity. Although the daughters reject their mother and attempt to perform the non-peripheral femininity, they fail at it due to the unacceptance and mockery from members of the upper-social class. Left without another choice, the daughters return to the mother's indigeneity world. The mother embraces them back in a benevolent and nurturing fashion despite being negated by their daughters earlier on. These plays besides depicting the mother-filial bond, also illustrate the discrimination Cholas endured and point out the relevance of their outfits as a marker of their identity, consequently as a visual sign of their identity.

On the other hand, the novel depicts her as a cruel and calculating woman. Novels such as *The Chaskañawi* (1947) by Carlos Medinaceli and *Potosi land* (1911) by Jaime Mendoza, show the Chola as a cold woman who seduces upper-class men. The men that fall into her scheme end up ruined financially and classless. Furthermore, the most prominent example of the discreditation of the Chola as a mother is in *La Niña de sus ojos* (1956) by Antonio Díaz Villamil. This novel, considered a classic of Bolivian literature, narrates the story of Domitila, the daughter of a Chola, who is sent from her childhood to a private boarding school. Her upbringing distances her from her Chola mother and positions her in a higher social class. Although culturally she pertains to the upper class, she faces rejection due to her genetic makeup. She is abandoned by her boyfriend, after he learns about her indigenous origins. Unable to succeed within the upper-class and no longer comfortable with the indigenous world of her parents, she leaves the city life and starts her new life as a teacher in the rural area to educate. This novel promotes the predominant discourse of the time: *mestizaje*, which sought to eliminate the cultural differences between the "white" and the "Indian," creating a third one: the mestizo. It was advocated that the "modernization" of the Indians was possible through instruction that inevitably led to ascription to the prevailing hegemonic values of the time.

Despite the opposing depictions of the Chola as mother, both genres converge in the rupture of the filial bond. In all cases, the children (mainly daughters) aspire to pertain to a higher social class and distance themselves from their indigeneity. The rupture of the maternal bond goes further than rejecting the mother as an individual, it conveys the refusal of their whole cultural identity and their liaison to the indigenous world and cosmovision. The outcome in both genres is similar in the sense that the daughters are not accepted by the upper-class society, but different in how they embrace or not their mothers in their return to the indigenous world. In the popular theater plays, the children embrace their mother and ask for forgiveness for distancing from her, but in the novel the child does not ask for forgiveness, the mother waits for them as the children go back to her, but in the novel the daughter still rejects her and returns to the indigenous world to "educate" it, to change it, not to be a part of it anymore. These considerations will be fundamental for the analysis of the mother Chola-daughter bond in the 21st century.

The rupture of the mother-daughter bond in contemporary comics

The literary oppositions of the 20th century regarding the mother-daughter bond led to questioning the maternal depiction of the Chola in the 21st century.

I examine two Bolivian contemporary comics in the manga style that illustrate the mother-daughter bond: *La Estrella y el Zorro* (2014) by Corven Icenail y Rafaela Rada and *Niña Cholita Andina* (2016) by Rafaela Rada. Both authors reside in La Paz, Bolivia. They are urban middle-class artists; Rafaela exclusively dedicates herself to the comic art while Corven writes fiction as well. Rada is one of the most popular comic strip creators in Bolivia as her portfolio includes more than 15 graphic novels whose topics range from the Chaco War to the family life of a Bolivian Otaku.

The manga *La Estrella y el Zorro* [The star and the fox] (2014) by Corven Icenail and Rafaela Rada takes place in a Bolivian rural area in the highlands. Wara is the main character, she is a Chola teenager who juggles taking care of the family's cattle and attending school. Her mother, a Chola whose full-time occupation is the farm, is constantly asking her to take on more responsibilities in it and shows blatant disregard for her education. Despite the lack of support, Wara stands out academically in her school led by German missionary nuns. The conundrum of the comic lies Wara's scholarship to Germany to study her bachelor's degree, and her hesitance of communicating it to her mother. Wara faces such a level of anxiety to inform her decision to leave the rural life for Germany that the nuns intervene to convince her mother of these plans.

Wara's mother, who is nameless throughout the comic, is not portrayed as a loving, understanding nor nurturing parent. The mother-daughter bond mirrors a business relationship, in which the mother acts as the boss, the farm is the livelihood and the worker is Wara. The absence of a paternal figure indicates the single parenthood of Wara's mother. In this sense, Wara's mother is clearly concerned to provide for her family as she is the only responsible for it. Despite the big responsibility, she is portrayed as rough, aggressive toward animals, loud and insensitive. Her communication with Wara is merely on cattle-hearing and the farm management duties. Performatively, she embodies violence and roughness as she yells and throws stones to animals to keep them away from her farm. Graphically, her roughness is conveyed through her bulkiness, thick neck, furious gazes and rugged and disgruntled facial features.

In this comic, Wara is the heroine. Her struggle is linked to the rural life to which she is confined; her mother acts as the jailer as she holds the keys, the permission, for her to leave the rural confinement. The ending shows Wara, victorious at the airport, heading to Germany to have a different life. The narrative favors Wara graphically and narratively. The separation and rejection of the mother and her indigenous world is celebrated, her triumph lies on the detachment from this reality, as this rural reality is deemed negative and looked down upon.

The second comic to analyze is *Niña Cholita Andina*, it narrates the story of Saturnina and her aspirations to become a model. Saturnina is a teenager who lives in the city of La Paz, and just like Wara, she helps her mother with work. She struggles to balance her work at the market stall with her modeling classes. Furthermore, in the modeling school she faces racism and rejection from her peers, and at home she faces the blatant discouragement of her mother. Despite the lack of support from both spheres, she ends up victorious as she is selected by a French promoter to be the ambassador of an important French hair products brand.

Saturnina's mother, unlike Wara's mother, who is stripped from her individuality by her lack of name, is named Mercedes and utilizes the nickname "Mecha." In the same way, Saturnina's mother is a single mother who provides for her daughter with her market stall. She wakes up early in the morning to start her business and ends her day late at night. Mercedes demands her daughter to help with the business. Her relationship with Saturnina is business-oriented and her interactions are unkind and hard-hearted. Graphically, Mercedes is drawn as short, bulky, with stark facial features, a scowling look, neglected skin and animal-like teeth. Her carelessness in her physical appearance contrasts with her daughter's graceful and slender presence. Mercedes' uncordial behavior accompanies her unkempt corporeal presentation.

Both comics have the same premise: the Chola daughter who needs to break free from the maternal ties to succeed in life. In both settings, rural and urban, the Chola mother reproduces an undesirable femininity which ought to be annulled for the heroine's victory. The dissociation between the mother and daughter is fundamental for the triumph of the daughters. This dissociation is presented in a trifold manner: narratively, graphically and performatively. Performatively as Wara and Saturnina are soft-spoken, have different international projects, different sensibilities and interests in contrast to their mothers. Graphically, both heroines are slender with smooth facial features, whereas their mothers are dehumanized and almost monstrous-like (Murillo 2020). Narratively, the plot favors the free spirit daughters and punishes the single working mother.

In the same fashion, the triumph in both comics involves the daughter's validation through a Western lens. The West validates the new Chola who steps away from her stereotypical occupations and adopts the Western values. In *Niña Cholita Andina*, the beauty canon is not challenged by Saturnina, but accepted as tolerated in the eyes of the French brand. Her "virgin" hair is the reason why Saturnina is selected. This reason evokes imagery of colonial practices and appropriation. Likewise, Wara seems to adopt Western values with her academic excellence and scholarship to Europe in contrast to the rural life that is provided by her mother and hometown. In this context, success is understood as the acquisition of Western knowledge, culture and values in the country of production. Both comics insinuate the impossibility of aligning the mother Cholas femininity to their new occupations (model and student). This incompatibility situates both femininities as opposites, one excluding the other, and in the end the triumphant femininity is represented in the daughters. In this sense, the adoption of the Western values and goals are celebrated while the perpetuation of the Chola as an outdated femininity is ingrained.

Both comics disparage the stereotypical Chola occupations while reducing the image of the Chola to them. Neither maternal character is multifaceted but follows a formulaic dehumanizing portrayal which shows lack of regard to single motherhood, or any other reason. The mother's story is absent in both cases, and its portrayal is reductionist. The narratives advocate for a new Chola whose ideals are like the westernized middle class. This westernized outlook of reality does not encompass the cultural identity of the authors, as neither of them are Cholas but middle to upper middle-class urban artists. In this sense, these comics, though they represent the Chola and include her in the Bolivian imaginary, do not speak for her. These narratives account for the mestizo middle-class national project which seeks for acculturation and adoption of Western values. This 20th-century national discourse aims for the erasure of non-Western cultural identities such as the Chola.

The Chola's heroic turn in "Super Cholita" and "Monstruo"

The notion of a Chola as a heroine would have been unthinkable due to her marginal situation within the political context and societal imagery of the 20th century, but it is a fact in the new millennium. In this section, I will explore two comics that present the Chola as a heroine: *Super Cholita* (2007) and *Monstruo* (2017), and their relationship with the political apparatus in formation during the Movimiento al Socialismo (MAS) governmental period.

First, I focus on the political context by paying a closer look into the social changes that Bolivia faced as part of a cultural and economic rupture within neoliberalism. Next, I will describe how *Super Cholita* and *Monstruo* portray what I describe as political disillusionment.

Political disenchantment

Since 2006, Evo Morales and the MAS party ruled Bolivia democratically. The elections of 2005, 2009 and 2014 were won by a great margin, more than 51% of the national vote. This government lasted almost 14 years and had a great impact in the country's economy, visibility and civil rights of indigenous people, anti-racist legislature and vitalization of indigenous languages. One of the most dramatic social transformations Bolivia witnessed in the 21st century is the reaffirmation of indigenous identity propelled by the MAS government. Such enhanced indigenous discourses produced popular support during the first years of governance. However, such support decreased over time. In 2016, after three presidential terms, Morales wanted to run for a fourth time. This candidacy would violate the Political Constitution (2009) and the 2016 referendum.[1] This decision showed a lack of respect toward the law and the population's vote, which fueled an intensified Anti-Morales and anti-MAS movement. In Farthing's words,

> After 2016, Morales's disrespect for the law fused with Bolivia's painful history of authoritarian rule to create a powerful anti-Morales movement that encompassed not only light-skinned middle and upper-middle classes, but also people propelled into the middle classes by MAS's redistributive policies.
> (2020, p. 5)

The disenchantment with the MAS party and Evo Morales is palpable in these comics, and their depiction of the Cholas. In the following pages, I will address the expression of discontent in *Super Cholita*.

Undoubtedly, the Bolivian comic that elicited the most media attention and notoriety on a national and international scale has been *Super Cholita* by Santos Callisaya and Rolando Valdez. The reason for the popularity lies in the heroine's societal identity as an underdog in the socio-political arena. This manga-style comic features a Chola named Francisca Pizarro Mamani. Aesthetically, she is young, able bodied, healthy and eager to defend Bolivia. Her mission is "to protect the needy and defend the Bolivian way of life." Her superpower is the ability to fly, using her shawl as a cape. Her kryptonite is "relleno de papa," a typical Bolivian food which consists of mashed potatoes wrapped around a meaty filling.

Her adventures take place in recognizable Bolivian landmarks such as Sucre, Tiahuanaco and Lake Titicaca, and the object of her mission is always related to Bolivian cultural heritage, history or even its cuisine. Fernández L'Hoeste (2013) argues that this heroine becomes the vehicle to punish and denounce US policies in Bolivia (p. 70). and identifies "Bolivianity" as a key element embodied in the heroine. He explains that Francisca personifies "Bolivianity" in her physical appearance, as well as in her behavior while using the aesthetics of manga:

> Super Cholita incarnates *bolivianidad* to the max. Aside from embodying Bolivianess in her attired and general appearance, the most relevant facet of Super Cholita with respect to identity is how she manages to act out Bolivianess, rather than just embody it physically.
>
> (p. 74)

It should be noted that the traditional manga style somewhat effaces *Super Cholita*'s Aymara phenotypic appearance. Her ethnic and cultural identity are visually revealed through her clothing and hair style. Fashion is a conventional way to perform cultural identity, dress is considered "a coded sensory system of non-verbal communication" (McGuire, 1995, p. 1). In this sense, *Super Cholita*'s fashion and hairstyle unequivocally convey "Bolivianness." This national character is the result of the romanticizing of the indigenous population as understood by the authors.

References to Bolivian national character are distinctive of this comic, and all her adventures are littered with elements of Bolivian culture. For example, in episode two, she comes to the rescue after the theft of the *charango*, a typical Andean instrument that is very popular in Bolivia: and in episode four she defends Bolivian cultural heritage from alien hands by saving the iconic Puerta del Sol in Tiwanaku. This Bolivianness is also portrayed through the character's visual presentation, as well as her performativity and her quests. These displays of national character contribute to its popularity with Bolivian audiences while confounding readers who are unfamiliar with Bolivian history and culture.

The political stance of *Super Cholita* is addressed in the comic. In the publications of 2013–2014 the former presidents Gonzalo Sánchez de Lozada (1993–1997,

2002–2003) and Evo Morales are secondary characters. The first is portrayed as a villain and the latter as an ally. *Super Cholita*'s political attitudes seem to mirror those of the Bolivian indigenous population. In this sense, the "gringo" Sánchez de Lozada was seen as a villain while Morales was celebrated for being the first indigenous president and his effort for the revitalization of the indigenous population was celebrated.

Super Cholita's affiliation with Evo Morales is explicit in the first strips. This edition shows a smiling Morales asking her for help with the country, and Super Cholita jokingly replying that she does not do miracles. The tone is amicable, and the facial features are relaxed and comfortable. However, a shift in *Super Cholita*'s political stance will be witnessed in 2018. In August, Santos Callisaya posted an image of Super Cholita defending the Bolivian Constitution next to an aggrandized and menacing image of Evo Morales. The image depicts Super Cholita in a fighting pose with her fists ready to fight, next to a small book, titled "Political Constitution of Bolivia."

This scene has to be understood within the 2018 political context. Morales had intended to run for the fourth time and his candidacy would be in direct violation of this law as it indicates a maximum of three consecutive presidential terms for a person. The book is small in comparison to Morales, who has frightened eyes and a mortified expression.

The image shows Evo Morales as the biggest figure, with a murky smile and grand hands trying to grab the constitution. Super Cholita is in between the constitution and the grasping hands of Morales. Her body position and facial expression indicate that she is in defense-mode, ready to protect the constitution from the president.

This disenchantment with the MAS government and Evo Morales is also made explicit in other comics, using similar methods. The 2017 *Monstruo* by Gustavo Terrazas was selected and published by the city governmental office of Cochabamba along with other governmental offices such as Casa de la Cultura as part of the third municipal contest of comics strips. The topic for this contest was the local myths, short stories and legends. The comic starts featuring a decrepit one-story building, the next vignette shows the inside of a bar. The silhouette of a young big-bosomed Chola holding a *uypulla* (Quichua pottery jar) in front of two inebriated men, follows. One man, wearing a blue and turquoise cap with the inscription MAS, pushes his hand in the jar with a *tutuma*.[2] The effects of the *chicha*[3] are evident in the next vignettes through their lustful gaze at the waitress' legs. The scene shows the man walking alone away from the bar. He arrives at his humble abode where there is a bed with a toddler and a baby sleeping on it, and a mattress on the floor with his Chola partner. He heads to the kitchen and after seeing the empty pot, returns to the sleeping woman and hits her. The next vignette shows the man reminiscing on the legs of the woman at the bar while pulling his pants down. The rape of the partner is clearly evoked. The woman's despairing facial expression indicates her resignation to this situation.

The following panel shows a morning landscape which indicates that it is the next day. Next, the woman seems sad while breastfeeding the infant while the man is sitting holding his head due to a hangover. Afterward, he goes through the Chola's skirt, and takes a couple of coins from her. In the next scene, he leaves home and heads to the bar. Later, in the bedroom everyone is lying together, the father and toddler on the bed and the mother and baby on a floor mattress. The baby starts crying and the angry father wakes up and grabs him with rage in his eyes. The mother goes to the baby's rescue, and the man starts punching her while she holds the baby. The toddler intervenes trying to stop the father from beating up the mother and he ends up on the floor knocked out by his own father. The woman cries in desperation. The next scenes show the mother holding both of their children in the forest, badly bruised, but together. The next vignette shows the father sleeping while some oil is being dripped over him, and a light matchstick. The last scene depicts the mother and children walking away from their homes in flames.

Monstruo portrays the Chola as a heroine, since she saves her family from the monster of her husband/partner. His death, his murder, is an act of self-defense to protect her family. She abandons her position as a victim of domestic violence to become a survivor and heroine to her family. She breaks free from the circle of domestic violence in a country where this type of violence is normalized. She is no longer a victim of multisided violence, understood by Menjívar as "structural, political, symbolic, and everyday violence that reinforces and undergirds the normalization of persistent impunity and violence in the lives of women" (Menjívar 2011; Menjívar and Walsh 2017, p. 223).

In addition, the comic graphically refers to Evo Morales and the MAS. First, the initial vignettes at the local bar show the drinking companion wearing a cap with the initials "MAS." The usage and blue color of this cap indicates political affiliation, as this is the color associated with the MAS party. The connection between the political party and the abusive behavior is explicit. Besides, the facial features of the drinking buddy are remarkably similar to Morales', who is depicted as a bad influence in the comic. Alcoholism and sexual violence are central to the appearance of this secondary character and seem to connect the affiliation of the political party to alcohol consumption, and later violent and sexist behavior.

Both comics reflect the political context with direct references to the presidency of Evo Morales (2006–2019). The longevity of Super Cholita allows the shift of attitude toward Morales to be revealed. In the first volume, Evo Morales was an ally, but in the latter version, Calisaya portrays Morales as the villain. The new antagonist position of Morales is expressed graphically by his stern facial features and his menacing hands trying to grab the constitution. In addition, Super Cholita looks as defiant as she would act in front of any other villain.

Both comics were written and designed by men, not Cholas. The comic industry in Bolivia is produced and consumed by middle and upper middle-class people. Both comics show the narrative of the Chola from the perspective of this social class, ignoring the self-identification of Cholas.

The anti-MAS movement is rooted in the middle class, also called "pititas" (Humerez Oscori 2020; Farthing 2020). This new narrative of the Chola and its disenchantment is an example of the subaltern narrative being told by a third party.

The subaltern, the Chola, does not speak for herself in these comics. It seems that the depiction of the Chola character in comics sets up an interrogation already posed by the Bolivian Chola feminist miner Domitila Chungara, who said "Si me permiten hablar" (If I may speak, 2013). The portrayal of Cholas that male middle-class men create in these comics is still entrenched in colonial practices that silence and position Chola women as the subaltern.

Conclusion

The depictions of the Chola examined in this chapter, which range from mother, daughter and heroine, reveal different narratives according to her performance within a mestizo political context. The motherly depictions show a rupture between what it considered to be the traditional Chola, and the new Chola. The new Chola, the daughter, affixes her femininity to a westernized one, and appropriates the values concomitant to this identity. This acculturation distances the mother from the daughter, annulling the filial bond in the process. The impossibility of the coexistence of both femininities, and the narrative triumph of the daughter's newfound femininity, indicate the caducity and dismissal of traditional Chola femininity, which is deemed archaic and irrelevant in the modern world.

In terms of the Chola as heroine, the depiction seems to project the new central role of the indigenous population within the 21st century, but the political shifts of the heroines indicate a mestizo agenda within a mestizo framework. Moreover, the depiction of the Chola does not emerge from the Chola population itself, but occurs through a third, middle-class party which dictates her narrative according to its own values. In this sense, thus far the Bolivian subaltern has not spoken for herself. Hopefully in the near future, she will tell her own story, in her own voice.

Notes

1 The referendum of 2016 elicited the response of the population in reference to the modification of the Political Constitution. In particular, it requested to extend the four-year presidential term, and allow for more reelections.
2 Quechua word for a receptacle used to drink beverages.
3 Fermented corn drink made in the Bolivian valleys.

Bibliography

Bhabha, H. K. (2012). *The location of culture*. Routledge.
Crabtree, J. (2020). "Assessing Evo's Bolivia: Inclusion, ethnicity, and class". *Latin American Research Review*, vol. 55, no. 2, pp. 379–390.
Farthing, L. (2020). In Bolivia, the right returns with a vengeance: The right-wing power grab in Bolivia has unleashed an authoritarian crackdown, racist violence, and a swift rollback of Evo Morales's policies. What is the path forward for reclaiming democracy?. *NACLA Report on the Americas*, vol. 52, no. 1, pp. 5–12.
Fernández L'Hoeste, H. (2013). *Súper Cholita* and Bolivian comics: In search of cultural and political hegemony. *International Journal of Comic Art*, vol. 15, no. 1, pp. 68–83.

Humerez Oscori, J. (2020). *Racialización del Poder. Dominación Jailona en Bolivia (2009–2020)*. Grupo Editorial Nina Katari.
Lehoucq, F. (2020). Bolivia's citizen revolt. *Journal of Democracy*, vol. 31, no. 3, 130–144.
McGuire, M. A. (1995). Introduction: Dress as expression of ethnic identity. In J. B. Eicher (Ed.), *Dress and ethnicity* (pp. 1–5). Berg Publishers.
Memmi, A. (2003). *The Colonizer and the Colonized (1957)* (trans. Howard Greenfeld). Boston, MA: Beacon, p. 103. (Original work published 1967).
Menjívar, C. (2011). *Enduring Violence: Ladina Women's Lives in Guatemala*. University of California Press.
Menjívar, C. & Walsh, S. D. (2017). The architecture of feminicide: The state, inequalities, and everyday gender violence in Honduras. *Latin American Research Review*, vol. 52, no. 2, pp. 221–240.
Mohanty, C. (1988). Under Western eyes: Feminist scholarship and colonial discourses. *Feminist Review*, vol. 30, no. 1, 61–88.
Murillo, M. (2018). The clothes (re)maketh the woman sartorial empowerment in contemporary Bolivian comics. *International Journal of Comic Art*, 430–452.
Murillo, M. (2020). The monstrous portrayal of the maternal Bolivian chola in contemporary comics. In S. Langsdale & E. R. Coody (Eds.), *Monstrous women in comics* (pp. 135–151).
Rada, R. (2016). *Nina Cholita Andina*. La Paz. Axcido.
Rada, R., & Corven, I. (2014). *La Estrella y el Zorro*. La Paz. Axcido.
Said, E. W. (2012). Culture and imperialism. Vintage.
Spivak, G. C. (2003). Can the subaltern speak? *Die Philosophin*, vol. 14, no. 27, 42–58.
Valdéz, R., & Callisaya, S. (2016). *Las aventuras de Super Cholita*. TuKiosko Editorial.

11
EMANCIPATED BEHAVIOR

The body and art in the work of Águeda Noriega and Ale Torres

Carla Sagástegui Heredia

The participation of women in the history of Peruvian comics goes back just to the last forty years, when they were recently integrated as readers, as creators and even as characters. Since the commercialization of the comic book in Lima in 1940, the context favored the marginalization of women from the circuit of children, family, and political comics, mainly because until the 1960s more than half of Peruvian women could not read or write (Padua, 1979), so it was published and imported for male readers or sometimes projected for a family audience. In addition, since the comic was born in the newspaper industry and it was a labor sector biased toward males, especially in Peru, the incorporation of women in the production of comics occurred outside of the most powerful and widely distributed newspapers and magazines, as far as the end of the 1970s (Sagástegui, 2016).

Because women were incorporated into comics within publications shedding critical light on social problems, as in the rest of the world, their work was born and remained critical and reflexive about being a woman and an artist. Hereafter, I will describe how the female characters of two contemporary cartoonists, Águeda Noriega (b. 1974) and Ale Torres (b. 1977) found in their art vocation the necessary approach to emancipate themselves – not without discomfort- from the role of mother and wife. That role, three decades ago, was the main concern embodied in the lack of agency in the characters of Marisa Godínez (n. 1950). The selection criteria for choosing Águeda and Ale (artistic names) were that they are cartoonists characterized by the graphic novelization of their comics, and that their work has been sustained over time since they began their artistic profession at the beginning of this century.

Since their characters are good examples of women fighting for their liberation, the main concept will be the "emancipated behavior" (Barrancos, 2020). Barrancos has explained how, in the 19th century, many underage Argentine women used marriage as a way for emancipating themselves from patriarchal violence without

DOI: 10.4324/9781003333296-14

foreseeing that a bigger hell awaited them after the one they had left behind. This paradox has led Barrancos to focus on two questions related to "emancipation" that illuminate the multiple rationalities involved, and that will be reviewed in the selected comics of these authors:

1. It is necessary to admit that female emancipation can be far from being whole, mostly being partial and only referring to one aspect and not to all the rules that these female actors must abide. A concept of totality, Barrancos emphasizes, supposes that there is a single organizing plane for all aspects, an integral emancipation, when it really is about "emancipated behaviors."
2. The "emancipation" can only be used as a concept in a situated way, that is, within the conditions of possibility of gender constructs, which cannot be absolute because points of view, ideas and values always intersect in each society according to a set of temporal events. As we will see in the comics of Águeda and Ale, the emancipatory marriage is denounced for failing in that role, and a century later has been substituted by art as an occupation that encourages an emancipatory behavior, but not an integral emancipation.

Marisa Godínez: bodies without agency

In the 1970s context of the Latin American dictatorships, the comic became a tool of resistance that fought by the side of the people (Catalá et al., 2017). During the *de facto* government of Francisco Morales Bermúdez (1975–1980), liberal president of the second phase of the Revolutionary Government of the Armed Force (1968–1975), the artistic comic rose against all political censorship, emerged in various opposition media, and increasingly explored the inner and symbolic world of its characters, as in the work of Juan Acevedo or Dare Dovidjenko in the magazine *Monos y Monadas* (1978) (Sagástegui, 2003). Concurrently, women began to gain greater access to basic education, university studies and professional labor, and the new students, writers and journalists formed the first feminist organizations, still active today (Orvig, 2004, p. 18).

During that decade, graphic humor took on the format of protest newspapers or magazines, and occupied a central place in the newsstands. The magazine that devoted most criticism against the government was *Monos y Monadas*. In this magazine, writers and cartoonists disappointed in the government after the social reforms were dismantled converged. Among them were only two women: María Zöellner, with a humor column; and Marisa Godínez (Marisa), with her surreal comics. In the case of Marisa, her motherhood coincided with the fact that the father of her children, the cartoonist Juan Acevedo, was part of the editorial board of the magazine. It was ironically due to these circumstances that Marisa, summoned to draw, represented the role of mother that in those times the Peruvian society imposed on the body of women. The first aesthetic line that Marisa developed gave a surrealistic body to the main character within the most significant emancipatory context in the history of Peruvian women.

"Feliz día de la Madre" [Happy Mother's Day] (Figure 11.1) is an example of how the surrealist bodies of Marisa translate to us the negative inscription of social norms in the bodies of women. Before her work, the Peruvian comics had never drawn a woman differently from the racist macho strokes or erotic figures which remained as anonymous women happy to expose their sexuality and reinforce male power. Marisa's comic begins with the exposition of the different gazes of the mother and three of her children, the four characters that in a certain way form just one: each gaze perceives the territory through which they move in their own particular way. The woman watches the road and holds the weight of three different children. The woman's gaze toward the road is a maternal gesture, as well as the confidence and security of the children when holding on to her. The youngest, climbing on the head of his mother, looks attentively ahead. The second daughter, sitting on the shoulders of her older brother, holds to her mother's ears, and watches the smiling landscape. The older one who goes on the back of her mother, hugs her seeking protection; he is the only one who is somewhat scared. It is an image of bodies that, despite the various looks that make it up, project a single body that contains them, a family without a father and with a barefoot mother.

FIGURE 11.1 Happy Mother's Day (Villar 166).

Source: Villar, Alfredo (editor). Bumm! Historieta y humor gráfico en el Perú: 1978–1992. Lima: Reservoir Books, Penguin Random House Grupo Editorial, 2016.

The landscape opens in the next panel and we see that they follow a lost path that leads to a small fair of electrical appliances called "Feliz día" [Happy Day]. When the woman and her children arrive, they are welcomed with joy by the fair entertainer. As a result, the mother returns dragging the three largest and heaviest artifacts with ropes tied to her feet and around her waist, in addition to continuing with her children on the road in what we already know will be long. The narrative does not describe an emancipated behavior, and even less so does it describe the dream achieved, according to gender conventions, in motherhood. Instead, the narrative shows us how our society inscribes over the female bodies the dreaded experience of living under unfair social norms and roles.

In the first stage of Marisa's work, her main characters lack agency. The etymology of the word *protagonist* suddenly does not fit, since the meaning of the Greek *agon* is nothing other than the human impulse to fight. To agonize is not to die, but to fight for life when death claims us, says Alberto Pérez Galindo (1980). Can a woman without agency be a protagonist? A valid question insofar in Marisa's comics each character is reduced to a mechanical execution, without any human vitality in the eyes of the characters. A singular omission, if we take into account that in the history of comics and animated cartoons an old and recognized resource to show the emotions is playing with the brightness of the eyes. It is this first stage of Marisa's work when the greatest distress produced by the pitch-black eyes becomes a way of looking at the invisible pains of women's daily lives.

Taking away any glint, during the reading of the family tree, we can confirm that the agency was not at loss, that it had been hauled out by the domestic ties, which turned the woman's body into the very root of the family tree, petrified, without any freedom. A slight smile in the first panel warns us that perhaps her eyes would not have been like that in a previous moment in which the family institution buried and held you. Faced with a force that the process represents as natural, that of putting down roots, recovering the agency of women, does it imply the cutting of the tree? Is it possible to recover the agency of these women? These questions reached Marisa's personal world when she joined the feminist movement, as she discovered that sharing readings and information with other women, could carry out a process of collective awakening capable of ending violence and taking down the conservative gender roles. The impact of liberation on Marisa produced in her a new aesthetic which leads her to test of a different graphic narrative, contrary to the graphic estrangement and literary uneasiness that characterized her surrealist work. She wanted to show women how to love each other with the whole body with simple and childish illustrations. For many years, Marisa was part of the project of writing and illustrating brochures for the workshops aimed at precariously literate women that took place in poor neighborhoods.

The body and consciousness

Three decades later, many of the women characters in Águeda Noriega and Ale Torres' comics are currently examples of emancipated behaviors, staged through their decision-making as artists. It is worth clarifying that it is not the subjectivity of both authors to which the characters refer to themselves in their comics. They are usually historical characters in the case of Águeda and fictional ones in the work of Ale Torres. They create in different media and materials, from the mural to the comic strip, but their main work is published in fanzines. A publication that, with the limitations and possibilities of its artisanal confection and independence, caused a significant change by developing its own language and an emotional and affective graphic critic of the social system (Shane Greene, 2017, p. 33). The fanzine, as part of the underground punk culture in Peru, was established in the 1990s through the influence of a circuit of anarchist and socialist musicians, which endowed comics with an emancipating power of rupture compared to the aesthetic characteristic of the commercial comic of entertainment and adventures.

The potential for creativity of the fanzine arose in the midst of an internal and cruel war against the Sendero Luminoso [Shining Path] Communist Party. As a graphic medium it was recognized for its disturbing words, images, and bodies, with the violence necessary to confront the bodies that the state and the society of those years wanted to invisibilize, such as those killed in armed confrontations or because of their sexual diversity. For all these reasons, the fanzine, progressively more sophisticated, became a support for artistic freedom which allowed different subjectivities to experiment with comics themselves. The fanzine puts a stop to the tradition of drawing erotic women as a sign of sexual freedom, and became an alternative tradition of emancipatory purposes centered on the recognition of bodies other than the male, in bodies who had been victims of violence, of racism. During this process, the woman's body ceased to be the one denounced by Marisa, one without agency, and was replaced by a diversification of possibilities thanks to the increasing number of female comic authors, which began to grow exponentially. This allowed them to learn quickly that comics were an art where the possibility of emancipation l was accessible for them as well as for their female characters.

The women of the first cartoonist

Águeda Noriega studied Philosophy at the National University of San Marcos. Her decision to become a professional cartoonist was made after she published her work on the comics magazine *La Inocente Hecatombe* (2002). Since then, Águeda unleashed her artistic production as an illustrator and cartoonist. Águeda's comics can be gathered into two big genres. One is the comic strip, starring Alter Ego (Noriega, 2012), a humorous cartoon version of herself and the first female protagonist in a Peruvian comic strip, the other is the novelized comic, usually published in her own fanzine named *Agathós* (Noriega, 2011, 2015). In these comics the main characters are recognized writers, artists, and singular women, focused on their desire for emancipation. Águeda gave the name *Agathós* to the fanzine because it refers to the Greek adjective for the behavior of a person based on her virtues. Two or three fictionalized comics make up each issue and are supported

FIGURE 11.2 Camille (Águeda s/n).

Source: Noriega, A. (año). Agathos, Lima, AgueDet Publicaciones.

by the illustration of a texture that simulates engraving, a technique widely used in the first publications of cartoons and comics in major newspapers and magazines around the turn of the 19th century (Leonardini, 2003). A time that coincides with the decades that the main characters in Águeda's narrative usually lived.

Each story condenses the attempts of emancipation of the female main characters focused on fulfilling both art and marriage. An example of this can be found in the second issue of *Agathós*: "Camille" (Noriega, 2011) is a comic that summarizes the tragic story of Camille Claudel because of her tragic love for Auguste Rodin (Figure 11.2). This piece is focused on the sensations, the perceptions of the world, and the affections suffered by Camille after a nervous breakdown that led her to destroy all of her sculptures and ended up with her being locked up in a mental institution for the last thirty years of her life. The comic begins with Camille wondering what it would be like if she could go back to sculpting. This passion leads her to remember herself as a woman with her hair up, somewhat tired, modeling the figure of a fallen man. The next panel shows her in the foreground across the page, with the wave-sculpted stone and a rasp in her hand. She dresses in white, while people around her are dressed in black in direct opposition; these are characters who are opposed to her wishes to form a family or not, to be a sculptor and to be able to sculpt projects with her lover. First her mother appears, arguing that she does not fulfill the role of mother and wife because she is a sculptor. And then Rodin, refusing to have a child with her. At the other bottom side of the page are the faces of two art critics also in black. One of them denying that she is capable of having made her pieces and attributing them to Rodin and the other one accepting that they are hers but rejecting them because of their open sensuality.

She claims Rodin is her destined partner so that they can develop great sculptural projects together, amalgamating art and the erotic love that exists between them. But with her face falling into darkness, Rodin refuses and she casts him out. Little by little her hair is released panel by panel. She compares her sculptures, Rodin's *Kiss*, to her Sakountala, in which the king recognizes his beloved and the son he had with her. Camille abandons herself to the darkness of confinement and decides to abhor men for the contempt they show for her work. Águeda resorts to a scene in which Camille cannot return from the darkness without distorting her wild eye, which, like a Spanish fan, expands and fades until turning into the waves that she sculpted in the stone. The comic ends when she, divided in half between shadow (the black) and light (the white), turns into tree branches and flourishes rooted under the surface, with the wavy-textured sculpture in which the lovers embrace leaning for the dance. The sad story finishes with her being abandoned in a madhouse. A woman who tried to be an artist, mother and lover at the same time but instead of fighting for her emancipation clamored for her lover as if he were a dominant and organizer "totality" of all aspects of Camille's life. And yet, her work as sculptor earned her recognition as an artist before her unfortunate confinement. After her death in the mental institution, her remains were abandoned by her family and then lost after the building was reformed. Camille's decision was difficult to make, because she was raised in a society that offered marriage as the only way for emancipation, and the man whom she loved did not want to marry or have children with her.

In the next issue of *Agathós*, Águeda explored the Brontë sisters, the three British novelists from the 19th century who first under male pseudonyms, and then using their own names, wrote books still considered today popular classics pieces of literature and often adapted to the cinema such as *Jane Eyre* (1847) or *Wuthering Heights* (1847). "La fuerza de tres" ("The Force of Three," 2015) a fiction created by Águeda, seems to capture a moment in the lives of the three sisters when, under pressure from their father and brother, they agreed to emancipate as women from their male relatives and to be writers and teachers rather than marry to escape from the desolate place where they lived (Figure 11.3). Unlike Camille, the sisters chose to become financially emancipated and Charlotte, after saying goodbye to her sisters, resolved to see the world and free herself, knowing that they had to stay. This comic has as a 19th-century theme in common with Camille: the incompatibility between being a married woman and being an artist. Although the comic does not show it, Charlotte dies a year after marrying, having abandoned her career as a writer against her will.

The most radical transgression that Águeda carries out is a fabulous emancipation that transcends freedom, in which a powerful imagination, an intense female creativity processed as madness implies the transformation of "the bodies" of the protagonist. "Penelope" (Noriega, 2011), based on the story by Gladys Cámere

FIGURE 11.3 La fuerza de tres (Águeda s/n).

Source: Noriega, A. (año). Agathos, Lima, AgueDet Publicaciones.

(1997) tells the story of a cat that lives in the house of a rich woman and describes the good life she has. We even perceive her carpeted path, just as she does, that leads her from the bedroom in which she was, to the room in which the owner of her house cuddles her. This contact lulls her into an erotic dream with illustrations of nude humans by Aubrey Beardsley (1872–1898). Tired of the privileges that keep her locked up, she decides to emancipate herself and discover free life. She walks through the streets that host the migrant poverty of the slums of old Lima. And suddenly, when she compares herself to the street cats, the cat remembers that she was a human woman first: sensual, highly desired, drawn like the reclining nudes in a 19th-century painting, and known as "La Gata." So far, liberation seems to have awakened a consciousness that lived hidden under an extreme distortion of reality. She continues to remember, how one day she really became that cat, how she was found in a garbage can and picked up for being Siamese. The man who picks her up takes her to her mistress, who chooses the name Penelope for her. After that, a new memory is presented: in an erotic scene in which the sheet that covers her has the shape of a vulva, she remembers how she became physically a cat (her paws and her mustache appear in various panels). She becomes aware and she wakes up in a hospital and hears a lady tell the man who picked her up from the garbage dump, who is a doctor in this reality, that Penelope is a woman who has been picked up from a garbage dump and taken to a psychiatric hospital for believing she is a cat. And although she does not have the strength to oppose it, she considers that it will continue to be a lie that she is a human. A deep transgression in which the woman wants to emancipate herself from being human and she manages to convince herself that she can sustain her life like a cat. The open question that remains is what must have happened to her as a human to reject her nature.

The main purpose of Águeda with *Agathós* is to make known to women and the general public "outstanding" biographical episodes (interview with the author, 2021, p. 4) of the life and work of valuable women who are not so well known outside the cultural field, but that she considers should be references of the women of the past to consolidate the conscience about the great effort that costs our freedom.

The bodies and art of Ale Torres

Ale Torres studied at the Trujillo Superior School of Fine Arts and produces short comics fictions starring women. One of her first works presents tiny women without conscience, but unlike Marisa who uses eyes without light, in "Mujer bonita" (Torres, 2014) the eyes of a woman that an organ grinder uses as a dancer, are exorbitant, accompanying a laugh feigned as the dogs surround her like prey. The gargantuan presence of the organ grinder forces us to think that she wants to save herself, like the women also shown in the comic who are carried in pet cages by men who walk next to a display case that exposes the sale of female breast prostheses. Is she really a woman? Is the obvious and final question, because before dancing she puts on each eye, a mouth, sews her breasts, puts on a wig, then dresses. In short, she is not really a woman, but rather constructs herself as one, to entertain men and dogs from her cage. No emancipated behavior is shown, but her exorbitant look and her laugh remain as an indelible indication of hidden emotions.

In "Baby" (Torres, 2010) the first approach to the relationship between emancipation and art is presented as a transgressive mechanism of order, when the client of a prostitute leaves his book of poems in her room. She is about to die from an advanced disease, as we infer from the panels showing her medication, but she has found in his poems a reason to fall in love, to live the illusion of helping him to publish the book, of being able to give him everything she has without worrying because it is in exchange: she would stop being a prostitute and would become a girlfriend. The poetry allows her to regain the feeling of love that she had forgotten, freeing her from the commercialization of her body, from her marginalized labor, although as Barrancos argues, it is not a question of integral emancipation (13). A colleague clarifies the message for her: she warns her that she is wasting the savings that should be meant for her health, but Baby is determined to change in the last moments of her life. Ironically, the story ends with her walking, looking happily, with a pair of second-hand clothes sellers passing by behind her, a harsh metaphor for the business of old and used things. "Nothing will ever be the same" concludes the comic with Baby smiling.

In "Day Dreaming" (Torres, 2016) (Figure 11.4), Ale starts the story by showing us in the first panel the protagonist's memories. "Day Dreaming" tells the process of a woman who must accept the end of a primarily sexual relationship. Hurt and with destructive thoughts, she is visited by a colleague dedicated to art like her, Barbie, who distracts her by bringing up in the conversation Mario Vargas Llosa's marriage with Isabel Preysler. Although she wants to talk about art with him, she gets distracted and returns to the ecstasy she experienced with her former partner. Barbie again distracts her, praising her murals and comparing them to Matisse's artwork, but she keeps thinking about the sexual encounters she has had after the fallout, which have not satisfied her. Barbie rebukes her. Only Vargas Llosa's ex-wife has the right to be depressed for having been abandoned and replaced by such a beautiful woman. Day reacts and declares that "suffering from love is so superficial." One day, she returns to the café where she was with Barbie and becomes aware of how much better she feels. The emancipation that art allows her has required Barbie's persistence. Her art allows the recovery of sexual desire for other bodies as a way to recover her own body. The need for awareness is extremely high in Ale's work, making visible new social norms and control of emotions. The protagonists, not in vain, belong to the social class that can afford to work in the fine arts market whenever they want. Finally, on "El día de la Marmota" ("Groundhog Day," Torres, 2018) Ale is inspired by Bill Murray's endearing film (in which the day repeats itself until the frustrated protagonist manages to feel empathy) to describe how the artist who stars in the comic, looking for a man who knows how to treat her as an artist without telling her how to manage her life and even her work, without even really having met her. She wonders what happens to men and yet she has sexual relations with each one despite their recommendation to get another job or to give her material for inspiration (Figure 11.5). Aware of this, the decorations in her

FIGURE 11.4 Day Dreaming (Torres 30).

Source: Torres, Ale. "Day Dreaming." Carboncito. N° 19 (2016): 110–113.

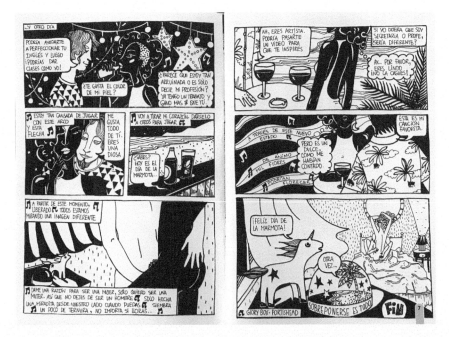

FIGURE 11.5 Feliz día de la Marmota (Torres 1).

Source: Torres, Ale. "El día de la Marmota." La Otra Damita. Amor (2018): 4–7.

room refer again to Groundhog Day. Like it or not, without a doubt we are seeing an emancipated behavior. Being an artist allows her to discriminate but at the same time she does not resolve her still-existing desire to find a stable partner; an enigma of the sphinx for both.

Ale's artistic proposal to access consciousness can be framed within the psychedelic aesthetic and particularly in the psychedelic experience that imagines it as lustful and sensual, hedonistic as it gets into the body through the effect of lysergic acid bringing a new notion of self-awareness and corporeality. It is an aesthetic result from a rethinking of the notions of perception, during the 1960s was taken as a tool of liberation and at the same time as one for escapism. Perhaps the same thing happens with Ale's characters, insofar as art can be interpreted as liberating her female characters from the bonds of marriage and motherhood that obscure the woman's conscience, or as a tool that allows them to pretend that they were liberated from those bonds but leaving latent the need to fill their absence.

Conclusion

Comics made by women and developed in the Peruvian fanzine circuit were born with a critical spirit of gender roles, attributes, and stereotypes. The work of Marisa

Godínez, during the 20th century, presents a woman without conscience due to her body being subjected, an act represented in a surreal way, and also because of the lack of light in her eyes, an image that greatly affects the emotions and feelings of the person who reads it carefully. At the beginning of the 21st century, Águeda Noriega, the first professional Peruvian cartoonist, publishes her fanzine *Agathós* in which she stages episodes where female artists from various fields must decide between their artistic career and their role as mother and wife, resulting in the choice for art as a form of liberation, at the same time as an impossible act to be able to reconcile both roles. These stories take place in the 19th century.

However, after studying a group of comics by Ale Torres, published as fanzines, we see that the incompatibility between art and the traditional role of mother and wife is seen as a balance that, ultimately, favors women, since they use art as a shield that allows sexual relations, but prevents them of a greater bonding with men, since they realize that they will not understand female artists, and thus this will cause depression and insecurity. It should be noted that this evolution goes through different aesthetic stages: surrealism, engraving, psychedelia. The children disappear, and the body of the protagonists gets free from sexual repression; so that in Águeda's work, the women can be shown naked and in Ale's comics women and men can be drawn having sex. Therefore, we can conclude that not only emancipatory behavior appears partially but increasingly in the comics characters of these authors, but also that drawing them for a fanzine has liberated them as cartoonists from the limitations and censorship that these publications would suffer in mainstream media.

References

Barrancos, D. (2020). Retando la norma: Mujeres emancipadas. *Mora*, N° 25, 11–20.
Cámere, G. (1997). *En primera persona*. Arteidea.
Catalá, J., Drinot, P., y Scorer, J. (2017). *Comics and memory in Latin America*. University of Pittsburgh Press.
Greene, S. (2017). *Punk y Revolución: 7 interpretaciones de la realidad subterránea*. Pesopluma.
Leonardini, N. (2003). *El grabado en el Perú republicano: diccionario histórico*. Universidad Nacional Mayor de San Marcos.
Noriega, A. (2011). *Camille*. In: *Agathos*. AgueDet Publicaciones.
Noriega, A. (2012). *Alter Ego*. El gato descalzo.
Noriega, A. (2015). *La fuerza de las tres*. In: *Agathos*. AgueDet Publicaciones.
Orvig, H. (2004). También antes hubo algo. Seminario nacional 25 años de feminismo en el Perú: historia, confluencias, perspectivas, pp. 18–23. Flora Tristán.
Padua, J. (1979). *Analfabetismo en tres países latinoamericanos. El analfabetismo en América Latina: Un estudio empírico con especial referencia a los casos de Perú, México y Argentina*. Ciudad de México: Colegio de México, pp. 57–166.
Pérez Galindo, A. (1980). *La Agonía de Mariátegui. La polémica con la Komintern*. Centro de Estudios y Promoción del Desarrollo.
Sagástegui, C. (2003). *Los primeros ochenta años de la historieta peruana (1887–1967)*. Lima, Instituto Cultural Peruano Norteamericano.

Sagástegui, C. (2016). Amando nuestro cuerpo. El género en la gráfica de Marisa Godínez. In Villar, A. (editor). *Bumm! Historieta y humor gráfico en el Perú: 1978–1992*. Lima, Reservoir Books, Penguin Random House Grupo Editorial, pp. 42–53.

Torres, A. (2010). Baby. In: Román, B. *et al.* (editor). *Venus Ataca. 10 historietistas peruanas*. Lima, Contracultura.

Torres, A. (2014). Mujer Bonita. *Carboncito*, N° 14 (2014), 1–5.

Torres, A. (2016). Day dreaming. *Carboncito*, N° 19 (2016), 110–113.

Torres, A. (2018). El día de la Marmota. *La Otra Damita. Amor*, 4–7.

12
COMICS AS A MEANS TO ILLUSTRATE SEXUAL DISSIDENCE

Guadalupe and *Poder Trans*

Janek Scholz

Introduction[1]

In their 2012 comic book *Guadalupe*, the Brazilian poet Angelica Freitas and the Brazilian comic artist Odyr tell the story of the 29-year-old Mexican woman Guadalupe. She lives with her rebel grandmother in Mexico City and is worried about how life is going to be in the future, as she is about to turn 30, but still not very clear about who she wants to be. There is also Minerva, a trans woman, who Guadalupe calls "her uncle." Minerva took care of the young protagonist when her parents went away to the United States without any notice, leaving the girl behind.

The following article aims at discussing examples of sexual dissidence in *Guadalupe*, analyzing the lives of the three women through a decolonial lens. Referring to decolonial concepts of feminism and transfeminism can be highly productive when reading the text and raises questions about what Leandro Colling calls *artivismo das dissidências sexuais e de gênero*, that is, the way, art and activism interact in a Latin American queer context. I will start with a brief introduction into the work of the two authors, to then continue with a discussion of sexual dissidence in *Guadalupe*, paying particular attention at the interplay of forms of sexual self-determination of the three women and Latin American decolonial thinking. The second part of the article will examine the concept of *artivismo* and its feasibility for the present text. To conclude, not only questions of advocacy will be discussed, especially cis-advocacy for transgender issues, but also the opportunities that come along with the medium of comics when talking about sexual dissidence.

Odyr and Angelica Freitas

Odyr Bernardi was born in 1967 in Pelotas, Brazil. He published several comic strips in newspapers and magazines, including *Folha de São Paulo*, *Le monde diplomatique*

DOI: 10.4324/9781003333296-15

Brasil, O Globo and others. His work has also been published in several edited volumes both in Brazil and in Argentina. Before publishing *Guadalupe* with Angelica Freitas in 2012, he launched his first comic book, *Copacabana* (Lobo & Odyr 2014), a co-production with Lobo who did the writing, in 2009. His comic book *A Revolução dos Bichos* [The Revolution of Animals] was published in 2018 – an adaptation of George Orwell's *Animal Farm*. The book gained the famous Troféu HQ Mix in 2019 for the best literary adaptation.

Angelica Freitas works mainly as a poet and translator from Spanish to Portuguese. She was born in 1973 in Pelotas, Brazil, and worked as a journalist in the first years of her career. She then started publishing poetry in edited volumes and launched her first book *Rilke Shake* in 2007. Her poems are translated to Spanish, English, German and French and are regularly published in international magazines like *Dia rio de Poesía* (Argentina), *Águas Furtadas* (Portugal), *Hilda* (Germany) and *Aufgabe* (USA). Her 2012 book *Um útero é do tamanho de um punho* [A uterus is the size of a fist] was a huge success and has been translated into several languages. In 2020, she launched the book *Canções de atormentar* [Songs of Torment]. *Guadalupe* was her first graphic novel/comic book.

It is important to point out that both authors worked on topics of sexual dissidence before. *Copacabana*, the 2009 comic book by Odyr and Lobo, tells the story of female prostitutes in Rio de Janeiro's famous neighborhood and a crime story they involuntarily get involved in.[2] The comic presents topics of love, fear, anger and hope, as well as the tension between economic needs and sexual self-determination, without falling back into clichés and prejudice.[3] Angelica Freitas' poems are generally very feminist, as the title of her book *Um útero é do tamanho de um punho* [A uterus is the size of a fist] already suggests. In the book, there are poems about women in several phases of their lives, including a poem about a trans woman, where the lyrical "I" writes a letter to the parents back home, telling them that Thailand is a beautiful spot where they even have elephants. Subsequently, she remembers scenes from her childhood and youth, when her father told her not to behave in such a girlish way, to finally reveal to her parents that she had a surgery and now is a woman for real. That such an association is somewhat problematic will be discussed later in the article.

Guadalupe has been discussed in three academic publications so far. On the one hand, David William Foster analyzes the gender and queer aspects of the comic book and stresses its "constant . . . antimasculine animosity" (Foster 2016, 121). Paulo da Luz Moreira on the other hand focuses on the Brazilian-Mexican entanglements and informs the readers about a journey to Mexico that Angelica Freitas undertook, before writing both Guadalupe and *Um útero é do tamanho de um punho*.

> Freitas was invited to a funeral with live music accompaniment, which is the trigger for a road trip in *Guadalupe*, whose protagonist's grandmother's last wish was to be buried with music in Oaxaca. Freitas never attended the funeral because she accompanied another friend on a visit to an abortion clinic in Mexico City. The hostility outside the clinic, where protesters

confronted patients and clinic workers left an impression on Freitas, who started at the time writing *Um útero é do tamanho de um punho [A Uterus Is the Size of a Fist]*.

(Moreira 2013, 165)

Moreira also discusses the evolution of the images of the comic. He cites Odyr who says that his imagination of the Mexican setting was half invented and half researched, as he did some research online, but also had several Mexican friends sending him photos and films to rely on (Moreira 2013, 166). Finally, Francesca Dennstedt uses *Guadalupe* to come to terms with her conception of a queer decolonial temporality and a "Latin American future" based on the *muxe*'s positionality between life and death. Hers is an intriguing approach that dialogues with the approach chosen in the present text, even though she dedicates huge parts of her article to terminological questions on the concepts of *queerness* versus *cuirness* – a debate that will not be taken into account in the present text.[4]

Guadalupe: sexual dissidence in Latin America

The comic book *Guadalupe* (Freitas & Odyr 2016), which the two aforementioned artists planned and realized together, has a rather complex plot. It tells the story of three women: Guadalupe, Minerva and Elvira. At a certain point in their lives, all of them struggled with the question of what it means to be a woman. Elvira, the mother of Minerva, lived her life as a rebel girl in the countryside, until she got married to an older man who wanted her to take responsibility as a housewife and mother. She gave in, mostly to please her parents and especially her father, but had some feelings for another woman, too. She even had a romantic relationship with that woman, Juanita. As her son grew older, he started behaving differently, which is why his father called him "um filho maricón," a "faggot son." To avoid any danger and harm toward her children, and after being threatened with death by her – equally betraying – husband because of her romantic affair with Juanita, Elvira decided to leave him and move to Mexico City together with her two kids. There, she moved back to her libertine behavior which is condensed in her interest in scooters and her rebellious way of driving them. Consequently, she dies in a traffic accident, even though it remains an unresolved question whether it was truly an accident or suicide.

Minerva, her child, took the chance of living in Mexico City to fully develop a proper gender identity and gender expression. Even though Guadalupe, Minerva's niece, refers to Minerva as her "uncle," the story leaves no doubt that she is a trans woman who formerly worked in a variety show, doing drag, but later on came out as trans and settled down, living a life as a female owner of a bookstore. Minerva took care of her niece Guadalupe, when the mother of the latter, Minerva's sister, unexpectedly left the country. Minerva's trans identity is known to her family and nobody seems to have any problems with it. Guadalupe might refer to Minerva as her "uncle" not because of disrespect or rejection, but due to the late coming out and her being used to having an uncle for the most part of her life.[5]

Finally, Guadalupe is at the advent of her 30th birthday and thinking a lot about what it means to be a woman in today's society. Her life is somewhat stable, even if she has no partner and does not fancy getting married and settling down soon. She is working in the bookstore of her "uncle" Minerva and feels that everything will continue like that forever, unless she does not make a radical change, leaving everything behind. Certainly, expectations of the society about what it means to be a woman are reflected here, for example when her friend Chino tells her that it is time for her to marry. While Elvira gave up her independent lifestyle for the sake of her parents and her children and submitted herself into a life as a housewife, Minerva gave up her flamboyant life as a star in the local variety show for the sake of her niece. Both women challenged society with their gender expression, but came to terms with societal expectations for the sake of other people. Now, it is Guadalupe – a representative of the next generation – who is concerned with the stereotypical life of a woman and the options that are left to live a different life. Her name, of course, is paradigmatic. Gloria Anzaldúa describes the transformation of Guadalupe from *Coatlalopeuh* to *la Virgen de Guadalupe*, including her condemnation by the Azteca-Mexica culture, that banned her from being a creator goddess, having both a light and a dark side, to being a creature of the underworld and thus depriving her of her powers (cf. Anzaldúa 2007, 49). The Christian Church continued with this split, making Guadalupe a chaste virgin.

> Today, *la Virgen de Guadalupe* is the single most potent religious, political and cultural image of the Chicano/*mexicano*. She, like my race, is a synthesis of the old world and the new, of the religion and culture of the two races in our psyche, the conquerors and the conquered. She is the symbol of the *mestizo* true to his or her Indian values.
>
> (Anzaldúa 2007, 52)

With the above-described three alternative forms of womanhood – lesbian and courageous, transgender and libertine and single and independent – the comic challenges heteronormative, cisnormative and patriarchal expectations. Still, the plot does not stop there. After the death of Elvira, Minerva and Guadalupe decide to carry the corpse to Elvira's hometown Oaxaca, in southern Mexico, both because it is the grandmother's natal soil, and because her only true moment of romantic love took place there. Juanita, the woman she fell in love with a long time ago is still alive and joins the funeral of Elvira. Before reaching their destination, though, the road trip is constantly in danger because of a henchman of Xyzótlan,[6] who tries to steal the dead body's soul for his master to avoid the latter losing influence in the pantheon of Mexican gods. As people resign to believe in the god's power, it is the henchman's task to find a soul that died only recently and bring it to his master. To prevent him from doing so and to fight the evil power of Xyzótlan, Minerva transforms into a super heroine at a certain point in the story, relying upon the superpowers of the *muxe*, a Mexican third gender.[7] Foster reads the fight between the Aztec/Toltec god and the three women as a fight between a world of toxic masculinity and a world of queer-feminist liberation. He writes: "The figure of Xyzótlan . . . and his nasty procuring agent . . . clearly function here as icons of an oppressive masculinism that is still a threat to the expanding feminist-queer world the main characters of *Guadalupe* represent." (Foster 2016, 123–124) He continues: "Xyzótlan unquestionably incarnates the abiding masculinism, including still-bed-rock heterosexism, of modern Mexican society. The god is loud and violent and he abuses his henchman both verbally and physically" (Foster 2016, 124).[8]

Even though David William Foster's analysis of *Guadalupe* is focusing mainly on sexual dissidence, it mistakes one key moment of the plot, as it is not Guadalupe who turns into the *muxe maravilha* and evokes the power of the Village People, as Foster claims (2016, 124 and 126), but Minerva. This is important, as it brings together modern concepts of gender identity/gender expression (i.e., transgender on the one hand and the Village People on the other) and precolonial forms of a gender systems that go far beyond Western binarism (i.e., *muxe*). Dennstedt also points to the "collision between the past . . . and the present" (2018, 42) which is represented by the *muxe maravilha*. According to Dennstedt, the (US-American!) present is represented by the Village People and Wonder Woman,[9] whereas "the ancient drug rituals, performed through eating a mushroom that reveals her *muxe-dad*" (Dennstedt 2018, 42) seem to represent a connection to a precolonial past. "The muxes [also] enact their Zapotecan past by adapting the traditional vela to the more recent necessities of making their gender/sexual dissidence visible" (Dennstedt 2018, 38). Those acts of decolonizing elements of modern pop culture and mixing them with traditional iconography are important in *Guadalupe*. Next to the references to Wonder Woman and the Village People, there is another reference to US-American pop culture, namely the fact that the invented "Mescal Comic Production" play with the name of the famous US-American comic label Marvel (cf. Foster 2016, 124).

Even though Dennstedt's article is primarily focusing on such moments of crossing temporalities in Guadalupe, it still misses one key image in which past, present and future merge, namely the mirror of *Popolancomelatle*. This mirror, that allows the owners to see their future 20 years from then, represents cyclical time in the comic book: On the one hand, it is a symbol of the past, namely the old Mexican deities whose influence decreases more and more, on the other hand, it shows the future that still can be changed in the present. Gloria Anzaldúa pays particular attention to the mirror, too. She writes, that the mirror is "the place where the souls of the dead live" (Anzaldúa 2007, 64) and that in ancient times it served to "reveal a vision concerning the future of the tribe and the will of the gods" (Anzaldúa 2007, 64). She puts the mirror and the act of seeing and being seen in direct contact with what she calls the *Coatlicue* state. *Coatlicue* is the "goddess of birth and death, [she] gives and takes away life; she is the incarnation of cosmic processes" (Anzaldúa 2007, 68).

> *Coatlicue* depicts the contradictory. In her figure, all the symbols important to the religion and philosophy of the Aztecs are integrated. Like Medusa, the Gorgon, she is a symbol of the fusion of opposites: the eagle and the serpent,

FIGURE 12.1 Angelica Freitas/Odyr: *Guadalupe* (2012), no page numbers.

heaven and the underworld, life and death, mobility and immobility, beauty and horror.

(Anzaldúa 2007, 69)

What does it mean, then, that Guadalupe throws the mirror away at the end of the story? On the one hand, it is a total break with the indigenous religion and beliefs; on the other, it is an act against binarism, as *Coatlicue*, according to Anzaldúa, represents both extremes of any spectrum and thus is an invitation for crossing the boundaries between one world and the other. The final panel of the comic book shows Guadalupe not only throwing the mirror away, but as a passenger on a boat or ship. It is, thus, a statement against conventionalism on several levels: On a first – more temporal – level, the mirror as a symbol for an indigenous past and a predetermined future, as well as a symbol for the *Coatlicue* state and thus for a binary system (including possible crossings) has no further authority. On a second level, which is more spatial, it is noteworthy that she is on a ship and thus neither in the big city, nor in the hinterland. Indeed, none of the two spaces represent a truly decolonial potential: one might assume that the city stands for colonialism and Western gender systems, whereas the countryside allows a more precolonial lifestyle within a non-binary gender system.[10] Quite the opposite is the case in the comic book, as it is precisely not the state or town of Oaxaca, where Minerva can live her life as a transwoman or *muxe* to the fullest, but Mexico City. Still, it is important to point out that the comic neither links the countryside exclusively to a precolonial past, where non-binary gender systems happened to be part of the societal structure,

FIGURE 12.2 Angelica Freitas/Odyr: *Guadalupe* (2012), no page numbers.

nor does it represent the metropolis as a place where exclusively modern gender systems are lived and accepted. Elvira queered – at least for some time – the Christian values of the countryside and the heteronormative patriarchal system. Minerva queers the modern cisnormative gender system of the metropolis and tries to reconnect to her indigenous past by consuming ritual magic mushrooms from a shaman.

Guadalupe, being on a ship, might be a symbol for something radically new to come, that lies neither in the past, nor in the present, neither in the countryside, nor in the metropolis. It is a different time and a different space – a queer time and space, maybe – that she, as the symbol of the *mestizo* (as Anzaldúa puts it), inaugurates in her act of throwing the mirror into the sea. It is a radical act that none of the previous generations fully achieved.

Anyway, it cannot be ignored that her act is a rather individual one, that goes against a communitarian idea of feminism as it was, for example, proclaimed by the Guatemalan feminist Lorena Cabnal. Indeed, none of the three women in Guadalupe can rely upon a strong local feminist community, except Minerva, connecting both to a Mexican *muxedad* and the international LGBTIQ-scene. The women in Guadalupe strongly question societal expectations, but are not part of the *levante* of activists that collectively and joyfully celebrate sexual dissidence and disobedience, as it will be discussed in the following chapter.

Sexual dissidence and comics: two ways of *artivismo*

Leandro Colling states that

> a maioria das pessoas e coletivos que integram o que estamos chamando de artivismos das dissidências sexuais e de gênero no Brasil da atualidade diz não à pulsão de morte, ao fracasso e à infelicidade e se constituiu em um *levante*

> . . . Nesse *levante*, desobedecer, às vezes inclusive com alegria, é um verbo muito mais apropriado do que fracassar.
>
> (Colling 2021, 112)[11]

What Colling calls a happy and positive disobedience is certainly one of the main tendencies of present queer movements in Latin America. Nevertheless, two forms of *artivismo* have to be distinguished. First, there is the typical form, that is defined by Colling and others: pieces of art that put the activism right in the center of the work and where the authors position themselves in a state of joyful disobedience (one might even call it a *gay* disobedience in the prior sense of the word *gay*). Those texts accuse social structures or certain behavior and offer an alternative thinking "que vai além da dicotomia tristeza ou alegria, porque os sentimentos se misturam e recombinam o tempo todo" (Colling 2021, 120).[12] Such pieces of art are usually produced independently in low numbers and consequently do not reach a huge audience, if not online. The second type of *artivismo* might be less obvious, but is still an important subcategory: texts like *Guadalupe* also accuse societal structures and stereotypes, but in a far less obvious or transgressive way. As they are published by a huge publishing house, in this case *Companhia das letras*, they do reach a broad audience, including people that never thought about sexual dissidence, feminism and trans issues before. Such readers are more likely to get engaged in debates about these topics, when the debates are not overly determined, but more subtle instead. So, a huge potential of these more mainstream texts might be that they are able to sensitize people to subversive topics. Still, a lot more caution is needed when reading these texts, especially when they treat topics that are not part of the author's personal experience and the author's position has not been made clear at the very beginning. That does not mean that advocacy as such is always problematic, but even the best intentions can lead to negative results.

In the case of *Guadalupe*, the comic talks about a trans woman (or *muxe*). Even though Minerva is depicted in a rather positive way and her family is somewhat at peace with her gender identity and gender expression, when Minerva is introduced as a former star of the local variety show it still evokes cliches about trans women working in the entertainment industry. Furthermore, when the comic talks about Minerva's time on stage, it somehow implies that instead of a trans woman, readers should read her as a crossdresser.[13] A tendency that is strengthened by the fact that Guadalupe misgenders Minerva throughout the whole book. This observation is reinforced by Angelica Freitas' aforementioned poem *mulher depois*. The woman in the poem says: "me operei e virei mulher" (Freitas 2012, 35)[14] – a sentence that implies that being a woman is necessarily connected to genitalia and that consequently every trans woman without a surgery still needs to be regarded as a man. This kind of false advocacy is problematic, as it reinforces typical gender stereotypes instead of deconstructing them, or, as Letícia Nascimento puts it: "A interrogação se nós, mulheres transsexuais e travestis, somos ou não mulheres, é um martelar constante, dúvida produzida pelo não enquadramento de nossas experiências dentro do CIStema colonial moderno de gênero" (Nascimento 2021, 17).[15] *Guadalupe* is certainly a book that has the potential to call into question Western expectations about how a woman has to behave in society, as both negative consequences of such expectations as well as alternative forms of behavior are discussed in the book in a subtle way, without neglecting that the story first and foremost is about a funny and entertaining road trip.

On the other hand, works that come from people that are deeply involved in social campaigns make the necessity for activism and social change much more visible. As the vocabulary and the visual language of such productions might be less flowery and as such texts or images are often produced independently, they usually reach a smaller audience and have difficulties in convincing the mainstream readers of their cause.[16] With the help of the Internet, the situation changed remarkably, though. Artists could now easily connect themselves with one another and create networks like the POC-CON, a queer comic festival in Brazil, that was inaugurated in 2019.[17] The festival grows bigger every year and is an important milestone for the visibility of queer comic artists and their work about sexual dissidence, including trans authors and their stories. Alongside these networks, social media like Facebook and Instagram help authors to directly get in touch with their audience and use their activist comics as a form of outreach whose visibility is no longer tied to a geographical region. Brazilian transgender artists that engage in such forms of self-publication are, to name only a few: Laerte,[18] Luiza Lemos[19] and Alice Pereira.[20] The work of these artists goes far beyond the representation of trans women in *Guadalupe* or *um útero é do tamanho de um punho*, as they put into question not only gender roles in society, but the connection of sex and gender as a whole and consequently claim that being a woman has nothing to do with having a vagina.

Another example which is certainly part of what Colling calls the *levante*, is a collection of comics on trans issues that have been published in Argentina in 2019, entitled *Poder Trans – Historieta Latinoamericana* (Aguirre et al, 2019).[21] The collection is the product of the *Convocatoria Latinoamericana de Historieta Trans 2018*. Twenty-two artists from both Argentina and Brazil participated in the book with stories that cover a wide range of topics, such as the relation toward the own body and the influence of hormones (pp. 27–28, 43–50 and 89–92), family and kinship (pp. 12, 108–115 and 122–123), sex (pp. 23–26), religion (pp. 71–80), hypocritical morals when it comes to marriage and monogamy (pp. 124–133), problems with local authorities and institutions (pp. 81–86) or even violence (pp. 8–9 and 129–131). Particularly, the vulnerability of the trans community, above all for trans women of color and for elderly trans people, is still extremely high and thus needs to be openly named and accused. *Guadalupe* fails to do that. With the figure of Minerva, Freitas and Odyr created a person that is not affected by any of these topics, even though the violence against the trans community and the numerous *transcídios*, the deliberate murder of a person for being trans, in Brazil and elsewhere, continue to be a huge problem on an individual, collective and institutional level.[22]

Alongside the vast topics that are treated in *Poder Trans* and that, of course, more or less influence the lives of any trans person in Latin America and around the world, the book also contains more didactic or educational pieces, be it about the distinction between gender identity, gender expression, sexual orientation and sexual characteristics (i.e., genitalia) and the plurality beyond any binarism (pp. 56–60 and 87–88), be it about the local history of sexual dissidence and the past acceptance and high social status of so called two-spirits (pp. 76–77 and 116–117) (see Figure 12.3).

With this second example, the impact of comics becomes obvious, when talking about sexual dissidence in a Latin American context. *Poder Trans* collects stories, that might be regarded uncomfortable, offensive or even abject for an audience that is not yet used to read stories and see bodies that go beyond the binary system that still dominates the common understanding of the world and, consequently, is an obvious case of the "prazer em transgredir . . . as normas de gênero e sexualidade" (Colling 2021, 120).[23] Comics like these are needed to fully express the complex reality of people that are regarded dissident and to accuse the offenses to which they are still exposed way too often. In this sense, these comics are highly transfeminist:

> O transfeminismo, entretanto, oferece um olhar diferente sobre o feminismo considerado padrão, assim como o feminismo negro, o feminismo lésbico, entre outras perspectivas, também oferecem. Nossas experiências como mulheres transsexuais e travestis são contribuições para o modo como entendemos o feminismo no campo das lutas políticas e das proposições teóricas.
> (Nascimento 2021, 21)[24]

Final remarks

There is no doubt that comics and queerness perfectly fit. Darieck Scott and Ramzi Fawaz write that "there is something queer about comics" (Scott and Fawaz 2018, 197) and that "comics are *formally* queer" (Scott and Fawaz 2018, 202). Hilary Chute even claims that "we might consider queerness part of the DNA of comics" (Chute 2017, 351). A first explanation for this can be found in Nina Eckhoff-Heindl's and Véronique Sina's edited volume on spaces between (the panels): "comics have the potential to destabilize and blur binary oppositions such as subject/object, nature/culture, man/woman, authentic/artificial, good/bad, abled/disabled, normal/abnormal or black/white" (Eckhoff-Heindl and Sina 2020, v). Scott and Fawaz provide an answer that focuses mainly on the effects that queer comics cause in the readers:

> Comics function . . . as queer orientation devices, productively directing readers toward deviant bodies that refuse to be fixed in one image or frame, toward new desires for fantasy worlds that rebel against the constraints of everyday life, and toward new kinds of counterpublic affiliations among readers who identify with the queer, deviant, maladjusted form called comics.
> (Scott and Fawaz 2018, 203)

Keeping this in mind, comics on sexual dissidence fulfil a double function in a Latin American context. Maria Lugones makes it quite clear that for a decolonial approach to sexuality and gender, a deconstruction of what she calls "the dark side of the gender system" is needed:

> The "dark side" of the gender system was and is thoroughly violent. We have began [sic] to see the deep reductions of anamales, anafemals, and "third" gender from their ubiquitous participation in ritual, decision making, economics; their reduction to animality, to forced sex with white colonizers, to such deep labour exploitation that often people died working.
> (Lugones 2008, 16)

She points to the acceptance of many precolonial societies toward fluid gender systems and diverse forms of gender expression[25] and promotes a "need for impure communit[ies]" (Lugones 2002, 58) that allow the individuals to fully develop an individual, changing, complex identity: "so it is the impulse to reject dichotomies and to live and embody that rejection that gives us some hope of standing together as people who recognize each other in our complexity" (Lugones 2002, 60). This complexity, that is undefinable and stands outside the order, goes hand in hand with decolonial approaches against binarism (cf. Segato 2016) and toward subversive, subaltern and bottom-up models of society.

Angelica Freitas' and Odyr's comic book *Guadalupe* (Freitas & Odyr 2016) is successful in discussing decolonial feminist approaches from Latin America, as it gives unexpected answers to the question of what it means to be a woman in a modern Mexican society, but apart from the feminist perspective, it recoils from discussing the question of what makes a person a woman und thus fails in comprehensively discussing trans issues. As a first step to get in touch with comics on sexual dissidence in Latin America, *Guadalupe* certainly is an important milestone and reaches a broad audience. When it comes to sexual dissidence, queerness/cuirness and impurity, though, the full potential of comics is only made use of when both the images and the language (and thus the topics) truly transgress societal expectations and gender norms in their complexity. There is no doubt, then, that comics as a medium has the potential to illustrate subversive approaches and alternative forms of community building and, thus, to take a clear stand against hatred, harassment and populist simplification that until today is present in a world that still suffers the influence of right-wing politics, heteronormativity and (neo-)colonialism.

Notes

1 As a preliminary remark, I feel the need to clearly position myself: I'm writing this text as a queer cis man from Europe and this fact puts me in a privileged position in many ways. When one talks about discrimination from a privileged position, the most important thing one can and have to do is listen. I listened and learned a lot in the past, thanks to many wonderful people, and I continue to listen and learn on a daily basis. So,

if anybody feels uncomfortable with what I've written about trans issues and/or Latin America, I would be more than happy to hearing from you: janek.scholz@uni-koeln.de.
2   For an extensive discussion of *Copacabana*, see Foster 2016, 96–105.
3   Both *Copacabana* and *Guadalupe* are drawn in a rather heavy handed black and white style, that is typical for Odyr. While in *Copacabana* the panels are often filled with black, as the background is usually shrouded in swaths or even whole blocks of black, in *Guadalupe* the atmosphere is much brighter and thus much lighter, as the panels focus mainly on the faces of the protagonists, except several eagle-eyed views on Mexico City. That allows Odyr to focus on the mimics of his protagonists without losing his brusque stroke.
4   Colling discusses the applicability of the word *queer* in a Latin American context, saying that local academics and activists are constantly giving local colors to the word *queer*, reframing it with positivity (Colling 2015, 248). A recent discussion of the terms *queer* and *cuir* is to be found in the first 2021 volume of *Periodicús*, entitled *Queer/Cuir Américas* (https://periodicos.ufba.br/index.php/revistaperiodicus/issue/view/2189).
5   Of course, this behavior is still somewhat problematic and one could ask if Guadalupe really supports Minerva's identity or if she is also mocking at her "uncle." Her comments on the changing names could imply such a mindset, even though the relationship between the two women is mostly positive, attentive and loving throughout the whole book.
6   The name of the invented god indicates that with him everything ends as it captures the last three letters of the Latin alphabet XYZ. The figure of Xyzótlan is inspired by the Toltec and Aztec god of the dead, Tezcatlipoca, who is known as a trickster and recognized by his mirror, that shows the future of a person. Both applies for Xyzótlan, too. With regard to Tezcatlipoca, I am deeply grateful to Jasmin Wrobel for sharing with me her vast expertise on Mexican mythology.
7   There are several newspaper reports on the *muxe*, for example, www.bbc.com/mundo/vert-tra-46374110 and www.goethe.de/ins/mx/es/kul/wir/50s/art/21587404.html.
     Media attention increased significantly after the Mexican and the British editions of VOGUE featured Estrella Vazquez on the cover in December 2019, cf. www.theguardian.com/world/2019/nov/21/vogue-cover-features-transgender-muxe-from-mexico-for-the-first-time.
8   It is noteworthy, though, that the victory of Minerva and the Village People over the powers of Xyzótlan also represents a fundamental break in the systems of beliefs. While precolonial indigenous deities lose their influence, modern icons gain a pseudo-religious status, which might be the effect of a global cultural colonialism that often has its origins in the United States.
9   Interestingly enough, Wonder Woman was long supposed to be a queer character which was officially confirmed by DC in 2016, making her an UN Honorary Ambassador for the Empowerment of Women and Girls (cf. Chute 2017, 349 and 388).
10 As it is precisely the city of Juchitán de Zaragoza in the state of Oaxaca that is often connected to the *muxe* (as for example the legend, told within the plot of *Guadalupe*, explains it, too).
11 English translation: "the majority of people and collectives that integrate what we are calling the artivisms of sexual and gender dissidence in Brazil today say no to the death drive, to failure and unhappiness and have constituted themselves in a *levante*. . . . In this *levante*, to disobey, sometimes even with joy, is a much more appropriate verb than to fail" (my translation).
12 English translation: "that goes beyond the dichotomy of sadness or joy, because feelings mix and recombine all the time" (my translation).
13 Indeed, both Foster and Dennstedt call Minerva a "transvestite."
14 English translation: "I had the surgery and turned a woman (my translation).
15 English translation: "the questioning of whether or not we transsexual and transvestite women are women is a constant hammering, a doubt produced by not framing our experiences within the modern colonial gender CIStem" (my translation).

16 One clear example is the Brazilian comic *Garota Siririca* (LoveLove6 2018), that treats topics like feminine masturbation and is rather explicit on a visual level.
17 https://poccon.com.br/ Co-Founder of the POC-CON and a central figure of the Brazilian queer comic scene is Mário César. He published several comic books on sexual dissidence, including *Ciranda da Solidão* (César 2013), *Purpura* (César & Cirne 2016) and the trilogy *Bendita Cura* (César 2018–2021). He also took part of the collection *Poder Trans* that will be discussed later on.
18 Cf. www.instagram.com/laertegenial/ and www.laerte.art.br/ Since the 1980s, Laerte is known as a successful comic artist on a national level. She now uses her popularity to help other trans artists to gain more visibility by sharing their work on her profile or timeline. Laerte also positions herself constantly in discussions about trans rights in Brazil (cf. Scholz and Wrobel 2021).
19 Cf. www.instagram.com/luizalemos39/.
20 Cf. www.instagram.com/alicepereiraart/ and http://alicepereira.iluria.com/.
21 The same publisher: *e(m)r;* launched the book *Historieta LGBTI* in 2017 (Aguirre et al. 2017), including comics on sexual dissidence from artists from Argentina, Colombia and Portugal. A similar project in Brazil is the book *Quadrinhos Queer* by Ellie Irineu et al. (2021).
22 In Brazil, one trans woman is murdered approximately every 48 hours. 175 trans people have been killed in 2020, 68% of the victims were black (cf. www.brasildefato.com.br/2021/01/29/brazil-transgender-murders-increased-41-in-2020/).
23 English translation: "pleasure in transgressing . . . the norms of gender and sexuality" (my translation).
24 English translation: "transfeminism, however, offers a different look on mainstream feminism, just as black feminism, lesbian feminism, and other perspectives also do. Our experiences as transsexual and transvestite women are contributions to the way we understand feminism in the field of political struggles and theoretical propositions" (my translation).
25 Lugones shows that the patriarchal-heterosexual power structure in many cases does not correspond to original models of social order, using the example of the Yoruba, where a non-gendered egalitarianism prevailed – the category "gender" was thus completely unknown and irrelevant for the social order (cf. Lugones 2008, 8). Furthermore, she presents indigenous groups in the Americas who lived a gynecratic egalitarianism, that is, who saw the origin of the world in a female force that organized all things and were thus often part of a more or less elaborate matriarchy. In addition, there was a relative openness of gender (self)determination: third gender and homosexuality were natural parts of the social spectrum (cf. Lugones 2008, 10–11).
26 Last access for all of the pages is August 26, 2021.

List of quoted texts

Comics

Aguirre, G. et al. (2017): *Historieta LGBTI*. Rosario: e(m)r.
Aguirre, G. et al. (2019): *Poder trans. Historieta latino-americana*. Rosario: e(m)r.
César, M. (2013): *Ciranda da Solidão*. São José do Rio Preto: Balão.
César, M. (2018–2021): *Bendita Cura 1–3*. São Paulo: Entre Quadros.
César, M. & Cirne, P. (2016): *Purpura*. São Paulo: SESI-SP.
Freitas, A. & Odyr (2012): *Guadalupe*. São Paulo: Companhia das Letras.
Irineu, E., Borges, G. & Smee, G. (eds.) (2021): *Quadrinhos Queer*. Florianópolis: Skript.
Lobo, S. & Odyr (2014): *Copacabana*. Lisbon: Polvo [= Portuguese Edition].
LoveLove6 (2018): *Garota Siririca Pocket*. Brasília: self-publishing.

Literature

Anzaldúa, G. (2007): *Borderlands – La Frontera. The New Mestiza*. San Francisco: Aunt Lute.
Chute, H. (2017): *Why comics, why queer*. New York City: Harper.
Colling, L. (2015): *Que os outros sejam o normal. Tensões entre movimento LGBT e ativismo queer*. Salvador: EDUFBA.
Colling, L. (2021): "Não ao fracasso. *Levantes* dos artivismos das dissidências sexuais e de gênero no Brasil", in: Luciana Moreira, Doris Wieser (eds.): *A flor de cuerpo. Representaciones del género y de las dissidências sexo-genéricas em Latinoamérica*. Madrid: Iberoamericana, pp. 103–125.
Dennstedt, F. (2018): "'Between Utopian Longings and Everyday Failures'. Imagining a Latin American Future", in: *Arizona Journal of Hispanic Cultural Studies*, Vol. 22, pp. 29–47.
Eckhoff-Heindl, N. & Sina, V. (eds.) (2020): *Spaces Between. Gender, Diversity and Identity in Comics*. Wiesbaden: Springer.
Foster, D. W. (2016): *El Eternauta, Daytripper, and Beyond. Graphic Narrative in Argentina and Brazil*. Austin: University of Texas Press.
Freitas, A. (2012): *Um útero é do tamanho de um punho*. São Paulo: Schwarcz.
Lugones, M. (2002): "Impure Communities", in: Philip Alperson (ed.): *Diversity and Community. An Interdisciplinary Reader*. Hoboken: Wiley-Blackwell, pp. 58–64.
Lugones, M. (2008): "The Coloniality of Gender", in: Duke Trinity College (ed.): *Worlds & Knowledges Otherwise*, Vol. 2, pp. 1–17. <https://globalstudies.trinity.duke.edu/sites/globalstudies.trinity.duke.edu/files/file-attachments/v2d2_Lugones.pdf>.
Moreira, P. da L. (2013): *Literary and Cultural Relations Between Brazil and Mexico. Deep Undercurrents*. New York City: Palgrave Macmillan.
Nascimento, L. (2021): *Transfeminismo*. São Paulo: Jandaíra.
Scholz, J. & Wrobel, J. (2021): "A representação da(s) identidade(s) trans na obra de Larte Coutinho", in: Luciana Moreira, Doris Wieser (eds.): *A flor de cuerpo. Representaciones del género y de las dissidências sexo-genéricas em Latinoamérica*. Madrid: Iberoamericana, pp. 277–303.
Scott, D. & Fawaz, R. (eds.) (2018): "Queer about Comics", in: *American Literature*, Vol. 90, Nr. 2, pp. 197–219.
Segato, R. (2016): "Koloniale/moderne Geschlechterverhältnisse zwischen Dualität und Binarismus", in: Lukas Schmidt, Sabine Schröder (eds.): *Entwicklungstheorien. Klassiker, Kritik und Alternativen*. Wien: Mandelbaum, pp. 386–390.

Websites[26]

http://alicepereira.iluria.com/
https://periodicos.ufba.br/index.php/revistaperiodicus/issue/view/2189
https://poccon.com.br/
www.bbc.com/mundo/vert-tra-46374110
www.goethe.de/ins/mx/es/kul/wir/50s/art/21587404.html
www.instagram.com/alicepereiraart/
www.instagram.com/laertegenial/
www.instagram.com/luizalemos39/
www.laerte.art.br/
www.theguardian.com/world/2019/nov/21/vogue-cover-features-transgender-muxe-from-mexico-for-the-first-time

13
PERVERTION THROUGH FUNNY COMICS

The case of Diego Parés' *Sr. and Sra. Rispo*[1]

Rodrigo O. Ottonello

> *No tengo una risa propia, voy copiando risas ajenas. Pero qué sé yo si detrás de todas las máscaras existe algo, no en mí, sino en todos.*
>
> —Parés, 2007b

Introduction: comics and sexual immorality

1.

The history of comics and the history of sexual immorality shared paths more than once, as in the sexual caricatures of Marie Antoinette at the verge of the French Revolution; as in the conversion of Harry Donenfeld from publisher of spicy and erotic magazines to the publisher of Superman; as when Hugh Hefner, at his peak at the end of the 1950s, signed for *Playboy* the talents of some of the greatest comic artists available (Jack Cole, Harvey Kurtzman and Bill Elder); as in the fanzines produced in San Francisco in the 1960s;, as in the post-Francoist Spain in the 1970s.

The infamous *The seduction of the innocent* (1954), written by Dr. Fredric Wertham and published in the United States, warned that comics, under the disguise of funny pages for kids, could be a perfect vehicle for depravation, as seen in Superman narcissism, Wonder Woman sadomasochism and Batman and Robin latent homosexuality. Wertham didn't say that all comics were inherently perverted, but claimed that such an anarchic and influential industry needed a more rigorous censorship. In 1955, after a harassment campaign of the press and a Senatorial hearing, Wertham's call was answered by all the major US publishers; from then on, comics became strictly chaste.

Soon after, a more radical take on the depravity of comics was offered by a group of artists and editors previously committed to horror and war comics, all of them greatly affected by the new censorship procedures adopted since 1955. The artisans of EC Comics (Kurtzman, Elder, Al Feldstein, Bill Gaines and Wally Wood, among others), reunited in the satirical magazine *Mad*, started to joke with the accusations, to treat all the major comic book characters as doomed in some way or another, to mock themselves as vicious and low men only useful for making small drawings good for no one and to portray their readers as pariahs eager to consume the trash that everybody else condemned. Comics were made *by*, *with* and *for* the unloved, the ones ardent in desires that nobody wanted, people so detached from the pleasures available for ordinary men that they only could find some fulfilment of their fantasies by treating childish fictions as sexual agents. Comics were presented as poison for innocent kids and pleasure for pathetic grown-up losers. Wood's sexual caricatures and comics featuring Walt Disney's characters and the comics and magazines of Robert Crumb became the Sistine Chapel of these visions. Such a depreciated image, nourished with equal doses of self-pity and joyful irony by most of the communities related to comics, was thereafter adopted by the general esteem, minus the pity and the irony.

2.

Satiric, sexually explicit and perverted comics, whatever is their importance for the general medium, were always a minor trend in the United States, shadowed by the massive industries of corporate funny animals and corporate superheroes. But in Argentina, while the once powerful local industries related to adventure and funny comics were melting (Vázquez, 2010), satiric, sexually explicit and perverted comics became the creative and commercial core of the medium, as if comics couldn't be another thing.

To tell the story of the most perverted Argentine comic ever published, Diego Parés' *Sr. and Sra. Rispo* (1990–2011), is necessary to tell a brief story about sexually frustrated grey men (see Figure 13.1 please place figure after ch 7/before Part II).

Rispo's ancestors and brothers: some sexual conflicts in Argentina, 1979–1999

3.

In 1979 Carlos Trillo and Horacio Altuna's *El Loco Chávez* was the most famous comic strip in Argentina, published daily, since 1975, in the back-page of *Clarín*, the best-selling national newspaper. Millions, every morning, eagerly read what happened next with Chávez, a handsome journalist of Buenos Aires always involved with gorgeous women. Men wanted to be as charming and determined as the gallant; women wanted to be as beautiful and free as the girls that drove him mad. Trillo, the most prolific and inventive writer in the history of Argentine comics, and Altuna, whose drawings mastered a perfect mix of ultra-realism and hyper-humor, were stars (they still are). But under success ran a darker mood.

Since 1976 Argentina was ruled by a terrible dictatorship that abducted, tortured, murdered and *disappeared* thousands of workers, union leaders, political dissidents, students, religious leaders, intellectuals and artists. Censorship was harsh and the slightest discontent could be dangerous. Many friends of Trillo and Altuna were exiled, living fearfully in their homes, or dead. In 1978 and 1979, two magazines, *Hum®* and *El Péndulo* –one dedicated to humor and the other to science fiction and fantasy– became the new centers that reunited many writers and artists willing to allegorize the turmoil while earning some money. Trillo and Altuna created *Las puertitas del señor López*, publishing it first in *El Péndulo* and then in *Hum®*. The new character was a kind of antithesis of the then still running and appealing Chávez.

López is a grey man in his late forties or early fifties, quiet, silent, ungraceful, a clerk with no hierarchy and a husband without love for his aged and moody wife. When the boredom of his existence becomes insufferable, he escapes to the closest bathroom, where after crossing the door he enters into an oneiric world reminiscent of the dreamy scenes in Federico Fellini's films. The magical realm is inhabited by young, beautiful, powerful and kind women shameless of being nude, and while López is there he allows himself to run after the girls and to confess the love and pain in his heart. The unfortunate man never accomplishes his desires, but, while dreaming, his desire, at least, can be expressed. Once he returns from the bathroom to everyday life, although his existence continues as grey as before, he is able to stand it.

Las puertitas del Sr. López was about the poetic inner life of a nobody equally unable to do wrong and to be heroic, about dreaming and masturbation as sole refuges against a cold world, about a time when institutions were so oppressive that even marriage could became a burden, a totalitarian contract that didn't contemplate divorce (ex-lovers who despised each other remained linked forever). López was a prisoner, a sad, impotent and fearful figure, representative of a time when men, in order to survive, needed to be silent, to look to the other side and to dream secretly. And women, like the dream girls, even if they were beautiful, were broken by sadness.

4.

Trillo and Altuna continued *López* until 1982. The Argentine dictatorship ended in 1983. Once democracy returned, with the abandonment of the State censorship and the legalization of divorce, Sr. López soon became a figure of the past, an image only relatable for shy men stuck in other times.

Since 1984 sex became omnipresent. Naked beautiful bodies were publicly visible in the covers of the magazines and in the billboards of the cinemas. Celebrities started to talk openly about their sexual life. Sex became an industry and all the other industries seemed to be selling sex: cigarettes, cars, holidays, the mandatory skirts for girls in private schools and everything that worth. In a certain sense, after the dark years, this sexual uncovering was a kind of relief. But very soon it was manifest that an active sexual life could be as frustrating as a repressed one.

In 1982, Altuna started his first solo work, *Ficcionario* (published in the Spanish *1984* magazine and later in the Argentine magazine *Fierro*). As Chávez and López, Beto, the new main character, has a black moustache, but he is neither sexy nor graceful, but a regular man. The comic is set in a dystopia where an authoritarian government rules over an impoverished population domesticated by means of unrestricted access to sex and drugs. Beto walks the streets, or travels in the train, and the people around are always copulating and intoxicated. Being a Latino immigrant and an industrial worker, Beto is permanently exposed to police brutality and bureaucratic corruption, and although he knows that sex is a sedative offered by the murderous government, he takes it, because it is all he has. The major comic magazines of the new democratic Argentina, *Fierro*, *Hum®* and *Sex-Hum®*, although full of sex, were darker than joyful.

Alfredo Grondona-White, maybe the most representative artist of the new democratic era, exposed this same situation under a somewhat different light: in his comics the nervousness and frivolity of the everyday life corrupts even the sexy bodies shining in clubs, beaches, malls and discotheques, as if something undefined and painful emerges even through the clearest lines. All the pleasures seemed to be frivolous and rotten.

5.

Diego Parés, the protagonist of our history, started his career working for *Sex-Hum®* in 1985; being a teenage, precocious artist, he was equally skilled drawing dramatic and highly realistic images and humoristic and simple caricatures. He was part of the democratic and sexual uncovering, but at the same time he was among the first of a new generation, the ones who were kids under the dictatorship and teenagers during the early democracy. For them sex was not impossible. For them sex was not a sedative. For them sex was not affected by the nervousness of the everyday life. Sex was not allegorical of other order of problems. Sex itself was the problem.[2]

In 1996, in page 9 of the second number of *¡Suélteme!* – magazine that congregated the most revulsive Argentine cartoonist of last decade of the 20th century (Parés included) – in the middle of four graphic jokes, appeared the following unsigned text:

False revolution 1: THE SEXUAL.

> *Since the mid-20th century, when it became a business to say that everything was in the verge of a change, unoccupied pen pushers and other opinion makers cyclically announced a pretended sexual revolution. In the meantime, the old in-and-out, in all its variations, was practiced with the same assiduity accustomed since Precambrian times.*
>
> *What it is true is not only that there wasn't any sexual revolution, but that its possibility is non-existent without a radical modification of the human anatomy of all of the world's population. For example: the massive loss of sexual difference (but this*

reminds us of the unlucky destiny of the Amazons); or the ternary differentiation; or a non-pathological and global androgyny or hermaphroditism.

We, those who enjoy a good and true revolution, yearn with hope for the coming of these changes.

This extraordinary manifesto is descriptive of a general situation. For the ones who were already sexually active during the dictatorship's years, the return of democracy could be experienced, in a certain sense, as a time of growing freedom, less vigilance and a much more ebullient sexual life, like a party some survivors gave to themselves. But the younger ones who became sexually active toward the end of the 1980s, who grew up in a society where the talking, offering and selling of sexual liberation was omnipresent, found that their sexual life was duller and more conflicted than ever, shadowed nonstop by a continuous flux of fantasies in the magazines and the screens that, instead of signaling a goal, was in itself an endless path of hyper-stimulation. Comics, like no other media, made this conflict one of their main themes.

In Argentina, during the 1990s, to be adept at comics was a kind of mild social disease, a symptom of isolation and malfunctioning, especially in the domains of sexual life. This vision increased at the same rate that Argentine comics became a rotten industry with no economic profits and thus – in times ruled by market success – without reasons for its existence. In the 1980s someone dedicated to comics could still be trying to break into some kind of business (as it happened in similar ventures, like newspapers, magazines and advertising agencies), but in the 1990s, whoever continued making comics without earning money, was just a sick person chasing sterile obsessions, maybe even a pervert.

Parés, during the 1990s, felt like that. The most popular Argentine comics of the decade, *Cazador* and *Cybersix*, were affected by similar problems.

6.

In 1992 La Urraca, the publishing house of *Hum®*, ventured into the North-American comic-book format with *Cazador*, a title by Jorge Lucas, Claudio Ramírez, Ariel Olivetti and Mauro Cascioli. Lucas created Cazador – a hyper-muscular masked man – following the aesthetic of the grim-and-gritty superheroes widely popular since Frank Miller's *The Dark Knight Returns* (1986), but the character soon became humorous, adopting the kind of satirical violence in the *Judge Dredd* fashion and, specially, in the North-American *Lobo* comics written by Keith Giffen and Alan Grant and drawn by Simon Bisley. But Cazador was uglier than his inspirations: he was deprived of any moral or sense of duty, and his main reasons to fight demons, corrupted politicians or alien invaders were his anger after being interrupted while consuming pornography or, on the same tone, his ardent desire to have sex with some exuberant woman in distress.

It was unmistakable, for any reader, that Cazador was a bully, a molester, even a rapist (see #6), but the joke was that the traditional Argentine culture and the mainstream North-American culture, both permanently satirized, were, under the disguise of goodness, even more vicious and cruel than the openly lazy and monstrous anti-hero. *Cazador*, greatly illustrated with gore images and powerful digital colors, was highly popular, being, during the 1990s, the sole successful Argentine comic in a market dominated by North-American superheroes and Japanese manga. It was a comic for the unloved and the resentful.

7.

In 1992, Trillo and Carlos Meglia created Cybersix, a character destined for the Italian market. Soon after, in 1993, the comic began to be published in Spanish, first in the anthology *Puertitas* and then in its own Argentine-published title. As in *Las puertitas del Sr. López*, we face another exhibition of Trillo's impressive tuning with the *zeitgeist*. Cybersix is a genetic experiment born in the laboratory of a Nazi scientist escaped to Latin America; she is also the only survivor after a great genocide and now, during the nights, she is a vampire in pursuit of other lab creatures, looking for their blood to obtain an artificial substance essential for her survival. The elements are typical of the super-hero comic, but Trillo and Meglia, free from the self-censorship of the North-American mainstream publishers, added a central sexual conflict. On one hand, Cybersix, a woman, lives her everyday life disguised as a man; she is trans. On the other hand, she is possessed by sexual desire, but she restrains herself of any relation because, since she is no human, she fears endangering herself or her mate with some terrible disease.

Fifteen years after *Sr. Lopez*, the sexual dilemmas written by Trillo are completely different: now sex, masterfully drawn and narrated by Meglia (who synthetized influences from the North-American comics, the Japanese manga and the European *ligne claire*) is everywhere, but there is no place for sexual diversity beyond the heterosexual norm (while disguised as a man, Cybersix is permanently bullied for being indifferent to the insinuations of a young and exuberant lady); and the pleasures of sex are accompanied with fears, maladies and stigmas (as it happened since the 1980s with the AIDS epidemic).

Cazador, Cybersix and Sr. and Sra. Rispo are creatures of a common time.

The many faces of Rispo, 1990–2013

8.

Parés was 20 years old and single when he started a comic about marriage at middle age. Maybe he was anticipating his fears. In 1990, published in *Sex-Hum®*, the first adventure of *Sr. y Sra. Rispo*, was titled "No one knows why they are married" (Parés, 2007a, pp. 16–17).

The drawings, synthetic and cartoonish, as well as the small characters, are immediately reminiscent of the comics by Manuel García Ferré, one of the dearest artists to many generations of Argentine children. Rispo and Sra. Rispo, almost identical to each other (except for Rispo's moustache), both wear the same glasses used by the highly popular Anteojito, Ferré's golden creature.

Parés' premise was quite simple: Rispo wants to have sex with his wife, but she is entertained with other men, so the unattended husband relieves himself with a doll. From here on Parés variations on the theme continued for decades.

Rispo looks like an unleashed version of Sr. López, deploying very wild impulses not in dreams, but in his everyday world, pants down and carrying an erection bigger than him. Although he is nobody, just another grey employee in suit and tie, he has no reasons to be restrained, since everything is a sexual invitation. Sometimes he craves after his wife, sometimes after another woman (specially his young niece), sometimes –both reluctantly and eager– he falls in the arms of a man (or animal) (Figure 13.2). Everything is possible. But the tragedy of Sr. Rispo is that even when he goes deep into his ardent will, up to the point of becoming a monster, he is always faced by a greater and more turbulent desire than his. His insatiable and ferocious wife (Sra. Rispo), his enormous and brutish adversary (Esteban Galíndez) or his treacherous friend (Horacio "the genius") are always involved in a greater orgy, in a greater debauchery from which he is totally excluded or, even worst, included like an impotent victim or a non-participant witness. Rispo is a predatory male subjugated in the course of his own game. As much as he tries, he always loses under a sharper and more violent lust.

Parés style over the first two years of the Rispos was clear and steady, suited to the professional standards of the comic strips published in newspapers, but at the service of stories only publishable in an adult-oriented magazine. With each new chapter, he became more daring, indulging his characters with rape, cannibalism, murder, mutilation and necrophilia. However, if *Sr. and Sra. Rispo* had ended after those early years, the stories wouldn't be enough to support a legend. The comics

FIGURE 13.2 Diego Parés, "Daily life," *El Sr. y la Sra. Rispo.* Illustration posted on Diego Parés' official Facebook site (2010).

that elevated the Rispos to cult status were still to come. And they wouldn't come until Parés descended to hell.

9.

Somewhere between 1991 and 1992 Parés became increasingly unsatisfied with his craft (Parés 1999, 2007a and 2017). His drawings were incredibly good, but not as good as the works of the masters of the past (García Ferré, A. Breccia, Hugo Pratt and Quino). At the same time, the works of his most admired contemporaries (Esteban Podetti, Pablo Fayó and Pablo Parés) were more spontaneous, funnier and more savage than his own. After ten years devoted to drawing, he was neither a peer among the greatest nor outstanding among the newest. Even if no other was his equal in love (and lust) to graphic-humor, the romance was not reciprocal. He needed to produce new images worthy to be seen, so he decided to become crazy and exploit all the putrefaction hidden in his mind (1999). To help himself, he started to consume large quantities of psychedelic and stimulant drugs (2007a). It's like the birth of a comic-book villain.

The premises of the following Rispos comics (most of them published by *Sex-Hum®*) were the same than before: unrestrained lust, violations, mutations and titanic hard-ons out of control. The difference was that now the gruesome didn't lie just in the actions, but in the quality of their graphic depiction.

Parés thought that *Sex-Hum®* was going to reject "Rispo draws himself" (Parés, 2007a, pp. 36–37), the first bloom of his new batch. Compared with his previous comics, these two pages look alien, even if the signature is the same. Gone are the solid and economic black and white vignettes from before. Gone is the classical cartoonish style. Now there is an explosion inside each panel and the characters are nervous and extremely ugly creatures suffering a non-stop mutation. Now there is a plague of details in every inch of space, as if Parés couldn't stop drawing. It looks like the rushed work of someone willingly possessed by demons. Parés was giving up all aim for perfection and equilibrium, exiling beauty out of his art and embracing nastiness and monstrosity. He was trying hard to be as repulsive as he could. Rispo's niece, once a beautiful little girl, looks now like a sexualized animal in a slaughterhouse. Rispo and Horacio are always sweating or crying in despair. It is a world where plasticity is painful. Everything is being torn apart by unnatural forces coming from undistinguishable directions.

10.

According to the dictum of Charles Baudelaire (1868, pp. 366–368) humor is always achieved by means of satanic attitudes (the will to expose someone's weakness) and satanic deformations (disguises, drugs, poisons, animalization, idolatry and profanity).

The tormented, funny and overpopulated quality of the Rispos comics produced circa 1993 pertains to a tradition of hellish illuminations rooted back beyond the paintings of Hieronymus Bosch, Pieter Brueghel the Elder and Giotto di Bondone. Parés delved in a subterranean guild of artists for whom, from the beginning, the first task of drawing was neither to portrait nor to represent, but to deform and alter reality (2007a, p. 96). The cartoonist's dilemma was how far he could go.

Who would be the first to succumb to the unbearable in those pages: the editors, the public or himself? Was it possible to go on forever?

The Rispo's original sexual riot was now accompanied by a graphic overflow, as if sex and drawing, when unrestrained, both rush to violence and madness. In the previous comics Rispo was beaten by the stronger desire of other subjects; since "Rispo draws himself," in addition, his own desire is revealed as a devouring force turned against him.

Parés seems to be deeply indebted to the 19th-century ideas about men, and specially artists, as decadent, insatiable, tormented and suicidal/murderous souls, in the lineage of the characters by Poe, Dostoevsky, Baudelaire, Rimbaud, Van Gogh, Conrad and Wilde, among others. Parés, however, doesn't diagnose this condition to all mankind. His lunatics, as Crumb's, aren't enlightened with a terrible truth, unacceptable by most; they are just clowns, ridiculous and pathetic people crying and laughing at the same time, perverts, deranged. Among the regular people the ones who desire monsters – or to be monsters (Figure 13.3).

In the great abyss of passions, as there is a place for tender lovers, angry lovers, platonic lovers, sadists, pedophiles (both platonic and angry) and so on, there is a place for the ones who just want those things perceived as horrible by everybody else. *Rispos* is a series of perversions told without judgement; perversion by itself, running wild.

FIGURE 13.3 Diego Parés, "Horacio," *El Sr. y la Sra. Rispo*. Illustration posted on Diego Parés' official Facebook site (2010).

11.

Perversion is funny horror. That's why perverts betray themselves laughing when everybody else is shocked, somber or nauseated.

Cartoons are funny monsters, creatures that would cause horror in this world (talking animals walking on two legs, deformed characters and so on).

Cartoon lovers and perverts are alike.

12.

Perversion is desire with a toll. In 1993, Rispo became darker with each new episode: he was locked in an asylum (Parés, 2007a, pp. 62–63), he died (pp. 66–67) and he beheld the aborted birth of monstrosity (pp. 68–69). Parés and Rispo were both going further at the cost of sanity.

The cartoonist, overwhelmed by drugs and hallucinations, finally collapsed. Parés dwelled in psychiatric hospitals and depressive rooms through the next five years. "Once out of the hospital – he said (p. 14) – I lost my drawing skills. They had vanished. I couldn't draw a single damned line. From them on, I think, Sr. and Sra. Rispo started to die."

The cartoonist, fortunately, survived.

The Rispos survived too.

13.

The star of Parés' most savage comics was Rispo, but the main character of the Rispos stories from 1994 to the end of the 20th century was his friend Horacio. While Rispo is an unchained perversion, Horacio – also a pervert – has a hinge for survival. Parés (2008) said that Horacio is a version of himself, while Rispo is drawn in a more unconscious way. "Horacio is good and evil, he alternates, he's ungraspable" (Parés, 2011d).

Horacio, a mad-melancholic scientist, deploys his desire only through pretexts, never acting as a driving force, always riding on somebody else's movements, being an instigator. He is the one who encourages Rispo to lose himself and who collects the debris of the turmoil; he seeds over Rispo's infertility (Parés, 2007a, pp. 68–69, 2011a). When he has no instigators, he just dooms in abandon, sadness and infinite masturbation. Horacio is fearful of the horrible torments from guilt (Parés, 2007a, p. 70), so he is the kind of vicious in need of someone worse in order to excuse himself (see Figure 13.4).

Parés drawing style was diverse over those years, but the stories starred by Horacio are drawn either more economically or more ornately than Rispo's, as if the scientist was both simpler and more real than his loony friend (2007a, pp. 48–49, 72–73 and 78–81; also three notable illustrations shared by Parés on his Facebook account). Horacio functions as mediation, pause and reflection amidst the whirl. In some sense, his bond with Rispo seems parallel to Parés' relationship with his characters.

Parés once tried to achieve, through his drawings, an ardor equal to Rispo's, but he couldn't endure it. To survive he became more distant, more aseptic and more laborious. Parés accepted that Rispo had a savage existence of his own, while he (a cartoonist) was only capable of being an eager, patient, obsessed, and scientific witness. Without the resources of dementia, the only way to portray Rispo was achieving mastery enough to draw the craziest things while being familiar, in the same way as it is familiar the candid photography of Basil Wolverton, tenderly held by his wife, Honor Lovette, while he is drawing Lena the Hyena, one of the ugliest cartoons ever done (Sadowski, 2019, p. 138).

14.

The return of Rispo, first circa 2001 and then, fully, between 2007 and 2011, was accompanied by a reformulation of Parés style. The hand of the artist behind the Rispos' savage years is clearly recognizable (2007a, pp. 86–87), but the drawings are more measured, as if he was trying to recollect and improve the classical cartoonish quality of the early years (pp. 88–89). The Rispos comics of the 21st century, from then on, exhibit a consolidated and consistent style; sometimes looser, as divertissements for fanzines (Parés, 2011b, 2013b), sometimes tighter, as very professional commissions for books or serious magazines (2009b, 2011a); they are always excellent.

Parés became able to exhibit at once maximum movement and maximum clarity, achieving pages worthy of the same kind of admiration inspired by Chester Gould's *Dick Tracy* or George Herriman's *Krazy Kat*. He produced equilibrated, dynamical and visually unforgettable comics. And he learned to reach craziness by pace and not by outcry. Although originally formed in the single panel tradition of graphic-humour, he became more focused on narrative. Before, each and every panel was demented; now, most of the panels could be as innocent as infantile comics (2010b), but put one after the other they build a demented rhythm of actions (2011a). In 1993, Parés was vomiting his delirium at the cost of sanity; in the 21st century, he realized that Gould and Herriman, in the golden age of funny comics, deployed their extremely crazy stories in major publications, being read and accepted everyday by millions, even earning money.

Nevertheless, the abyssal difference between Parés and Gould is that after three decades the former produced approximately three hundred pages of *Rispos*, while the latter published those same numbers every single year. *Dick Tracy* was eagerly demanded by the publishing industry and by the general public, while the Rispos apparitions were confined to declining magazines and non-lucrative fanzines for limited and specialized publics. The Rispos, quantitatively, represent a very small fraction of the many professional commissions completed by Parés in his long career; besides, they never were good business. They were produced by marginal and precarious work.

Parés (1999) acknowledged that while he was young, stimulated by his drawing abilities, he had dreams of a glorious destiny. His misjudgment, precisely, was to seek fortune in the domains of funny comics, an art being rapidly abandoned by industry, money, fame and public. Animation, in the northern side of the American continent, could still offer some place for ambitious craziness (as in Matt Groening's *The Simpsons* and John Kricfalusi's *Ren & Stimpy*), but within the comic field there was barely nothing. Parés continued because he couldn't stop, consciously pursuing an always-unsatisfied desire, producing as a worker of a non-existent industry.[3]

15.

In 2010, while he was producing a brilliant batch of Rispos comics (2009a, 2009b, 2010a, 2011a) and, at the same time, thanks to his protean drawing skills, while he was a recurring contributor for all the major Argentine magazines requiring illustrators, Parés became part of the prestigious back-page of the influential newspaper *La Nación*, a major recognition for an Argentine cartoonist.

His single-panel jokes for *La Nación*, still running under the title *Humor Petiso* (*Short Humour*), are innocent, clean and apt for general audiences. However, it's hard to miss, among the recurring characters, the apparition of alternate versions of Rispo and his wife (Parés, 2015, pp. 38 and 47): suits, haircuts, moustaches, glasses and physiognomies are more or less the same. What it's lost is Rispo's depravity, replaced by the intimidated expression of a generic man that goes under generic surnames, as Gómez (pp. 110–118) or García (p. 100). Gómez even looks like an alternate version of Trillo and Altuna's Sr. López; nevertheless, he is closer to Rispo.

López was grey and fearful, but he had some dignity. He was not rebellious, and he didn't have what he wanted, but at least he wasn't forced against his will. He had a bastion, even if only in his mind. On the contrary, Rispo and Gómez are beaten by overwhelming humiliation.

Rispo always loses because he can't restrain himself; he falls in each and every plot set against him (Parés 2009b, 2010a, 2011b). Gómez loses because he is absolutely obedient; he even consents to be a sacrificial victim for his abusive bosses (Parés 2015, p. 114). One by will, the other by submission, both accept everything and are crushed by its force.

16.

The graphic and narrative changes between Rispo in 1993 and Rispo in 2010 are accompanied by a modification in his personality: now he is able to self-censor. Anyhow, nothing changes. As he is unable to stop his desire, he is equally incapable to stop his self-repression. Rispo's repression comes neither after his actions (as for Horacio) nor as renouncement to action (as for Gómez); it is just a change in the course of the rush, a tide running back and still unstoppable. He seeks goodness as another thing among the many he desires voraciously; if he is restrained, it is only by the same unconscious and immoral force that drives his depravity.

In the world of the Rispos, instead of morality (desire conducted by regulation), there are stronger desires. Rispo's passion rolls back when he clashes against the overpowering will of Sra. Rispo. And she triumphs because, besides her own force, she has the ability to deviate his.

Although it is impossible to repress desire (especially one as wild as Rispo's), it is possible to instigate desires of self-mutilation. The effects of censorship are deployed not over desires, but over bodies, since it is possible to desire against the body as is not possible against desire. A censored body has not a lesser desire, but anyhow, sooner or later, it will find to have less power for achieving pleasure. Monogamy, for example, is not regulation over desire, but the accomplishment of some particular desire through some mutilation or confinement of the body that excludes absolutely any other pleasures (Parés, 2011b). Rispo goes from hostile and depraved to harmless and crippled through a continuous and interrupted exhilaration (2010a, 2013b).

Rispo's weakness is to be concerned just by his own desire, or in some cases, when force is not enough, by the will to turn someone else's desire into a positive response to his. Sra. Rispo and Horacio, both more ambitious, are concerned by Rispo's desire even though they are not interested in a relationship with him. Sra. Rispo and Horacio are masterminds of different complots aimed to exclude Rispo out of a selection of sexual intercourses. This kind of instigation of desires in the undesired is the defining prerogative of power.

To exclude is more than saying no; it's a way to not even say no and obliterate any possible proposition between certain desires. This kind of selection has correspondence with the procedures of moral conclusions, but it is just desire without any hint of altruism. Morality is a name for strategy, not for virtue. Sra. Rispo and Horacio don't moralize Rispo; they just tempt him with the pleasures of self-mutilation.

Morality, as comfort for the vanquished, only rises when Rispo, after performing self-mutilation, proclaims his victory. Morality is to desire what is imposed by mutilation. Morality is to be proud for being excluded from a selection of sexual intercourses. Morality promotes self-censorship. As the depraved rejoices in the mutilation of others, the moral man rejoices in his own impairment (Parés, 1999 and 2011b). These are not excluding attitudes.

17.

Rispo is a pervert and a victim. This doesn't mean equivalence. It's just a funny and terrible thing: there is a single image able to conjure both depravity and humiliation. It is the image of a dark haired little man wearing a black suit and a peculiar moustache, a tramp, a clerk, a bureaucrat, a policeman, a perfect nobody; in comics he looks like Altuna's López and Beto, like Hergé's Dupond and Dupont, like Landrú's characters, like the mask wore by Moore and Gibbons' V; he also resembles Charlie Chaplin, Edgar Allan Poe, Fernando Pessoa, Groucho Marx, Cantinflas, old Bob Dylan, some of The Village People, Salvador Dalí, Adolf Hitler and Jorge Rafael Videla. He wears the most regular outfit, but somehow he looks disguised. He effaces himself into a non-identity and he still remains highly singular. He is the recognizable embodiment of anonymity, the man in the multitude. Without changing his image Rispo is sometimes a joke, sometimes a regular man and sometimes a mass murderer. Gómez, on his side, is just a regular and one-dimensional man, but he participates, the same, in the pathos of the everyman (Figure 13.5).

While the number of men looking like the caricature of a grey nobody diminished since the end of the 20th century, Rispo and Gómez are still clearly recognizable as humorous personifications of the most common man. There's not a contemporary analogous suited for that role since the idea of a universal man is becoming an antiquity.

The man in suit and moustache is not everyman, but he might be any kind of man. He is an image without character, like a closed and unsigned envelope, like the ringing of a telephone in the pre-Caller ID era. He is a relic of a time when the

FIGURE 13.5 Diego Parés, "Tomorrow, there's no tomorrow." *El Sr. y la Sra. Rispo* blog (January 31, 2010).

destiny of men was undefined. He is a dress tailored to be worn under any upcoming future and among any other men. He contains multitudes.

Since the end of the 20th century the image of the suited grey man became exclusive to lawyers, politicians, TV hosts, businessmen and participants in civil ceremonies. Any other man in a suit is a clown. Now there is no possible confusion between bosses and low men aspiring to powers that will never be theirs. Except in cartoons and comics.

18. Rispo is comic, tragic and old-fashioned because he believes, as men have for millennia, that men are different to women. He believes that males are, at the same time, stronger and more oppressed than females; he believes that men have certain rights over women; and he believes that his desire is more ferocious and more monstrous than Sra. Rispo's desire. This is funny because Sra. Rispo looks exactly like him, except that she has no moustache and she wears a white dress instead of a black suit; their physiognomic differences are meaningless and Bety Rispo is perfectly able to wear a suit, a moustache and even a penis (she does it frequently). This is even more funny because Bety Rispo is always more ferocious and more monstrous than his husband, overpowering him time after time. In Rispo's world, women are more resourceful, subtler and more commanding than men; it's not because they are better. The difference is just historical: men take for granted powers that they are losing, while women, still subject to male dominance, are forced to be subtle even when their intentions are barbaric and predatory. Rispo is an embodiment of male rage and frustration in a collapsing patriarchal order. Bety Rispo is the embodiment of the masculine terror to an alpha male with a vagina.

19.

In *Correrías del Sr. y la Sra. Rispo*, it is revealed that our anti-heroes are brother and sister. The shocking notice comes while Bety Rispo is pregnant, so the upcoming child is a fruit of incest; no bigger transgression is possible. Everybody, starting with Horacio, turns against the Rispos, who thereafter are chased as unbearable beasts by angry mobs and institutional powers. The Rispos struggle, determined to birth their creature, fighting against everybody.

Correrías, published in 2011, is the second book of the Rispos and their first "graphic novel" (Parés abjures the expression and uses it only ironically). The first one, *El Sr. y la Sra. Rispo: ¡Dos caretas como vos!*, published in 2007, was a compilation of short stories. *Correrías* is partially constructed over some published pages (mainly in *Fierro* and *Barcelona* magazines), but all the episodes, now expanded, are entangled like the movements of an organic opus. It is a masterpiece of humor, of comics and of literature. Parés, now detoxed, trips through his drawings, exhibiting an astonishing virtuosity, a jaw-dropping skill to imagine crazy situations and a fluid and voracious talent to narrate by means of a variety of graphic resources only available for a savant of the history of comics with almost magical hands. Most of the story is drawn with the perfected professional cartoonish style developed by Parés since 2007, but all his other previous styles are also summoned for different episodes (hallucinations, backstage, incursions into the deep unconscious); it is a place for all the faces of the Rispos, as it is a place for all the faces of the comics and for all the faces of the history. It is a comic where everything could happen, it doesn't matter what. It is an explicit, joyful and infuriated celebration of that power: everything could be satirized; every person and every situation is a possible subject for jokes and destruction (in the satiric genre – as in Karl Kraus' *The Last*

Days of Mankind, as in Kurt Vonneguts' *Slaughterhouse 5* and as in Thomas Pynchon's *Gravity's Rainbow* – jokes and destruction are indiscernible).

Correrías ends with a big fat kill. Rispo and Bety, sick of being hunted, slaughter all mankind. Under the sovereignty of a despaired desire, no obstacle has a right to survive. While the incestuous couple is covered in blood, appreciating the hecatomb, Bety births their creature and Parés delivers a last joke, a last humiliation to Rispo. Even in the twilight of Armageddon, a new minor tragedy arises and, with that ridiculous discomfort, a new smile.

20.

Since *Correrías*, Parés published just a few of new Rispos. Maybe he didn't have an opportunity. Since then the Argentine economy has been suffering a devastating crisis, condemning half of the population to poverty. Since then, a new public sensibility to the exhibition of sexual violence (a consequence of the growing feminist movements to which Parés, in a very Rispo-like attitude, often reacts defensively) has been established. Maybe Parés has neither the time nor the will to commit himself to a work that will offer little economic profit while being potentially offensive. Or maybe the Rispos are just waiting to reemerge, once again stronger than their creator, as disturbing expressions of a ravaging, perverted and irrepressible desire.

Notes

1 I wrote this essay during the course of the COVID-19 pandemic and without proper access to public libraries and archives, so the scope of the research was severely limited. The work was only possible thanks to Brian Janchez, who generously gave me his own old magazines, and José María Gutiérrez, who facilitated me the access to the resources of the Archivo de Historieta y Humor Gráfico Argentinos of the Biblioteca Nacional Mariano Moreno.
2 In a recent study, Fabián Ludueña Romandini wrote: "lo sexual (que no es equivalente a la sexualidad), es una tortura para *Homo*" (2020: 31).
3 This condition is clearly visible in the vintage design adopted in 2011 for the publishing of *Correrías del S r. y la S ra. Rispo*.

Bibliography

Adanti, D., Diaz, D.J., Fayó, P., Migliardo, E., Parés, D., Parés, P., Podetti, E. & Sapia, P. (1996) "Agitación libertaria", *¡Suelteme!* No. 2, pp. 9–14.
Altuna, H. (1996) *Ficcionario*. La Urraca.
Baudelaire, C. (1868) *Œuvres complètes II. Curiosités esthétiques*. Michel Lévy Frères.
Lucas, J., Ramírez, C., Olivetti, A. y Cascioli, M. (1992–1997) *Cazador* (#1–36). La Urraca.
Ludueña Romandini, F. (2020) *Summa Cosmologiae. Breve tratado (politico) de inmortalidad. La comunidad de los espectros IV*. Miño y Dávila.
Parés, D. (1999) "Pandemonium", *¡Suelteme!* No. 5, pp. 23–26.
Parés, D. (2007a) *El sr. Y la sra. Rispo: ¡Dos caretas como vos!* Nobuko.
Parés, D. (2007b) "¡Mamá, Diego Parés me rompió todos los juguetes!" (an interview by Lucas Nine), *Sacapuntas* No. 7, pp. 3–12.
Parés, D. (2008) "Entrevista a Diego Parés – Dibujante de aquellos", *Tierra Freak*. https://tierrafreak.blogspot.com/2008/03/entrevista-diego-pars-dibujante-de.html

Parés, D. (2009a) "El sr. Y la sra. Rispo: Atomizados", *Fierro* No. 34, pp. 24–25.
Parés, D. (2009b) "Sr. y sra. Rispo: Jailhouse Blues", *Fierro* No. 38, pp. 38–39.
Parés, D. (2010a) "Sr. y sra. Rispo: Guerra Mundial", *Fierro* No. 39, pp. 9–11.
Parés, D. (2010b) "El sr y la sra. Rispo y Horacio en: ¡De canillita a subcampeón!", *Fierro* No. 40, pp. 29–32.
Parés, D. (2011a) *Correrías de el sr. y la sra. Rispo.* Llantodemundo.
Parés, D. (2011b) *La monogamia del sr. Rispo.* Musaraña.
Parés, D. (2011c) "Un possible prólogo para el libro de Rispo que sí sale", https://diego-pares.blogspot.com/2011/04/un-posible-prologo-para-el-libro-de.html
Parés, D. (2011d) "Lamentable", https://elsrylasrarispo.blogspot.com/2011/06/lamentable.html
Parés, D. (2012) *Sr. Rispo presenta: "El eternauta para principiantes."* Digital fanzine.
Parés, D. (2013a) *500 dibujos.* Musaraña – Llantodemundo.
Parés, D. (2013b) *El sr. y la sra. Rispo: una historieta a mano alzada.* Digital fanzine.
Parés, D. (2015) *Humor petiso. Las mujeres y los niños primero.* Edhasa.
Parés, D. (2016) "La belleza no es graciosa" (an interview by Nicolás Mavrakis), *Revista Paco.* https://revistapaco.com/diego-pares-la-belleza-no-es-graciosa/
Parés, D. (2017) "Hay que laburar, laburar, laburar" (an interview by Amadeo Gandolfo and Pablo Turnes), *Kamandi.* www.revistakamandi.com/2017/08/30/hay-que-laburar-laburar-laburar-una-entrevista-a-diego-pares/
Sadowski, G. (2019) *Brain Bats of Venus. The life and comics of Basil Wolverton. Volume Two, 1942–1952.* Fantagraphics.
Trillo, C. y Altuna, H. (2007) *Las puertitas del sr. López.* Clarín.
Trillo, C. y Meglia, C. (1995) *Cybersix. Las primeras historias.* Meridiana.
Vázquez, L. (2010) *El oficio de las viñetas. La industria de la historieta argentina.* Paidós.

INDEX

adaptation 8, 23, 208
agency capacity 46–48
Aguilar Fernández, Paloma 52
Angola Janga 12, 83, 85, 92–93, 95, 97–99, 105–106, 109–114
Arab Spring 47
Argentina 2–4, 6–9, 11–12, 21–23, 70, 76–77, 152, 154–155, 169–170, 208, 215, 222–223, 225
Argentine artists 76–78
Argentine comics 14, 77, 222, 225
artivismos 207, 213–214

Bakhtin, Mikhail 26, 84
Barcelona 61, 127, 172
Bartual, Roberto 39
battle of santiago 122
Baudelaire, Charles 228
Bermúdez, Francisco Morales 194
Bernardi, Odyr 207
Berone, Lucas 9, 77
Bioy Casares, Adolfo 24
blackness 12, 114–115
Black visualities 105; in Brazilian comics 107, 109, 111, 113, 115
Blanes, Jaume Peris 52, 58
Bolivia 2–4, 6–8, 11, 13, 185, 187–190
Bolivian comics 183, 185, 187, 189, 191
Borges, Jorge Luis 19, 23
Brazil 2–9, 11–13, 82–93, 97–99, 105–109, 111, 113–114, 169, 207–208, 215
Brazilian comics 12, 105–107, 109–111, 113–115
Brazilian history 92–93

Breccia, Alberto 22–23
Brescia, Pablo 22
Buenos Aires 7, 19, 22–23, 28, 127, 222
Burke, Peter 89
Bustos, Luis 55

Casale O'Ryan, Mariana 21–23
Catalá-Carrasco, Jorge L. 38
CETPA 106–107
Chaves Palacios, Julián 51
Chávez, Hugo 2
Chilean comics 54, 59, 63, 117, 119, 125–126, 129
Chilean graphic novels 122
Chute, Hillary 53
Cinelli, Juan Pablo 21
Colling, Leandro 213–214, 216
colonial gaze 167
comic art 176, 185
comic book artists 8, 92
comics 5–14, 51–56, 58–59, 62–64, 67–71, 75–79, 82–85, 87–93, 105–120, 122, 125–129, 149–151, 161–162, 166–170, 175–177, 183–199, 204–205, 215–217, 221–233, 235; history of 105, 168, 177, 196, 221, 235; production 12, 67–68, 70, 76, 79, 127, 170, 177, 193; scenes 7, 11, 166; studies 8–11, 111
comic scene 6, 8, 70
comic strips 22, 68–69, 75, 106–108, 110, 118–119, 152, 189, 197, 207, 227
comic theory 151
competitive funds 70–71, 79
contemporary Chilean comics 51, 117–118

contemporary comics 184–185
contemporary Mexico 35–36
Copacabana 208
Corbin, Alan 110
Correrías 235–236
Cruz, Nicolás 54
Cuarón, Alfonso 38
Cuartango 158
Cybersix 225–226

Day Dreaming 202
Desejo, Quarto de 110
dictatorship 19, 51–52, 54–55, 59, 61, 63–64, 69, 73–75, 82, 87–88, 118–119, 122–123, 126
Didi-Huberman, Georges 125
digital comics 71
Donato, Edgardo 23
D'Salete, Marcelo 97
Dunlap, Charles 4

Eisner, Will 42
emancipated behavior 193–197, 202, 204
emancipation 194, 197, 199–200, 202
escapes 56, 73, 91–92, 94, 151–152, 154–155, 158, 200, 223

false revolution 224
female comics artists 166, 168–169, 177
feminine territoriality 166–170, 172–173
feminism 109, 168, 207, 213–214
fiction 23, 54–55, 71, 77, 93–94, 97, 113, 122, 185, 200
Foster, David William 211
Freitas, Angelica 207–208, 214, 217
Fuentealba, Ricardo 151
funny comics 222–223, 225–235

Galizzi, Silvio 75
Gálvez, Pepe 61
García, Jorge 62–63
García Canclini, Néstor 10
Gardel, Carlos 23
Gilroy, P. 95
Girondo, Oliverio 26
Godínez, Marisa 193–194
Gombrowicz, Witold 26
Gorodischer, Julián 43
graphic activism 167, 172
graphic novels 7, 11–14, 36, 44, 62, 64, 70–71, 75–76, 109, 122, 124; in Brazil 109
graphic resistance 109
Guadalupe 14, 207–215, 217
Guijarro, Carlos 62

hacer historietas 9
Halconazo 35–39, 43, 45, 49
halcones 37–39
Hinojosa, Hugo 64
historias clandestinas 54, 59, 64, 123
historical comics 12, 67, 70, 75–78
historical events 35, 54–55, 74–75, 78, 124–125
historical graphic novels 67, 75–76; in Uruguay 67, 69–79
historical memory 48–49, 52
historicity 105, 114, 169
historiographic rigor 78
historiography 64, 79, 113
Hobsbawm, Eric 38, 49
homosexuality 221
Howard Miller, John 168

Icenail, Corven 185
iconic images 19, 21, 23, 25, 27–29
intertextuality 19, 21, 23

Joly, Maud 62

Kirby, Jack 110

La Estrella y el Zorro 185
Lagos, José Gabriel 69
Lange, Norah 26
Larra, Lola 120
Latin America 2–6, 8–13, 47, 52, 166, 169, 174, 176–177, 209, 214–215, 217
Latin American comics 2, 4–8, 10, 13–14, 149–151, 155, 161, 166, 168–170, 207, 209, 216–217
Latin American dictatorships 194
Lazzara, Michael J. 56
Le Goff 93
Leguisamo, Pablo "Roy" 75
Lenzi, Carlos César 23
L'Hoeste, Fernández 188
López, Alfonso 61

McCausland 170, 177
McGee, Bobby 88
Malloy, Sylvia 24
Malos tiempos 58
Mannheim, Karl 48
Manzi, Jorge 120
Maroh, Julie 168
Martín, Jaime 58–59
Martín-Cabrera, Luis 52
Martínez, Fidel 62
Masotta, Oscar 8

materiality 84–85, 93, 176
memory 11–13, 35–54, 56, 58–59, 62, 63–64, 82–93, 98–99, 118–120, 124–126, 128–129, 149–152, 154–162; comics 53; of trauma 51, 53, 54, 59, 62
Mexico City 36–37, 39–40, 45, 47, 49, 207–209, 212
Mexico City Historical Center 40, 42, 49
migrant bodies 152, 154–155
Miller, Daniel 87
Mil vidas más 61
Mitchell, William John Thomas. 53
Mora, Augusto 12, 35–36, 39–40, 43, 45–49
Morales, Evo 190
Moxey, Keith 53
Muñoz, David 56

Navascués, Javier de 23
never-ending struggle 11
Noriega, Águeda 197
Novus, Mundus 167

oblivion 49, 152, 156–157, 160–161
Ocampo, Silvina 24
Onetti, Juan Carlos 74
Operation Scarecrow 26

Panchulei 127, 166, 172–177
Paraizo, Mariana 151
Pardo, Jaime 158
Parés, Diego 14, 224–226, 228–233, 235–236
Parodi, Don Isidro 24
Penguin Revolution 119, 121
Penna, Luli 91
Perón, Juan Domingo 19
Perramus 22
Peruzzo, Nicolás 76, 78
pervertion 223–235
Pinturas de guerra 59
Plaza, Vicho 151
political disenchantment 187
politics of memory 51–53, 162
positive disobedience 214
poultry inspector 19, 21–22, 24–26, 28
Prado, Miguelanxo 24
Pratt, Hugo 23

Rada, Rafaela 185
Reguillo, Rossana 48
Rispos comics 228, 231–232

Rodríguez, Javier 54
Rojas, Sergio 162

Sábat, Hermenegildo 23
sadomasochism 221
Santullo, Rodolfo 69, 71, 73–77
Sasturain, Juan 22
Segar, Elzie Crisler 168
self-determination 170
Sem Dó 85
sexual dissidence 11, 13–14, 207–209, 211, 213–217
sexual immorality 221
sexual life 223, 225
Smolderen, Thierry 151
social harmony 111
social mobilization 46, 117, 122–123, 127, 129
social outburst 117, 125, 128, 172
Soriano, Osvaldo 22
Soruco Sologuren, Ximena 183
Spain 6, 8, 11–12, 51, 63, 84, 176
Spanish comics 12, 61, 62
student movements 35–49
subalternity 183, 185, 187, 189, 191

Torres, Ale 13, 193, 196–197, 201, 205
torture 53, 59, 61, 74, 128
Trabado 125
Trillo, Carlos 23
Turnes, Pablo 23

Uruguay 2, 4, 7–8, 11–12, 67–79
Uruguayan comics 68, 76–77
Uruguayan strip, periodization 68

violence 11–12, 42–43, 56–59, 62–63, 111, 150, 152, 154–155, 168, 170, 172, 190, 196–197, 215; against civilians 56; against women 61
visual narrative 78, 96
Vollenweider, Nacha 152

Waldseemüller, Martin 167
Wertham, Fredric 221
Williams, Raymond 83
witness 53, 55, 57, 59, 149–151, 156, 161, 231
Wrobel, Jasmin 94

#YoSoy132 Movement 35, 43, 45–49

Zitarrosa, Alfredo 73
zoetrope 88, 91